From
P O R
Las Vegas

by Mary Herczog

Macmillan • USA

ABOUT THE AUTHOR

Mary Herczog lives in Los Angeles and works in the film industry. She is the author of *Frommer's New Orleans* and contributed to *Frommer's Los Angeles*. She still isn't sure when to hold and when to hit in Blackjack.

IDG BOOKS WORLDWIDE, INC.

An International Data Group Company
919 E. Hillsdale Blvd.
Suite 400
Foster City, CA 94404

Find us online at **www.frommers.com**

ISBN 0-02-862631-1
ISSN 10903-5472

Editor: Naomi P. Kraus
Production Editor: Robyn Burnett
Photo Editor: Richard Fox
Design by Michele Laseau
Staff Cartographers: John Decamillis, Roberta Stockwell
Front cover photo: Luxor Sphinx
Page creation by John Bitter, Natalie Evans, Sean Monkhouse, and Angel Perez

SPECIAL SALES

For general information on IDG Books Worldwide's books in the U.S., please call our Consumer Customer Service department at 1-800-762-2974. For reseller information, including discounts, bulk sales, customized editions, and premium sales, please call our Reseller Customer Service department at 1-800-434-3422.

Manufactured in the United States of America

5 4 3 2 1

Contents

List of Maps

AN INVITATION TO THE READER

In researching this book, we discovered many wonderful places—hotels, restaurants, shops, and more. We're sure you'll find others. Please tell us about them, so we can share the information with your fellow travelers in upcoming editions. If you were disappointed with a recommendation, we'd love to know that, too. Please write to:

Frommer's Portable Las Vegas
IDG Travel
1633 Broadway
New York, NY 10019

AN ADDITIONAL NOTE

Please be advised that travel information is subject to change at any time—and this is especially true of prices. We therefore suggest that you write or call ahead for confirmation when making your travel plans. The authors, editors, and publisher cannot be held responsible for the experiences of readers while traveling. Your safety is important to us, however, so we encourage you to stay alert and be aware of your surroundings. Keep a close eye on cameras, purses, and wallets, all favorite targets of thieves and pickpockets.

WHAT THE SYMBOLS MEAN
✪ Frommer's Favorites

Our favorite places and experiences—outstanding for quality, value, or both.

The following abbreviations are used for credit cards:

AE	American Express	EU	Eurocard
CB	Carte Blanche	JCB	Japan Credit Bank
DC	Diners Club	MC	MasterCard
DISC	Discover	V	Visa
ER	enRoute		

FIND FROMMER'S ONLINE

Arthur Frommer's Budget Travel Online (**www.frommers.com**) offers more than 6,000 pages of up-to-the-minute travel information—including the latest bargains and candid, personal articles updated daily by Arthur Frommer himself. No other Web site offers such comprehensive and timely coverage of the world of travel.

Introducing Las Vegas

*A*s often as you might have seen it on TV or in a movie, there is nothing that prepares you for that first sight of Las Vegas. The skyline is hyperreality, a mélange of the Statue of Liberty, a giant lion, a pyramid and a Sphinx, and preternaturally glittering buildings. At night, it's so bright you can actually get disoriented—and suffer from a sensory overload that can reduce you to hapless tears or fits of giggles. And that's without setting foot inside a casino, where the shouts from the craps tables, the crash of coins from the slots, and general roar combine into either the greatest adrenaline rush of your life or the eleventh pit of hell.

Las Vegas is a true original; there is nothing like it in America or arguably the world. In other cities, hotels are built near the major attractions. Here, the hotels are the major attractions. For that matter, what other city has a skyline made up almost entirely of buildings from other cities' skylines? Las Vegas can be whatever a visitor wants, and for a few days, a visitor can be whatever he or she wants. Just be prepared to leave all touchstones with reality behind. Here you will rise at noon and gorge on endless amounts of rich food at 3am. You will watch your money grow or (more probably) shrink. You will watch a volcano explode and pirates fight the British. And after a while, it will all seem pretty normal. This is not a cultural vacation, okay? Save the thoughts of museums and historical sights for the real New York, Egypt, Paris, and Venice. Vegas is about fun. Go have some. Go have too much. It won't be hard.

The result of all this is that once you go to Vegas, you will want to come back again, if only to make sure you didn't dream it all. Yes, it's noisy and chaotic. Yes, it's gotten more and more like Disneyland for adults. Yes, it's a shrine to greed and the love of filthy lucre. Yes, there is little ambience and even less "culture." Yes, someone lacking self-discipline can come to great grief. But in its own way, Vegas is every bit as amazing as the nearby Grand Canyon, and every bit as much a must-see. It's one of the Seven Wonders of the Artificial World. And everyone should experience it at least once—you might find yourself coming back for more.

1 Frommer's Favorite Las Vegas Experiences

- **A Stroll on the Strip After Dark.** You haven't really seen Las Vegas until you've seen it at night. This neon wonderland is the world's greatest sound-and-light show. Begin at the Luxor and work your way down past the incredible New York New York. If your strength holds out, you will end at Circus Circus, where live acrobat acts take place overhead while you gamble. Make plenty of stops en route to take in the ship battle at Treasure Island, see the Mirage volcano erupt, and, most of all, marvel at the choreographed water fountain ballet at Bellagio.

- **Casino-Hopping on the Strip.** The interior of each lavish new hotel-casino is more outrageous and giggle-inducing than the last. Just when you think they can't possibly top themselves, they do. From Venice to ancient Egypt, from a rain forest to a pirate's lair, from King Arthur's castle to New York City, it is still all, totally, completely, and uniquely Las Vegas. See chapter 7 for our reviews.

- **The Penny Slots at the Gold Spike.** Where even the most budget-conscious traveler can gamble for hours. See chapter 7.

- **A Creative Adventures Tour.** Char Cruze of **Creative Adventures** (☎ **702/361-5565**) provides personalized tours unlike anything offered by a commercial tour company, full of riveting stories and incredible facts about both natural and artificial local wonders.

- **A Dinner Show at Caesars Magical Empire.** A solid dinner plus hours of entertainment, including your own personal magic show, make this one of the best values in Vegas, and a heck of a good time. See "Las Vegas Attractions" in chapter 6.

- **Buffets.** They may no longer be the very best of bargains, as the cheaper ones do not provide food as good as the more pricey ones, but there is something about the endless mounds of food that just screams "Vegas" to us. We've covered the best in chapter 5.

- **Cirque du Soleil's O and Mystère.** You haven't really seen Cirque du Soleil until you've seen it in a showroom equipped with state-of-the-art sound-and-lighting systems, and a seemingly infinite budget for sets, costumes, and high-tech special effects. It's an enchantment. See chapter 9.

- **An Evening in Glitter Gulch.** Set aside an evening to tour the Downtown hotels and take in the overhead light show of the Fremont Street Experience. Unlike the lengthy and exhausting

---

Favorite Vegas Movies from the Former Mayor of Las Vegas

Jan Laverty was the mayor of Las Vegas until 1999.

- *Ocean's Eleven*
- *Viva Las Vegas*

(10 Other Vegas Movies the Mayor Didn't Pick & Possible Reasons Why)

- *Leaving Las Vegas.* Alcoholics and hookers are not good role models.
- *One from the Heart.* Shot on a soundstage rather than in Las Vegas.
- *Vegas Vacation.* Griswald family not typical Vegas tourists.
- *Casino.* Puts the squeeze on heads rather than on wallets.
- *They Came to Rob Las Vegas.* The title says it all.
- *The Electric Horseman.* Robert Redford successfully steals valuable horse from casino.
- *Indecent Proposal.* Robert Redford successfully wins a million dollars from casino.
- *Fear and Loathing in Las Vegas.* Bad Craziness not the kind of image the Tourist Commission wishes to promote.
- *Showgirls.* Need we say more?
- *Honeymoon in Vegas.* Beats us. Who doesn't love Flying Elvii?

Strip, you can hit 17 casinos in about 5 minutes. See chapters 7 and 9.

- **The Liberace Museum.** It's not the Smithsonian, but then again, the Smithsonian doesn't have rhinestones like these. Nowhere else but here. See "Las Vegas Attractions" in chapter 6.
- **Your Favorite Headliners.** As soon as you arrive in town, pick up a show guide and see who's playing during your stay. For the top showrooms, see chapter 9.
- **The Grand Canal Shops at the Venetian and the Shopping Forum at Caesars Palace.** Take what Napoléon called "the greatest drawing room in Europe," replicate it and add shops, and you've got the Venetian shopping experience—St. Mark's Square, canals, gondolas, and all. Then there is Caesars' arcade replicating an ancient Roman streetscape, with classical piazzas

and opulent fountains. Don't miss the scary Audio-Animatronic statues as they come to glorious, cheesy life. See "Hotel Shopping Arcades" in chapter 8.

- **The Dolphins at the Mirage.** Actually, a most un-Vegas experience. Zone out as you watch these gorgeous mammals frolic in their cool blue pool. If you are really lucky, they will play ball with you. See "Las Vegas Attractions" in chapter 6.

Planning a Trip to Las Vegas

*B*efore any trip, you need to do a bit of advance planning. When should I go? Should I take a package deal or make my own hotel and airline reservations? Will there be a major convention in town during my visit? We'll answer these and other questions for you in this chapter, but you might want to read through the sightseeing and excursions in chapter 6 for some ideas on how to spend your time if you tire of gambling.

1 Visitor Information

For advance information, call or write the **Las Vegas Convention and Visitors Authority,** 3150 Paradise Rd., Las Vegas, NV 89109 (☎ **800/332-5333** or 702/892-0711; www.lasvegas24hours.com). They can send you a comprehensive packet of brochures, a map, a show guide, an events calendar, and an attractions list; help you find a hotel that meets your specifications (and even make reservations); and tell you if a major convention is scheduled during the time you would like to visit Las Vegas. Or stop by when you're in town. They're open Monday to Friday 7am to 5pm and Saturday and Sunday 8:30am to 5pm.

Another excellent information source is the **Las Vegas Chamber of Commerce,** 711 E. Desert Inn Rd., Las Vegas, NV 89109 (☎ **702/735-1616**). Ask them to send you their *Visitor's Guide,* which contains extensive information about accommodations, attractions, excursions, children's activities, and more. They can answer all your Las Vegas questions, including those about weddings and divorces. They're open Monday to Friday 8:30am to 5pm.

And for information on all of Nevada, including Las Vegas, contact the **Nevada Commission on Tourism** (☎ **800/638-2328**). They have a comprehensive information packet on Nevada.

If you're surfing the Net, you can get information about Las Vegas from these Web sites:

- The **"Official" Las Vegas Leisure Guide and Resource Directory:** www.pcap.com
- **Las Vegas Hack Attack** is written by area taxi drivers who "know all the inside scoops": www.lasvegastaxi.com
- **Las Vegas Online:** www.lvol.com
- *Las Vegas Weekly,* an online version of the weekly alternative magazine (formerly known as *Scope*): www.scopemag.com
- *Las Vegas Review Journal* is the largest paper in town: www. lvrj.com
- *What's On Magazine,* the local tourist paper: www. whats-on.com
- *Vegas 4 Visitors* is an opinionated Web site with reviews for tourists: www.vegas4visitors.com

2   When to Go

Since most of a Las Vegas vacation is usually spent indoors, you can have a good time here year-round. The most pleasant seasons are spring and fall, especially if you want to experience the great outdoors. Weekdays are slightly less crowded than weekends. Holidays are always a mob scene and come accompanied by high hotel prices. Hotel prices also skyrocket when big conventions and special events are taking place. The slowest times of the year are June and July, the week before Christmas, and the week after New Year's. If a major convention is to be held during your trip, you might want to change your date.

One thing you'll hear again and again is that even though Las Vegas gets very hot, the dry desert heat is not unbearable. This is true. Generally, the humidity averages a low 22%, and even on very hot days there's apt to be a breeze. Also, except on the hottest summer days, there's relief at night when temperatures often drop as much as 20°. But it can also get quite cold, especially in the winter, when at night it can drop to 30°F and lower. The breeze can also become a cold, biting, strong wind of up to 40 miles per hour and more. If you aren't traveling in the height of summer, bring a wrap. Also, remember your sunscreen and hat—even if it's not all that hot, you can burn very easily and very fast. (You should see all the lobster-red people in the casinos at night.)

Las Vegas's Average Temperatures (°F)

	Jan	Feb	Mar	Apr	May	June	July	Aug	Sept	Oct	Nov	Dec
Average	44	50	57	66	74	84	91	88	81	67	54	47
Avg. High	55	62	69	79	88	99	105	103	96	82	67	58
Avg. Low	33	39	44	53	60	68	76	74	65	53	41	36

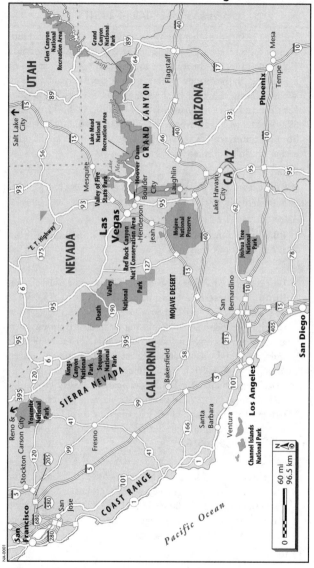

LAS VEGAS CALENDAR OF EVENTS

You may be surprised that Las Vegas does not offer as many annual events as most tourist cities. The reason is Las Vegas's very raison d'être: the gaming industry. This town wants its visitors spending their money in the casinos, not off at Renaissance fairs and parades. When in town, check the local paper and call the **Las Vegas Convention and Visitors Authority** (☎ **800/332-5333** or 702/ 892-0711), **Las Vegas Events** (☎ **702/731-2115**), or the **Chamber of Commerce** (☎ **702/735-1616**) to find out about other events scheduled during your visit.

January
- **PBA Classic.** The **Showboat Hotel,** 2800 Fremont St. (☎ **800/ 826-2800**), hosts this major bowling tournament every January.

March
- **PBA Invitational.** Another major annual bowling tournament, also at the Showboat Hotel.

April
- **World Series of Poker.** This famed 21-day event takes place at **Binion's Horseshoe Casino,** 128 Fremont St. (☎ **702/ 382-1600**), in late April and early May, with high-stakes gamblers and show-biz personalities competing for six-figure purses. There are daily events with entry stakes ranging from $125 to $5,000. To enter the World Championship Event (purse $1 million), players must put up $10,000. It costs nothing to go watch the action.
- **TruGreen-ChemLawn Las Vegas Senior Classic.** This 4-day event in mid- to late April or early May takes place at the **Tournament Players Club (TPC),** The Canyons, 9851 Canyon Run Dr., in nearby Summerlin. For details and driving information, call ☎ **702/382-6616.**

September
- **Oktoberfest.** This boisterous autumn holiday is celebrated from mid-September through the end of October at the Mount Charleston Resort (☎ **800/955-1314** or 702/872-5408) with music, folk dancers, sing-alongs around a roaring fire, special decorations, and Bavarian cookouts.

October
- **PGA Tour Las Vegas Invitational.** This 5-day championship event, played on three local courses, is televised by ESPN. For details, call ☎ **702/382-6616.**

Major Convention Dates for 2000

Listed below are Las Vegas's major annual conventions with projected attendance figures for 2000.

Consumer Electronics Show
Jan 6–9   100,000

Men's Apparel Guild in California (MAGIC)
Feb 2–7   90,000

Western Shoe Associates
Feb 4–7   30,000

Associated Surplus Dealers
Feb 27–Mar 2   32,000

National Association of Broadcasters (NAB)
Apr 10–13   115,000

Networld/Interop
May 11–15   60,000

Western Shoe Associates
Aug 8–11   30,000

Men's Apparel Guild in California (MAGIC)
Aug 29–31   90,000

Professional Golfers Association
Sept 11–13   36,000

National Mining Convention
Oct 9–12   75,000

Softbank Comdex
Nov 13–17   225,000

December
- **National Finals Rodeo.** This is the Super Bowl of rodeos, attended by close to 170,000 people each year. The top 15 male rodeo stars compete in six different events: calf roping, steer wrestling, bull riding, team roping, saddle bronco riding, and bareback riding. And the top 15 women compete in barrel racing. An all-around "Cowboy of the Year" is chosen. In connection with this event, hotels book country stars in their showrooms, and there's a cowboy shopping spree—the NFR Cowboy Christmas Gift Show, a trade show for western gear—at Cashman Field.

The NFR runs for 10 days during the first 2 weeks of December at the 17,000-seat Thomas and Mack Center of the University of Nevada–Las Vegas (UNLV). Order tickets as far in advance as possible (☎ **702/895-3900**).

- **Las Vegas Bowl Week.** A championship football event in mid-December pits the winners of the Mid-American Conference against the winners of the Big West Conference. The action takes place at the 32,000-seat Sam Boyd Stadium. Call ☎ **702/895-3900** for ticket information.

- **Western Athletic Conference (WAC) Football Championship.** This collegiate championship event takes place the first week in December. Call ☎ **792/731-5595** for ticket information. Ticket prices range from $15 to $100.

- **New Year's Eve.** This is a biggie (reserve your hotel room early). Downtown, Fremont Street is closed to traffic between Third and Main streets, and there's a big block party with two dramatic countdowns to midnight (the first is at 9pm, midnight on the East Coast). Of course, there are fireworks. Naturally, New Year's Eve 1999 promises to be a blowout like never before. Act and plan accordingly (though by the time you read this, all hotel rooms may be gone anyway).

3 Tips for Travelers with Special Needs

For Travelers with Disabilities   Las Vegas is fairly well equipped for the disabled, with virtually every hotel having handicapped rooms, ramps, and other requirements. On the other hand, the distance between each hotel (particularly on the Strip) makes a vehicle of some sort virtually mandatory for most of the disabled. Additionally, the casinos can be quite difficult to maneuver in, particularly for a guest with a wheelchair, since they are crowded, and the machines and tables are often laid out close together, with chairs and such further blocking easy access.

While each hotel should be able to give you an idea of how accessible it is, consider also writing or calling the **Independent Living Program,** 6039 Eldora, Suite F, Las Vegas, NV 89146 (☎ **702/889-4216**). They can recommend hotels and restaurants that meet your needs, help you find a personal attendant, advise about transportation, and answer all questions.

In addition, the **Nevada Commission on Tourism** (☎ **800/638-2328**) offers a free accommodations guide to Las Vegas hotels that includes access information.

For Gay & Lesbian Travelers The **Las Vegas Bugle,** a biweekly magazine serving the gay community, provides information about bars, workshops, local politics, support groups, shops, events, and more. A subscription costs $20 for 12 issues. For details call ☎ **702/369-6260.** See also listings for gay bars in chapter 9. Check out **Gay Vegas** at **www.gayvegas.com,** which has helpful advice on lodging, restaurants, and nightlife.

For Seniors Don't be shy about asking for discounts, but always carry some kind of identification, such as a driver's license, that shows your date of birth. Also, mention the fact that you're a senior citizen when you first make your travel reservations.

Members of the **American Association of Retired Persons (AARP),** 601 E St. NW, Washington, DC 20049 (☎ **800/424-3410** or 202/434-2277), get discounts not only on hotels but on airfares and car rentals, too. AARP offers members a wide range of special benefits, including *Modern Maturity* magazine and a monthly newsletter.

For Families Las Vegas in the '90s is discussed in the "Especially for Kids" suggestions in chapter 6.

Children under 12, and in many cases even older, stay free in their parents' rooms in most hotels. Look for establishments that have pools and other recreational facilities (see "Family-Friendly Hotels" in chapter 4).

For Women Las Vegas, thanks to the crowds, is as safe as any other big city for a woman traveling alone. Women on their own should take the usual precautions, and should be wary of hustlers or drunken businessmen who may mistake them for "working girls." Many of the big hotels (all Mirage hotels, for example) have security guards stationed at the elevators at night to prevent anyone other than guests from going up to the room floors. *Always* double lock your door and deadbolt it to prevent intruders from entering.

4 Getting There

BY AIR
THE MAJOR AIRLINES

The following airlines have regularly scheduled flights into Las Vegas (some of these are regional carriers, so they may not all fly from your point of origin): **Air Canada** (☎ 800/776-3000), **Alaska Airlines** (☎ 800/426-0333), **America West** (☎ 800/235-9292), **American/American Eagle** (☎ 800/433-7300), **American Trans Air** (☎ 800/543-3708), **Canadian International** (☎ 800/426-7000),

Condor (☎ 800/524-6975), **Continental** (☎ 800/525-0280), **Delta/Skywest** (☎ 800/221-1212), **Frontier** (☎ 800/432-1359), **Hawaiian** (☎ 800/367-5320), **Kiwi** (☎ 800/538-5494), **Midway** (☎ 888/226-4392), **Midwest Express** (☎ 800/452-2022), **Northwest** (☎ 800/225-2525), **Reno Air** (☎ 800/736-6247), **Southwest** (☎ 800/435-9792), **Sun Country** (☎ 800/359-6786), **TWA** (☎ 800/221-2000), **United** (☎ 800/241-6522), **US Airways** (☎ 800/428-4322), and **Western Pacific** (☎ 800/930-3030).

The newest low-cost airline on the Las Vegas scene, **National Airlines** (☎ 888/757-5387), debuted in 1999 and has its hub at McCarran Airport. It offers nonstop service to several major U.S. cities and offers free unlimited stopovers in Vegas on its transcontinental flights.

THE LAS VEGAS AIRPORT

Las Vegas is served by **McCarran International Airport,** 5757 Wayne Newton Blvd. (☎ **702/261-5743;** TDD 702/261-3111; www.mccarren.com). It's just a few minutes' drive from the southern end of the Strip. This big, modern airport—with a brand-new $500 million dollar expansion—is rather unique in that it includes a casino area with more than 1,000 slot machines. Although these are reputed to offer lower paybacks than hotel casinos (the airport has a captive audience and doesn't need to lure repeat customers), it's hard to resist throwing in a few quarters while waiting for luggage to arrive. **Bell Trans** (☎ **702/739-7990** or fax 702/384-2283) runs 20-passenger minibuses daily between the airport and all major Las Vegas hotels and motels almost around the clock (4:30am to 2am). There are several other companies that run similar ventures—just stand outside on the curb and one will be flagged down for you. Buses from the airport leave about every 10 minutes. For departure from your hotel, call at least 2 hours in advance (though often you can just flag one down outside any major hotel). The cost is $3.50 per person each way to Strip and Convention Center area hotels, $4.75 to Downtown properties (any place north of the Sahara Hotel and west of I-15).

Even less expensive are **Citizen's Area Transit (CAT)** buses (☎ **702/CAT-RIDE**). The no. 108 bus departs from the airport and will take you to the Stratosphere, where you can transfer to the 301, which stops close to most Strip and Convention Center area hotels. The no. 109 bus goes from the airport to the Downtown Transportation Center at Casino Center Boulevard and Stewart

Driving Distances to Las Vegas (in miles)

Chicago	1,766	New York City	2,564
Dallas	1,230	Phoenix	286
Denver	759	Salt Lake City	421
Los Angeles	269	San Francisco	586

Avenue. The fare is $1.50, 50¢ for seniors and children. *Note:* If you have heavy luggage, you should know that you might have a long walk from the bus stop to your door (even if it's right in front of your hotel).

All of the major car-rental companies are represented in Las Vegas, if you choose to rent one while you are in town. For a list of agencies and more information on getting a good deal on a rental, see "Getting Around by Car" in chapter 3.

BY CAR

The main highway connecting Las Vegas with the rest of the country is I-15; it links Montana, Idaho, and Utah with southern California. The drive from Los Angeles is quite popular, and thanks to the narrow two-lane highway, can get very crowded on Friday and Sunday afternoons with hopeful weekend gamblers making their way to and from Vegas. (By the way, as soon as you cross the state line, there are three casinos ready to handle your immediate gambling needs, with two more about 20 minutes up the road, 30 miles before you get to Las Vegas.)

From the East Coast, take I-70 or I-80 west to Kingman, Arizona, and then U.S. 93 north to Downtown Las Vegas (Fremont Street). From the south, take I-10 west to Phoenix and then U.S. 93 north to Las Vegas. From San Francisco, take I-80 east to Reno and then U.S. 95 south to Las Vegas. If you're driving to Las Vegas, be sure to read the driving precautions in "Getting Around" in chapter 3.

PACKAGE DEALS

For popular destinations like Las Vegas, packages are a smart way to go because they save you a lot of money. In many cases, a package that includes airfare, hotel, and transportation to and from the airport will cost you less than just the hotel alone would have, had you booked it yourself. That's because packages are sold in bulk to tour operators—who resell them to the public at a cost that drastically undercuts standard rates.

whether you travel midweek or on the weekend, and other factors. Since even an advance-purchase round-trip fare between New York and Las Vegas can easily be $100 or $200 more than a package deal, it seems almost insane not to book one.

FINDING A PACKAGE DEAL

The best place to start your search for a package is the travel section of your local Sunday newspaper. Other package dealers include **Liberty Travel** (☎ **888/271-1584** to be connected with the agent closest to you; www.libertytravel.com), one of the biggest packagers in the Northeast, and **American Express Vacations** (☎ **800/241-1700;** www.leisureweb.com) Check out its **Last Minute Travel Bargains** site, offered in conjunction with **Continental Airlines** (www6.americanexpress.com/travel/lastminutetravel/default.asp), with deeply discounted vacation packages and reduced airline fares. **Northwest Airlines** (www.nwa.com), offers a similar service. Posted on Northwest's Web site every Wednesday, its **Cyber Saver Bargain Alerts** offer special hotel rates, package deals, and discounted airline fares.

Another good resource is the airlines themselves, which often package their flights together with accommodations. **National Airlines** (☎ 888/757-5387), a new low-cost carrier based in Las Vegas, is partially backed by Harrah's Entertainment, Inc. Although vacation packages for 2000 had not been set at press time, National will offer discount packages that include stays at either Harrah's or the Rio Suites.

At press time, a **Delta Dream Vacation** (☎ 800/872-7786) package leaving from New York could cost as little as $362 per person based on double occupancy, including round-trip coach air transportation, 2 nights at your choice of several major casino hotels, a rental car for 24 hours, airport transfers, and bonus discounts and admissions. **Southwest Airlines** (☎ 800/423-5683) was offering round-trip airfare from Los Angeles with 2 nights at several different hotels complete with ground transportation; per person based on double occupancy.

Other airlines that offer some excellent packages to Las Vegas include **American Airlines FlyAway Vacations** (☎ 800/321-2121), **America West Vacations** (☎ 800/442-5013), and **US Airways Vacations** (☎ 800/455-0123).

The biggest hotel chains, casinos, and resorts also offer package deals. If you already know where you want to stay, call the resort itself and ask if they can offer land/air packages.

Getting to Know Las Vegas

*L*ocated in the southernmost precincts of a wide, pancake-flat valley, Las Vegas is the biggest city in the state of Nevada. Treeless mountains form a scenic backdrop to hotels awash in neon glitter. For tourism purposes, the city is quite compact.

1 Orientation

VISITOR INFORMATION

All major Las Vegas hotels provide comprehensive tourist information at their reception and/or sightseeing and show desks. Other good information sources are: the **Las Vegas Convention and Visitors Authority,** 3150 Paradise Rd., Las Vegas, NV 89109 (☎ **800/332-5333** or 702/892-0711; www.lasvegas24hours.com), open Monday to Friday 8am to 6pm, Saturday and Sunday 8am to 5pm; the **Las Vegas Chamber of Commerce,** 711 E. Desert Inn Rd., Las Vegas, NV 89109 (☎ **702/735-1616**), open Monday to Friday 8am to 5pm; and, for information on all of Nevada, including Las Vegas, the **Nevada Commission on Tourism** (☎ **800/638-2328**), open 24 hours.

FOR TROUBLED TRAVELERS

The **Traveler's Aid Society** is a social-service organization geared to helping travelers in difficult straits. Their services might include reuniting families separated while traveling, feeding people stranded without cash, or even emotional counseling. If you're in trouble, seek them out. In Las Vegas there is a Traveler's Aid office at McCarran International Airport (☎ **702/798-1742**). It's open daily 8am to 5pm. Similar services are provided by **Help of Southern Nevada,** 953-35B E. Sahara Ave. (Suite 208), at Maryland Parkway in the Commercial Center (☎ **702/369-4357**). Hours are Monday to Friday 8am to 4pm.

CITY LAYOUT

There are two main areas of Las Vegas: the **Strip** and **Downtown.** For many people, that's all there is to Las Vegas. But there is actually more to the town than that; maybe not as glitzy and glamorous—okay, definitely not—but you will find still more casino action on Paradise Road and in east Las Vegas, mainstream and alternative culture shopping on Maryland Parkway, and different restaurant choices all over the city. Confining yourself to the Strip and Downtown is fine for the first-time visitor, but repeat customers (and you will be) should get out there and explore. Las Vegas Boulevard South (the Strip) is Ground Zero for addresses; anything crossing it will start with 1 East and 1 West (and go up from there) at that point.

THE STRIP

The Strip is probably the most famous 3½-mile stretch of highway in the nation. Officially Las Vegas Boulevard South, it contains most of the top hotels in town and offers almost all of the major showroom entertainment. We divide the Strip into three sections: **South Strip** can be roughly defined as the portion of the Strip south of Harmon Avenue, including the MGM Grand, the Monte Carlo, New York New York, and the Luxor hotels. **Mid-Strip** is a long stretch of the street between Harmon Avenue and Spring Mountain Road, including Caesars, the Mirage and Treasure Island, Bally's, the Flamingo Hilton, and Harrah's. **North Strip** stretches north from Stardust Road all the way to the Stratosphere Tower and includes the Stardust, Sahara, Riviera, Desert Inn, and Circus Circus. It's on the Strip where first-time visitors will, and probably should, spend the bulk of their time. If mobility is a problem, then it's probably the South and Mid-Strip locations that are the best bets.

EAST OF THE STRIP/CONVENTION CENTER

This area has grown up around the Las Vegas Convention Center. Las Vegas is one of the nation's top convention cities, attracting more than 2.9 million conventioneers each year. The major hotel in this section is the Las Vegas Hilton, but in recent years Marriott has built Residence Inn and Courtyard properties here, and the Hard Rock Hotel has opened. You'll find many excellent smaller hotels and motels southward along Paradise Road. All of these offer close proximity to the Strip.

DOWNTOWN

Also known as **"Glitter Gulch"** (narrower streets make the neon seem brighter), downtown Las Vegas, which is centered on Fremont Street between Main and 9th streets, was the first section of the city to develop hotels and casinos. With the exception of the Golden

Las Vegas at a Glance

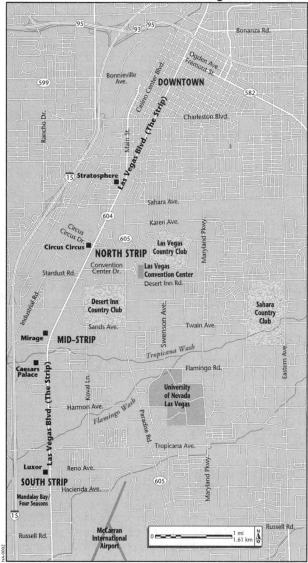

Nugget, which looks like it belongs in Monte Carlo, this area has traditionally been more casual than the Strip. But with the advent of the **Fremont Street Experience** (see chapter 6 for details), Downtown is experiencing a revitalization. The area is clean, the crowds low-key and friendly, and the light show overhead as silly as anything on the Strip. Don't overlook it. Las Vegas Boulevard runs all the way into Fremont Street Downtown (about a 5-minute drive from the Stratosphere if traffic is good).

BETWEEN THE STRIP & DOWNTOWN

The area between the Strip and Downtown is a seedy stretch dotted with tacky wedding chapels, bail-bond operations, pawnshops, and cheap motels.

However, the area known as the **Gateway District** (roughly north and south of Charleston Boulevard to the west of Las Vegas Boulevard South) is slowly but surely gaining a name for itself as an actual artists' colony. Studios, small cafes, and other signs of life are springing up, and it is hoped this movement will last.

2 Getting Around

It shouldn't be too hard to navigate your way around. For the most part, you won't have to.

BY CAR

We highly recommend a rental car for Vegas tourists. The Strip is generally too spread out for walking, Downtown is too far away for a cheap cab ride, and public transportation is ineffective at best. Plus, further visits call for exploration in still more parts of the city, and a car brings freedom. You should note that places with addresses some 60 blocks east or west from the Strip are actually less than a 10-minute drive—provided there is no traffic. However, if you plan to confine yourself to one part of the Strip (or one cruise down to it) or to Downtown, your feet will suffice.

Note: If you can, avoid driving during peak rush hours, especially if you have to make a show curtain. The city's growing population means a proportionate increase in the number of cars, and so traffic is getting worse, and it's harder and harder to get around town with any certain swiftness. Parking is usually a pleasure, since all casino hotels offer valet service. That means that for a mere $1 tip you can park right at the door (though the valet usually fills up on busy nights). Furthermore, though bus tours are available to nearby

Alert

The area northeast of Harmon and Koval has had increased gang activity of late and should be avoided or at least approached with caution.

---

attractions, a car lets you explore at your own pace rather than according to a tour schedule.

RENTING A CAR   All of the major car-rental companies are represented in Las Vegas. We like **Allstate** (☎ **800/634-6186** or 702/736-6148), the least expensive of the airport-based car-rental agencies. Besides the usual mix, their fleet of more than 1,500 vehicles includes an inventory of 15 passenger vans, four-wheel-drives, Jeeps, minivans, sports cars, and convertibles. We've found this local family-owned company (the largest independent operator in Las Vegas) friendly and competent, with an invariably charming staff at the airport. They're open 24 hours. And they've agreed to offer our readers a **20% discount off regular rental rates** at any Allstate location (just show the agent your copy of this book).

National companies with outlets in Las Vegas include **Alamo** (☎ 800/327-9633), **Avis** (☎ 800/367-2847), **Budget** (☎ 800/922-2899), **Dollar** (☎ 800/842-2054), **Enterprise** (☎ 800/325-8007), **Hertz** (☎ 800/654-3131), **National** (☎ 800/227-7368), and **Thrifty** (☎ 800/367-2277).

DRIVING SAFETY   Since driving on the outskirts of Las Vegas—for example, coming from California—involves desert driving, you must take certain precautions. It's a good idea to check your tires, water, and oil before leaving. Take at least 5 gallons of water in a clean container that can be used for either drinking or the radiator. Pay attention to road signs that suggest when to turn off your car's air conditioner. And don't push your luck with gas—it may be 35 miles, or more, between stations. If your car overheats, do not remove the radiator cap until the engine has cooled, and then remove it very slowly. Add water to within an inch of the top of the radiator.

BY TAXI

Since cabs line up in front of all major hotels, an easy way to get around town is by taxi. Cabs charge $2.20 at the meter drop and 30¢ for each additional one-fifth of a mile. A taxi from the airport to the Strip will run you $8 to $12, from the airport to Downtown $15 to $18, and between the Strip and Downtown about $7 to $10. You can often save money by sharing a cab with someone going to the same destination (up to five people can ride for the same fare).

If you want to call a taxi, any of the following companies can provide one: **Desert Cab Company** (☎ 702/376-2688), **Whittlesea Blue Cab** (☎ 702/384-6111), and **Yellow/Checker Cab/Star Company** (☎ 702/873-2000).

FAST FACTS: Las Vegas

Ambulances   See "Emergencies," below.

Area Code   **702.**

Baby-sitters   Contact **Around the Clock Child Care** (☎ 800/ 798-6768 or 702/365-1040). In business since 1985, this reputable company clears its sitters with the health department, the sheriff, and the FBI, and carefully screens references. Charges are $40 for 4 hours for one or two children, $8 for each additional hour, with surcharges for additional children and on holidays. Sitters are on call 7 days a week, 24 hours a day, and they will come to your hotel. Call at least 2 hours in advance.

Banks   Banks are generally open 9 or 10am to 5pm and sometimes 6pm, and most have Saturday hours. See also "Cash & Credit," below.

Car Rentals   See "Getting Around," above.

Cash & Credit   It's extremely easy, too easy, to obtain cash in Las Vegas. Most casino cashiers will cash personal checks and can exchange foreign currency, and just about every casino has an ATM, or a machine that will provide cash on a wide variety of credit cards.

Climate   See "When to Go" in chapter 2. For local weather information call ☎ **702/248-4800.**

Conventions   Las Vegas is one of America's top convention destinations. Much of the action takes place at the **Las Vegas Convention Center,** 3150 Paradise Rd., Las Vegas, NV 89109 (☎ **702/892-0711**). The largest single-level convention center in the world, its 1.3 million square feet includes 89 meeting rooms. And this immense facility is augmented by the **Cashman Field Center,** 850 Las Vegas Blvd. N., Las Vegas, NV 89101 (☎ **702/**

386-7100). Under the same auspices, Cashman provides another 98,100 square feet of convention space.

Dentists & Doctors   Hotels usually have lists of dentists and doctors should you need one. In addition, they are listed in the Centel Yellow Pages.

For dentist referrals you can also call the **Clark County Dental Society** (☎ **702/255-7873**), weekdays 9am to noon and 1 to 5pm; when the office is closed, a recording will tell you who to call for emergency service.

For physician referrals call **Desert Springs Hospital** (☎ **800/ 842-5439** or 702/733-6875). Hours are Monday to Friday 8am to 5pm.

Drugstores   **Sav-on** is a large 24-hour drugstore and pharmacy close to the Strip at 1360 E. Flamingo Rd., at Maryland Parkway (☎ **702/731-5373** for the pharmacy, 702/737-0595 for general merchandise). **White Cross Drugs,** 1700 Las Vegas Blvd. S. (☎ **702/382-1733**), open daily 7am to 1am, will make pharmacy deliveries to your hotel during the day.

Dry Cleaners   Things spill, and silk stains. When in need, come to **Steiner Cleaners,** 1131 E. Tropicana, corner of Maryland Parkway, in the Vons Shopping Center (☎ **702/736-7474**), open Monday to Friday 7am to 6:30pm, Saturday 8am to 6pm. Not only did they clean all the costumes for the movie *Casino,* but they were Liberace's personal dry cleaner for years.

Emergencies   Dial ☎ **911** to contact the police or fire departments or to call an ambulance.

Emergency services are available 24 hours a day at **University Medical Center,** 1800 W. Charleston Blvd., at Shadow Lane (☎ **702/383-2661**); the emergency room entrance is on the corner of Hastings and Rose streets. **Sunrise Hospital and Medical Center,** 3186 Maryland Pkwy., between Desert Inn Road and Sahara Avenue (☎ **702/731-8080**), also has a 24-hour emergency room. For more minor problems, if you are on the Strip, the Imperial Palace has a 24-hour urgent care facility, the **Resorts Medical Center,** an independently run facility on the 8th floor, with doctors and X-ray machines; it's located at 3535 Las Vegas Blvd. S., between the Sands and Flamingo (☎ **702/731-3311**).

Emergency **hotlines** include the Rape Crisis Center (☎ **702/ 366-1640**), Suicide Prevention (☎ **702/731-2990**), and Poison Emergencies (☎ **800/446-6179**).

Highway Conditions   For recorded information, call ☎ **702/ 486-3116.**

Libraries   The largest in town is the **Clark County Library branch** at 1401 Flamingo Rd., at Escondido Street, on the southeast corner (☎ **702/733-7810**). Hours are Monday to Thursday 9am to 9pm, Friday and Saturday 9am to 5pm, Sunday 1 to 5pm.

Liquor & Gambling Laws   You must be 21 to drink or gamble. There are no closing hours in Las Vegas for the sale or consumption of alcohol, even on Sunday.

Parking   Valet parking is one of the great pleasures of Las Vegas and well worth the dollar tip (given when the car is returned) to save walking a city block from the far reaches of a hotel parking lot, particularly when the temperature is over 100°. Another summer plus: The valet will turn on your air-conditioning so that you don't have to get in an "oven on wheels."

Police   For nonemergencies call ☎ **702/795-3111.** For emergencies call ☎ **911.**

Post Office   The most convenient post office is immediately behind the Stardust Hotel at 3100 Industrial Rd., between Sahara Avenue and Spring Mountain Road (☎ **800/297-5543**). It's open Monday to Friday 8:30am to 5pm. You can also mail letters and packages at your hotel, and there's a full-service U.S. Post Office in the Forum Shops in Caesars Palace.

Safety   In Las Vegas, vast amounts of money are always on display, and criminals find many easy marks. Don't be one of them. At gaming tables and slot machines, men should keep wallets well concealed and out of the reach of pickpockets, and women should keep handbags in plain sight (on laps). Outside casinos, popular spots for pickpockets and thieves are restaurants and outdoor shows, such as the volcano at the Mirage or at the Treasure Island pirate battle. Stay alert. Unless your hotel room has an in-room safe, check your valuables in a safety-deposit box at the front desk.

Taxes   Clark County hotel room tax is 9%, the sales tax is 7%.

Time Zone   Las Vegas is in the Pacific time zone, 3 hours earlier than the East Coast, 2 hours earlier than the Midwest. For exact local time call ☎ **702/248-4800.**

Weddings   Las Vegas is one of the easiest places in the world to tie the knot. There's no blood test or waiting period, the ceremony and license are inexpensive, chapels are open around the clock, and your honeymoon destination is right at hand. More than 101,000 marriages are performed here each year. Get a license Downtown at the Clark County Marriage License Bureau, 200 S. 3rd St., at Bridger Avenue (☎ **702/455-3156**). Open Monday to Thursday 8am to midnight, and from 8am Friday through midnight Sunday. On legal holidays they're open 24 hours. The cost of a marriage license is $35; the cost of the ceremony, another $35.

4

Accommodations

*I*f there's one thing Vegas has, it's hotels. Big hotels. Here you'll find the 10 largest hotels in the United States, if not in the world. And rooms: 120,000 rooms, to be exact—or at least exact at this writing. Every 5 minutes, or so it seems, someone is putting up a new giant hotel, or adding another 1,000 rooms to an already existing one. So finding a place to stay in Vegas should be the least of your worries. Or is it?

When a convention, a fight, or some other big event is happening—and these things are always happening—darn near all of those 120,000 rooms are going to be sold out. (Over the course of last year, the occupancy rate for hotel rooms in Las Vegas ran at about 90%.) A last-minute Vegas vacation can turn into a housing nightmare.

But, the bottom line is that with a few, sometimes subtle, differences, a hotel room is a hotel room is a hotel room. After you factor in location, price, and whether you have a pirate-loving kid, there isn't that much difference between rooms, except for perhaps size and the quality of their surprisingly similar furnishings. Price isn't even always a guideline; prices in Vegas are anything but fixed, so you will notice wild ranges (the same room can routinely go for anywhere from $60 to $250, depending on demand), and even that range is negotiable if it's a slow time (though such times are less and less common thanks to the influx of conventions).

1 Best Bets

- **Best for Conventioneers/Business Travelers:** The **Las Vegas Hilton,** 3000 Paradise Rd. (☎ **800/732-7117**), adjacent to the Las Vegas Convention Center and the setting for many on-premises conventions, offers extensive facilities along with helpful services such as a full business center.
- **Best Elegant Hotel:** Country club elegance is the keynote of the **Desert Inn Country Club Resort and Casino,** 3145 Las Vegas Blvd. S. (☎ **800/634-9606**). In its European-style casino, gaming tables are comfortably spaced; the glitzy glow of neon is

replaced by the glitter of crystal chandeliers; and the scarcity of slot and video poker machines eliminates the usual noisy jangle of coins. Extensive facilities are complemented by attentive personal service.

- **Best Luxury Resort:** Many of the new hotels are duking it out for this title, but we are throwing the vote to the **Four Seasons,** 3960 Las Vegas Blvd. S. (☎ **877/632-5200**), because their size and experience in luxury makes them the only true claimant to the throne.

- **Best Swimming Pool:** If you want lushly landscaped areas surrounding amorphously shaped pools with water fountains and slides, plus a rather festive atmosphere, head to the **Mirage,** 3400 Las Vegas Blvd. S. (☎ **800/627-6667**). Much more Vegas, however, is the **Tropicana Resort & Casino,** 3801 Las Vegas Blvd. S. (☎ **800/634-4000**), where you'll also find a swim-up bar/ blackjack table.

- **Best Health Club:** The club at the **Mirage** (see above) is probably the best equipped, offering a full complement of machines— some with individual TVs (headphones are supplied), free weights, attendants who soothe you with iced towels and drinks, a thoroughly equipped locker room, and comfortable lounges in which to rest up after your workout.

- **Best Hotel Dining/Entertainment:** Foodies will work up a good case of gout trying all new haute cuisine options at **Bellagio,** which has a branch of Le Cirque, Circo and Aqua, plus restaurants by Todd English (Olives) and Julian Serrano (Picasso).

- **Best Interior:** For totally different reasons, it's a tie between **New York New York Hotel & Casino's,** 3790 Las Vegas Blvd. S. (☎ **800/693-6763**), jaw-dropping attention to detail; the **Mirage's,** 3400 Las Vegas Blvd. S. (☎ **800/627-6667**), relaxing tropical rainforest; and the **Venetian's,** 3355 Las Vegas Blvd. S. (☎ **888/2-VENICE**), authentic re-creation of Venice, down to its architecture, detailed statues, murals, and yes, water-filled canals with gondolas.

- **Best for Families: The MGM Grand,** 3799 Las Vegas Blvd. S (☎ **800/929-1111**), is still a hit with families, despite backing away from more child-friendly details like its original Oz theme and downscaling its amusement park. Then there is also the classic: **Circus Circus Hotel/Casino,** 2880 Las Vegas Blvd. S. (☎ **800/444-CIRC**), with ongoing circus acts, a vast video-game arcade, a carnival midway, and a full amusement park.

- **Best Rooms:** On the strip, the **Venetian's** new 700-square-foot extravaganzas, with separate sitting and bedroom areas, full of all sorts of special details, win the day. Downtown, they're at the **Golden Nugget,** 129 E. Fremont St. (☎ **800/634-3454**), which look almost identical to the Mirage's rooms, though the latter are done in more earth tones, while golds are the hallmark of the former.

- **Best Bathrooms:** This one definitely is won by **Mandalay Bay,** 3950 Las Vegas Blvd. S. (☎ **877/632-7000**), whose spacious setup features copious amounts of glass and marble, plus double sinks and a deep soaking tub—it's a wonder anyone ever leaves them to go to the casino.

- **Best Casinos:** Our favorite places to gamble are anywhere we might win. But we also like the **Mirage** (lively, beautiful, and not overwhelming), **Caesars Palace** (because the cocktail waitresses are dressed in togas), **New York New York** (because of the aforementioned attention to detail; it almost makes losing fun!), and **Main Street Station,** 200 N. Main St. (☎ **800/465-0711**) (because it's about the most smoke-free casino in town, and because it's pretty).

- **Best Downtown Hotel:** It's a tie. The upscale **Golden Nugget** (see above) is exceptionally appealing in every aspect. The **Main Street Station** (see above), which has done a terrific job of renovating an older space, now evokes turn-of-the century San Francisco, with great Victorian details everywhere, solidly good restaurants, and surprisingly nice rooms for an inexpensive price.

- **Best Views:** From high-floor rooms at the **Stratosphere Las Vegas,** 2000 Las Vegas Blvd. S. (☎ **800/99-TOWER**), you can see the entire city, while the **Four Seasons** Strip-side rooms give you the entire Las Vegas Boulevard panorama from the southernmost end.

2 South Strip

VERY EXPENSIVE

✪ **Four Seasons.** 3960 Las Vegas Blvd. S., Las Vegas, NV 89119. ☎ **877/632-5200** or 702/632-5000. Fax 702/632-5222. 424 units. AC TV TEL MINIBAR. $200–$500 standard; $400 and way up for suites. Free parking.

As various mammoth Vegas hotels attempt to position themselves as luxury resorts, insisting that service and fine cotton sheets can be done on a mass scale, very quietly a true luxury resort—in some people's eyes, *the* luxury resort—has moved in. The Four Seasons is

Reservations Services

If you get harried when you have to haggle, use a free service offered by **Reservations Plus,** 2275 A Renaissance Dr., Las Vegas, NV 89119 (☎ **800/805-9528;** fax 702/795-8767). They'll find you a hotel room in your price range that meets your specific requirements. Because they book rooms in volume, they are able to get discounted rates. Not only can they book rooms but they can arrange packages (including meals, transportation, tours, show tickets, car rentals, and other features) and group rates.

The **Las Vegas Convention and Visitors Authority** also runs a room reservations hotline (☎ **800/332-5334**) that can be helpful. They can apprise you of room availability, quote rates, contact a hotel for you, and tell you when major conventions will be in town.

For those of you hooked up to the Internet, there is a variety of online reservations systems that can help you get a room and make all the appropriate travel arrangements for you.

- **www.180096hotel.com**
- **www.lasvegashotel.com**
- **www.lasvegasreservations.com**
- **www.lasvegasrooms.com**
- **www.lvholidays.com**

A couple of words of warning: Make sure they don't try to book you into a hotel you've never heard of. Try to stick with the big names or ones listed in this book. Always get your information in writing and then make some phone calls just to confirm that you really have the reservations that they say they've made for you.

located on the top five floors of Mandalay Bay, but in many ways, it's light-years away. A separate driveway and portico entrance, plus entire registration area, sets you up immediately. This is the one fancy hotel in town where you are not greeted with the clash and clang of slots, and the general hubbub that is the soundtrack to Vegas. Inside the Four Seasons, all is calm and quiet. But it's really the best of both worlds—all you have to do is walk through a door and instantly you are in Mandalay Bay, with access to its casino and nightlife. The difference is quite shocking.

The rooms don't look like much at first—slightly bland but good taste—but when you sink down into the furniture you know their budget was much higher. The beds have feather pillows and down comforters, robes are plush, amenities really, really nice. Strip views (the most expensive rooms), being the farthest south of any hotel, are the best on the Strip, giving you the whole panorama. Service is superb, and needs anticipated so quickly, you are tempted to sink to the floor in the lobby because you know someone will have a chair under your rear before you land. Children are encouraged and spoiled. Once you factor in all the freebies (gym/spa access, pool cabanas, various other amenities), not to mention the service and the blessed peace, the difference between the Four Seasons and Bellagio in price is nothing.

Dining: There are two restaurants and two lounges, one of which serves afternoon tea.

Amenities: 24-hour room service, safe, iron and ironing board, voice mail, hair dryers, bathrobes, daily newspaper, VCRs, laundry, dry cleaning, complimentary shoe shine, turndown service, complimentary children's amenities and services, gym, concierge, business center, lounge area for late departure, banquet and meeting facilities. The Four Seasons has its own pool, and guests also have full access to Mandalay Bay's pool area.

EXPENSIVE

✪ **Mandalay Bay.** 3950 Las Vegas Blvd. S., at Hacienda. Las Vegas, NV 89119. ☎ **877/632-7000** or 702/632-7000. Fax 702/632-7119. http://www.mandalaybay.com. 3,309 units. A/C TV TEL. $99–$149 standard double; $169 and up for suites; $149 and up for House of Blues Signature Rooms. Extra person $20. AE, CB, DC, DISC, JCB, MC, V. Free self- and valet parking.

The Mandalay Bay may well prove to be our favorite new hotel. Why? Well, we love that the lobby (impossibly high ceilings, calm, gleaming with marble, and housing a large aquarium) and the other public areas really do seem more like an actual resort hotel than just a Vegas version of one. You don't have to walk through the casino to get to any of these public areas or the guest room elevators, the pool area is spiffy, and the whole thing is less overwhelming than some of the neighboring behemoths.

The rooms are perhaps the best on the Strip (king rooms are more attractive than doubles), spacious and subdued in decor. Tropical influence seems to be limited to faux leopard skin chairs by the work table, and plantation shutter doors to closets and the bathroom. King beds have large carved headboard posts and firm mattresses. The bathrooms are the crowning glory—certainly the best on the Strip and maybe the best in Vegas. Downright large,

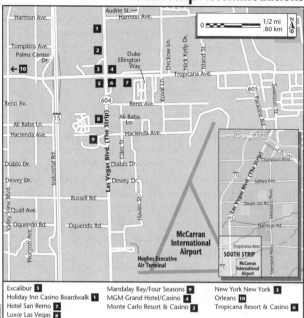

Excalibur **5**
Holiday Inn Casino Boardwalk **1**
Hotel San Remo **7**
Luxor Las Vegas **8**

Mandalay Bay/Four Seasons **9**
MGM Grand Hotel/Casino **4**
Monte Carlo Resort & Casino **2**

New York New York **3**
Orleans **10**
Tropicana Resort & Casino **6**

with impressive, slightly sunken tub, glassed-in shower, double sinks, separate water closet, fab amenities and lots of them. If only they included bathrobes.

The pool area is a major plus here—it has no less than four pools, including a touted wave pool. As of this writing, the waves couldn't be turned on full force, as the pool was too short and surfers went crashing into the concrete lip at the end. The problem may have been worked out by the time you read this, but plan instead to bob gently in miniwaves, or better still, float happily in the lazy river. Service overall is pretty good, and those pool area employees are the best in Vegas. A monorail system connects the hotel with Luxor and Excalibur.

Dining/Diversions: The restaurants in Mandalay Bay feature some of the most innovative interiors in Vegas, each one more whimsical and imaginative than the last. Even if you don't eat there, drop in and poke around. Choose from **Aureole,** the **Border Grill, Red Square, China Grill café, Trattoria del Lupo, Shanghai Lilly's, rumjungle, Raffles Café, House of Blues,** and **Zen Sum.**

Amenities: Iron and ironing board, 24-hour room service, data port, turndown on request, hair dryers, dry cleaning and laundry, concierge, boutiques, baby-sitting, business center, safe-deposit boxes, wedding chapel, salon, conference center, 12,000-seat sports and entertainment complex, health club and spa, four pools plus lazy river (boogie and surf board rental available).

✪ **MGM Grand Hotel/Casino.** 3799 Las Vegas Blvd. S., at Tropicana Ave., Las Vegas, NV 89109. ☎ **800/929-1111** or 702/891-7777. Fax 702/891-1030. www.mgmgrand.com. 5,005 units. A/C TV TEL. $59–$169 standard double; $99–$2,500 suite. Extra person $25. Children under 12 stay free in parents' room. AE, DC, DISC, MC, V. Free self- and valet parking.

The MGM Grand has recently completed one of the most amusing renovations in Vegas. When it first opened, the billion-dollar property, spread over 114 acres, had a *Wizard of Oz* theme. The outside was a shocking shade of emerald green, some door handles had "Oz" on them, rainbows were everywhere, and right in the center was a giant Animatronic reenactment of MGM's most famous movie. Outside was a theme park, which initially charged an exorbitant entry fee.

That has changed. The outside is still green, but now the MGM Grand is the City of Entertainment, which means the theme is *all* MGM movies, not just one specific film beloved by children. Gone is the Oz attraction (though it may reappear at a later date in a different, less prominent part of the hotel), replaced by a Rain Forest Cafe and Studio 54, both of which are accessed through an ornate circular domed room, full of replicated '30s glamour, glitz, and gilded statues. Obviously, this is all more appealing to adults.

The TV monitors in the lobby remain, but the area is now immediately accessible from outside. The redesign will attempt to create some more intimate corners, and has already made navigating the still immense place somewhat easier. And the staff, confirms a recent guest, couldn't be more helpful and friendly. The place still seems most popular with families, who must not mind how they are no longer openly catered to. Throughout, the theme of the City of Entertainment is repeated, as old movies are evoked in the decor (though considerable green and the odd rainbow still remain). In certain areas (like the restaurant row), the look is meant to suggest a behind-the-scenes view of a film studio back lot.

The rooms are being renovated, scheduled for completion sometime in 2000. Currently, they are decorated in four distinct motifs. Most glamorous are the Hollywood rooms furnished in two-tone wood pieces (bird's-eye maple on cherry), with gold-flecked walls (hung with prints of Humphrey Bogart, Marilyn Monroe, and Vivien Leigh as Scarlett) and gilded moldings. Oz-themed rooms still have emerald-green rugs and upholstery, silver-and-gold star-motif wallpaper, and walls are hung with paintings of Dorothy and friends. The Casablanca rooms are decorated in earth tones with shimmery fabrics and artworks that depict Moroccan scenes. And the cheerful Old South rooms feature 18th-century–style furnishings and faux-silk beige damask walls hung with paintings of Southern belles and scenes from *Gone with the Wind.* All rooms offer gorgeous marble baths.

Opening by the time you read this will be a 30,000-square-foot lion habitat with adult lions and cubs you can hold and have a photo taken with.

Dining/Diversions: MGM houses the most prestigious assemblage of dining rooms of any hotel in town. A number of cutting-edge stars in the Las Vegas culinary galaxy—the **Wolfgang Puck Café,** Emeril Lagasse's **New Orleans Fish House,** and Mark Miller's **Coyote Cafe**—along with buffet offerings and the **Rain Forest Cafe** are described in chapter 5. There are a number of other restaurants and lounges as well.

Amenities: 24-hour room service; foreign currency exchange; guest relations desk; shoe shine (in men's rooms); casino; MGM Grand Adventures Theme Park; full-service health spa and health club; full-service beauty salon; 30,000-square-foot video arcade (including virtual-reality games); carnival midway with 33 games of skill; business center; florist; shopping arcade; two wedding chapels (in the theme park); show/sports event ticket desks; car-rental desk; sightseeing/tour desks; monorail to Bally's runs 9am to 1am; a new shopping center will include high-ticket stores like DKNY.

The **MGM Grand Youth Center** is a first-rate facility for children ages 3 to 16, (☎ **702/891-3200** for details and prices).

Monte Carlo Resort & Casino. 3770 Las Vegas Blvd. S., between Flamingo Rd. and Tropicana Ave., Las Vegas, NV 89109. ☎ **800/311-8999** or 702/730-7777. Fax 702/730-7250. www.monte-carlo.com. 3,002 units. A/C TV TEL. Sun–Thurs $49–$179 double, Fri–Sat $109–$269 double; $149–$339 suite. Extra person $15. Children under 12 stay free in parents' room. AE, CB, DC, DISC, MC, V. Free self- and valet parking.

When it was built, the massive Monte Carlo was the world's seventh largest hotel. It gets somewhat overlooked by its more high-profile, more theme-intensive brethren, but guests who stay here come away most pleased with the experience. It comes off more as a European casino hotel (before Bellagio usurped that position), fronted by Corinthian colonnades, triumphal arches, splashing fountains, and allegorical (and slightly naughty) statuary, with an entranceway opening onto a bustling casino. A separate entrance in the rear of the hotel leads to a splendid marble-floored, crystal-chandeliered lobby evocative of a European grand hotel. Palladian windows behind the registration desk overlook a salient feature: the hotel's 20,000-acre pool area, a lushly landscaped miniature water park with a 4,800-foot wave pool, a surf pond, waterfalls, and a "river" for tubing.

Spacious rooms with big marble baths exude a warmly traditional European feel with rich cherrywood furnishings and vivid floral-print fabrics and carpeting. Cable TVs are equipped with hotel information channels, keno, and pay-movie options. A concierge level for VIPs is on the 32nd floor.

Dining/Diversions: The Monte Carlo's **Pub & Brewery** and **Dragon Noodle Co.** are described in chapter 5. In addition, there is now a branch of the classic Downtown French restaurant **Andre's,** reviewed in chapter 5, in the hotel.

Amenities: 24-hour room service, foreign currency exchange, shoe shine, limo rental, casino, car-rental desk, four tennis courts, sightseeing/tour/show desk, barber/beauty salon, vast swimming pool, kiddie pool, whirlpool, water attractions (see above), wedding chapel, full business center, large video-game arcade, large shopping arcade.

✪ **New York New York Hotel & Casino.** 3790 Las Vegas Blvd. S., at Tropicana Ave., Las Vegas, NV 89109. ☎ **800/693-6763** or 702/740-6969. Fax 702/740-6920. www.nynyhotelcasino.com. 2,033 units. A/C TV TEL. Sun–Thurs from $59 double, Fri–Sat from $109 double. Extra person $20. AE, CB, DC, DISC, MC, V. Free self- and valet parking.

Just when you think Las Vegas has it all and has done it all, they go and do something like this. New York New York is just plain spectacular. Even the jaded and horrified have to admit it. You can't miss the hotel; it's that little (Hah!) building on the corner of the Strip and Tropicana that looks like the New York City skyline: the Empire State Building, the Chrysler Building, the Public Library, down to the 150-foot Statue of Liberty and Ellis Island, all built to approximately one-third scale. And as if that weren't enough, they threw in a roller coaster running around the outside and into the hotel and casino itself.

And inside, it all gets better. There are details everywhere—so many, in fact, that the typical expression on the face of casino-goers

👪 Family-Friendly Hotels

As repeatedly mentioned in their individual listings, most of the hotels are backing away from being perceived as a place for families. Still, anything with a serious theme and/or outlets for kids, as the following all have, is probably better than a regular hotel.

Circus Circus Hotel/Casino (*see p. 54*) Centrally located on the Strip, this is our first choice if you're traveling with the kids. The hotel's mezzanine level offers ongoing circus acts daily from 11am to midnight, dozens of carnival games, and an arcade with more than 300 video and pinball games. And behind the hotel is a full amusement park.

Excalibur (*see p. 35*) Also owned by Circus Circus, Excalibur features a whole floor of midway games, a large video-game arcade, crafts demonstrations, free shows for kids (puppets, jugglers, magicians), and thrill cinemas. It has child-oriented eateries and shows (details in chapter 10).

Luxor Las Vegas (*see p. 36*) Another Circus Circus property. Kids will enjoy VirtuaLand, an 18,000-square-foot video-game arcade that showcases Sega's latest game technologies. Another big attraction here is the "Secrets of the Luxor Pyramid," a high-tech adventure/thrill ride using motion simulators and IMAX film.

MGM Grand Hotel/Casino (*see p. 30*) This resort is backed by a 33-acre theme park and houses a state-of-the-art video-game arcade and carnival midway. A unique offering here is a youth center for hotel guests ages 3 to 16, with separate sections for different age groups. Its facilities range from a playhouse and tumbling mats for toddlers to extensive arts-and-crafts equipment for the older kids. They also have a terrific new pool area and the whole property still seems popular with families.

is slack-jawed wonder. If you enter the casino via the Brooklyn Bridge (the walkway from the Strip), you find yourself in a replica of Greenwich Village, down to the cobblestones, the manhole covers, the tenement buildings, and the graffiti. (Yes, they even re-created that. You should see the subway station.) The main casino area is done as Central Park, complete with trees, babbling brooks, streetlamps, and footbridges. The change carts are little Yellow Cabs. The reception area and lobby are done in belle epoque, art deco, golden age of Manhattan style; you feel like breaking out into a

1930s musical number while standing there. It really is impossible to adequately describe the sheer mind-blowing enormity of the thing. So we are just going to leave it at *Wow!* The word *subtle* was obviously not in the lexicon of the designers. It's hard to see how Vegas can ever top this, but then again that's been said before.

Rooms are housed in different towers, each with a New York–inspired name. There are 64 different styles of rooms, and they are all smashing. Each essentially is done up in a hard-core art deco style: various shades of inlaid wood, rounded tops to the armoires and headboards, usually shades of brown and wood colors. However, some of the rooms are downright tiny (just like New York again!), and in those rooms all this massively detailed decoration could be overwhelming, if not suffocating. The bathrooms are also small, but have black marble–topped sinks, which again lend a glamorous '20s image.

Dining/Diversions: The **Motown Cafe** is described in chapter 5. Other restaurants include **Il Fornaio, Chin-Chin,** and **Gallagher's Steak House.**

Amenities: Concierge, courtesy limo, currency exchange, dry cleaning, express checkout, laundry, newspaper delivery, room service, safety-deposit boxes, video rentals, beauty salon, car rental, casino, arcade, pool, tour desk. The spa is smaller than average and merely adequate, but at $15 a day it is slightly cheaper than other major hotels.

Tropicana Resort & Casino. 3801 Las Vegas Blvd. S., at Tropicana Ave., Las Vegas, NV 89109. ☎ **800/634-4000** or 702/739-2222. Fax 702/739-2469. www.tropicanalv.com. 1,874 units. A/C TV TEL. $79–$229 double. Extra person $15. Children under 18 stay free in parents' room. AE, CB, DC, DISC, MC, V. Free self- and valet parking.

This longtime denizen of the Strip is looking great since a major renovation in 1995. The entranceway is now a colorful Caribbean village facade; there are nightly laser light shows on the Outer Island corner facing the Strip; pedestrian skywalks across the Strip link the Trop with the MGM Grand, the Excalibur, and the Luxor; and the resort's resident bird and wildlife population has dramatically increased. The Trop today comprises a lush landscape of manicured lawns, towering palms, oleanders, weeping willows, and crepe myrtles. There are dozens of waterfalls, thousands of exotic flowers, lagoons, and koi ponds. And flamingos, finches, black swans, mandarin ducks, African crown cranes, cockatoos, macaws, toucans, and Brazilian parrots live on the grounds (and occasionally make it a bit messy with guano). There's even a wildlife walk (home to pygmy marmosets, boa constrictors, and others) inside the resort itself.

Rooms in the Paradise Tower are traditional, with French provincial furnishings and turn-of-the-century wallpapers. They're a bit bland, but within easy walking distance of the casino and restaurants. Island Tower rooms, more befitting a tropical resort, are decorated with splashy print bedspreads and bamboo furnishings; some have beds with mirrored walls and ceilings. They are also, however, a major hike from the casino and parking lots. Bathrooms in the tower rooms are clean and come with roomy bathtubs. As for the motel-like Garden Rooms, the Trop would do itself a world of PR good if they were demolished ASAP. All Trop rooms have sofas and safes; TVs offer Spectravision movies, account review, video checkout, and channels for in-house information.

Dining: Restaurants include **Mizuno's, El Gaucho, Papagayo's, Savanna,** and **Peitro's. Calypso's,** the Trop's 24-hour coffee shop, is the most cheerful in town.

Amenities: 24-hour room service, shoe shine, casino, health club (a range of machines, treadmills, exercise bikes, steam, sauna, whirlpool, massage, and tanning room), video-game arcade, tour and show desks, wedding chapel, car-rental desk, beauty salon and barbershop, business center, travel agent, shops, and three swimming pools, including one with a swim-up bar/blackjack table.

MODERATE

Excalibur. 3850 Las Vegas Blvd. S., at Tropicana Ave., Las Vegas, NV 89109. ☎ **800/937-7777** or 702/597-7777. Fax 702/597-7040. www.excalibur-casino.com. 4,032 units. A/C TV TEL. $49–$119 for up to 4 people. Children under 17 stay free in parents' room; children over 17 pay $12. Rates are higher during holidays and convention periods. AE, CB, DC, DISC, MC, V. Free self- and valet parking.

Now this is kitsch. One of the largest resort hotels in the world, Excalibur (a.k.a. "the Realm") is a gleaming white, turreted castle complete with moat, drawbridge, battlements, and lofty towers. And it's huger than huge. Apparently, the creators thought there were a lot of Arthur and Guinevere wannabes out there. And they are probably right; but do we really need a medieval, forest-themed, knights-running-amok hotel in which to act out our fantasies?

And it is hilarious. What it is not, is comfortable, which is actually historically accurate, since big castles were not traditionally warm, cozy, inviting places. Excalibur is just too darn big, a chaotic frenzy at all times. Even the must-see factor fades quickly.

The rooms maintain the Arthurian motif with walls papered to look like stone castle interiors with the knightly motif continued throughout, but not nearly enough to make this a fantasy theme room. Dang. Guests who have stayed in Tower 2 have complained about the noise from the roller coaster across the street at New York New York. It shuts down at 11pm, so early birds should probably stay in a different part of the hotel.

Dining/Diversions: Restaurants include **Camelot, Nitro Grill, Sir Galahad's, Regale Italian Eatery,** and the **Sherwood Forest Cafe.**

Amenities: 24-hour room service, free gaming lessons, shoe shine, foreign currency exchange, casino, tour and show desks, state-of-the-art video-game arcade, wedding chapel (you can marry in medieval attire), unisex hairdresser, car-rental desk, a parking lot that can accommodate RVs, shops (see chapter 8). There are two large, beautifully landscaped swimming pools complete with waterfalls and water slides and an adjoining 16-seat whirlpool spa.

Hotel San Remo. 115 E. Tropicana Ave., just east of the Strip, Las Vegas, NV. ☎ **800/522-7366** or 702/739-9000. Fax 702/736-1120. $49–$169 double. A/C TV TEL. AE, CB, DC, DISC, JCB, MC, V. Free self- and valet parking.

Located right behind the Tropicana, this is a good Strip alternative, since it puts you right at one of the most active corners, for a much better rate than usually found on the Strip. Plus, they always seem to have a $4 prime rib deal going on, which is very Vegas indeed. The rooms are quite nice, done in a French Provincial style, and are larger than normal. Some come with convertible sofas and dressing areas, and 40% of tower rooms even have balconies. The "minisuites" are larger than the standard rooms by half, adding a sitting area and desks.

Dining/Diversions: Restaurants include **Luigi's Deli, Paparazzi's Grille,** and **Ristorante Dei Fiori.**

Amenities: 24-hour room service, laundry service, bell desk, show desk, gift shop, casino, pool with poolside service.

✪ Luxor Las Vegas. 3900 Las Vegas Blvd. S., between Reno and Hacienda aves., Las Vegas, NV 81119. ☎ **800/288-1000** or 702/262-4000. Fax 702/262-4452. www.luxor.com. 4,400 units. A/C TV TEL. Sun–Thurs $49–$259 double, Fri–Sat $99–$299 double; $99–$329 whirlpool suite, $500–$800 for other suites. Extra person $15. Children under 12 stay free in parents' room. AE, CB, DC, DISC, MC, V. Free self- and valet parking.

The Luxor has just completed a $300 million renovation and expansion. Cheese fans will be disappointed to learn that the Egyptian fantasma that set the pace for all others isn't all that tacky anymore. Oh sure, the main hotel is still a 30-story bronze pyramid, complete with a really tall 315,000-watt light beam at the top. (The Luxor says that's because the Egyptians believed their souls would travel up from heaven in a beam of light; we think it's really because it gives them something to brag about: "The most powerful beam on earth!") Sure, replicas of Cleopatra's Needle and the Sphinx still grace the outside, but the interior redesign has been made much more inviting, classier, and functional.

The rooms have had a freshening up in the pyramid and are due to have an extensive remodeling throughout 1999. High-speed "inclinator" elevators run on a 39° angle, making the ride up to your room a bit of a thrill. Sloped window walls remind you that you're in a pyramid. *Note:* In the pyramid, most baths have showers only, no tubs. The rooms are probably better in the new tower. Featuring fine art deco and Egyptian furnishings, they were full of nice touches. This is one of the few rooms in Las Vegas that stands out.

Dining/Diversions: The Luxor's **Pharaoh's Pheast** buffet is discussed in chapter 5. Other restaurants include **Isis,** the **Sacred Sea Room,** the **Luxor Steakhouse, La Salsa,** and the 24-hour **Pyramid Café.**

Amenities: 24-hour room service; hair dryers; foreign currency exchange; shoe shine; casino; full-service unisex hair salon; 24-hour spa and health club (with a full range of machines, free weights, steam, sauna, and whirlpool; massage, facials, herbal wraps, and other beauty treatments available); VirtuaLand, an 18,000-square-foot video arcade that showcases Sega's latest game technologies; car-rental desk; tour/show/sightseeing desks, five swimming pools.

INEXPENSIVE

✪ **Orleans.** 4500 W. Tropicana Ave., west of the Strip and I-15, Las Vegas, NV 89103. ☎ **800/ORLEANS** or 702/365-7111. Fax 702/365-7505. www. orleanscasino.com. 840 units. A/C TV TEL. $39–$89 standard double; $175–$225 one-bedroom suite. AE, DC, DISC, MC, V. Free self- and valet parking.

The Orleans is owned by the same company that owns the Barbary and Gold Coast casinos. It's a little out of the way, and there is virtually nothing around it, but with a 12-screen movie complex, complete with food court and day care center, this is an attractive option to staying on the hectic Strip. Plus, there is a shuttle that runs continuously to the Barbary Coast on the Strip. If the prices hold true (as always, quotes vary), this hotel is one of the best bargains in town, despite the location. The rooms are particularly nice and the largest standard rooms in town, so the hotel claims. They all have a definite New Orleans French feel. They are L-shaped with a seating alcove by the windows, and come complete with slightly turn-of-the-century–style overstuffed chair and sofa. The one drawback is that all these furnishings, and the busy floral decorating theme, make the room, particularly down by the seating area in front of the bathrooms, seem crowded. Still, it's meant to evoke a cozy, warm Victorian parlor, which traditionally is very over-crowded, so maybe it's successful after all.

Dining/Diversions: Restaurants include **Vito's, Canal St. Grill,** and **Don Miguel's.**

Amenities: Room service, safety-deposit boxes, courtesy bus to/from airport and the Strip, casino, beauty salon, business center, game room/arcade, 70-lane bowling alley, wedding chapel, 40,000 square feet of meeting space (with more on the way), two medium-sized pools with grass and cabanas.

3 Mid-Strip

VERY EXPENSIVE

Bally's Las Vegas. 3645 Las Vegas Blvd. S., at Flamingo Rd., Las Vegas, NV 89109. ☎ **800/634-3434** or 702/739-4111. Fax 702/794-2413. www.ballyslv.com. 2,814 units. A/C TV TEL. $95–$135 double, $35 more for concierge floor (including breakfast); $300–$2,500 suite. Extra person $15. Children 18 and under stay free in parents' room. AE, CB, DC, JCB, MC, V. Free self- and valet parking.

Bally's recently completed a $72 million renovation, which included the construction of a monorail that whisks passengers from its downstairs shopping level (a bit of a hike from the casino) to the MGM Grand. More noticeable is its elaborate new facade, a plaza containing four 200-foot people movers that transport visitors to and from the Strip via a neon-lit arch surrounded by cascading waters and lush landscaping. Light, sound, and water shows take place here every 20 minutes after dark.

The minute you step from its glittering entranceway into its light and airy casino, you'll notice that Bally's is one of the most cheerful hotels on the Strip. Large rooms are decorated in teal, mauve, and earth tones. All have sofas. TVs offer video checkout, not to mention cash-advance capability for your credit card. The 22nd floor is a concierge level.

Dining/Diversions: Restaurants include **Seasons, Bally's Steakhouse, Al Dente, Las Olas,** and **Chang's.**

Amenities: 24-hour room service, guest services desk, shoe shine, foreign currency exchange, casino, tour and show desks, car-rental desk, small video-game arcade, shopping arcade (see chapter 8), wedding chapel, men's and women's hair salons, state-of-the-art health spa and fitness center, eight night-lit tennis courts and pro shop (lessons available), two basketball courts, and a large swimming pool.

○ **Bellagio.** 3600 Las Vegas Blvd. S., at the corner of Flamingo Rd., Las Vegas, NV 89109. ☎ **888/987-6667** or 702/693-7444. Fax 702/693-8346. www.bellagiolasvegas.com. 3,270 units. A/C TV TEL. $129–$499 double. Extra person $30. AE, CB, DC, DISC, MC, V. Free self- and valet parking.

Steve Wynn, the man who more or less began the modern Vegas era with the Mirage, ushers in the new post-Vegas-is-for-families elegance epoch with his $1.6 billion luxury resort. What did he—and you—get for that money? Well, for starters, though it is named for a certain charming Lake Como village, Bellagio is not, thankfully, as theme intensive as some of its nearest competition. There is an 8-acre Lake Como stand-in out front, complete with a dazzling choreographed water ballet extravaganza, plus the simulated front of an Italian lakeside village, while the pool area is sort of Hearst Castle Romanesque, but that's about it. Just as well. This is not much like a getaway to a peaceful, romantic Italian village. But it is exactly like going to a big, grand, state-of-the-art Vegas hotel. To expect more probably isn't fair, but then again, they tried to set the tone with those dreamy, soft-focus TV ads. Nothing with a casino stuck in the middle of it can be that serene and restful.

But does it work as a luxury hotel? Sort of. It certainly is much closer to a European casino hotel than a Vegas one and fabulous touches abound. The rooms are nice—oh, very nice, nicer than the Mirage even, but maybe just not quite nice enough for the price. Furnishings are plush (good beds with quality linens, armoire with TV, comfy chair), the roomy bathrooms even more so (marble and glass plus good-smelling soap—it works every time), but it's all still just a slightly more luxurious, and busy, variation on what's found over at the Mirage. Strip-side rooms, while featuring a much-desired view of the water fountains, don't quite muffle the booms said fountains make as they explode. Still, service is top-notch, despite the size of the place, full of eager-to-please, nonpatronizing help. What does all this add up to? The ultimate in the new Vegas luxury resort experience, certainly, and if it doesn't quite work, that's probably more the fault of the initial concept than the hotel itself.

Dining/Diversions: Just about all the best new restaurants are found in Bellagio. Including, **Le Cirque, Circo, Aqua, Olives Picasso,** and **Prime.**

The man who brought us a free pirate show and a volcano explosion now brings us a water ballet, courtesy of a dancing fountain with jets timed to a rotating list of nine songs (everything from pop to Sinatra to Broadway to opera). This sounds cheesy, but it absolutely is not. It's really quite delightful and even witty (no, really), and is the best free show in Vegas.

Amenities: 24-hour room service, concierge, hair dryers, shoe shine, laundry and dry cleaning, video arcade, twice daily maid service, business center, beauty salon. Free monorail travels between Bellagio and Monte Carlo nearly around the clock, six swimming pools, health club and spa and a shopping arcade, **Via Bellagio.**

✪ **Caesars Palace.** 3570 Las Vegas Blvd. S., just north of Flamingo Rd., Las Vegas, NV 89109. ☎ **800/634-6661** or 702/731-7110. Fax 702/731-6636. www.caesars.com. 2,471 units. A/C TV TEL. From $99 standard double, $109–$500 "run of house deluxe" double; $549–$1,000 suite. Extra person $20. Children under 12 stay free in parents' room. AE, CB, DC, DISC, MC, V. Free self- and valet parking.

Since 1966, Caesars has stood as simultaneously the ultimate in Vegas luxury and the nadir (or pinnacle, depending on your values) of Las Vegas cheese. It's the most Vegas-style hotel you'll find. Or at least it was. Caesars has completed a massive $300 million renovation, inside and out. Don't worry, the Roman theme remains. But as with everything else in Vegas, it has been upgraded to, let's say, a nicer neighborhood in Rome.

Past or future, Caesars remains spectacular. From the Roman temples, heroic arches, golden charioteers, and 50-foot Italian cypresses of its entrance, to the overwhelming interiors, it's the spectacle that every good Vegas hotel should be.

Accommodations occupy (ultimately) four towers, and there are too many decorator schemes to describe here. You'll likely enjoy a lavish bath with marble floor, European fixtures, and oversized marble tubs (about half are whirlpools). (*Note:* Some of the rooms have lavish tubs in the middle of the room, which can be uncomfortable if you wish to shower and don't want this to turn into a spectator sport.) Art in the rooms keeps to the Greco-Roman theme (some have classical sculptures in niches); furnishings tend to neoclassic styles; Roman columns, pilasters, and pediments are common. Many rooms have four-poster beds with mirrored ceilings, and all are equipped with three phones (bedside, bath, and desk), cable

Mid-Strip Accommodations

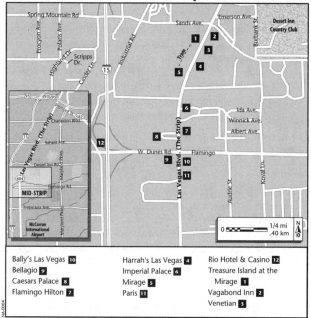

Bally's Las Vegas **10**	Harrah's Las Vegas **4**	Rio Hotel & Casino **12**
Bellagio **9**	Imperial Palace **6**	Treasure Island at the
Caesars Palace **8**	Mirage **5**	Mirage **1**
Flamingo Hilton **7**	Paris **11**	Vagabond Inn **2**
		Venetian **3**

TVs with HBO, a gaming instruction channel (with cameo appearances by hotel headliners like Natalie Cole and Johnny Mathis), and in-house information stations. All rooms have private safes, hair dryers, irons and ironing boards, and lighted closets.

Dining/Diversions: Caesars has a well-deserved reputation for superior in-house restaurants. There are nine in the hotel, plus dining facilities in the Forum shopping area. All are highly recommended.

Amenities: 24-hour room service, shoe shine, complimentary gaming lessons, valet and dry cleaning services, three casinos, two extensive shopping arcades (see chapter 8), state-of-the-art video arcade, American Express office, show desks, car-rental desk, three swimming pools, health club and spa.

Paris-Las Vegas Casino Resort. 3655 Las Vegas Blvd. S., Las Vegas, NV 89109. ☎ **888/BONJOUR.** 2,916 units. $119–$269 double; $350 and way up for suites. AE, MC. V.

Starting in September 1999, you don't have to wait until springtime to enjoy Paris. Las Vegas has thoughtfully provided it for you for all seasons, including a 50-story replica of the Eiffel Tower. Rooms will be French Regency style, probably not good enough for Louis XIV, but just fine for you and me. There will also be a European health spa, a 2-acre rooftop swimming pool, a copy of the Rue de la Paix, similarly lined with shops and restaurants, plus the largest ballroom in Vegas in their convention area. There's no word yet on whether the staff has been trained to act rude if your grammar isn't perfectly correct. An indoor walkway will connect it to Bally's next door.

✪ **The Venetian.** 3355 Las Vegas Blvd. S., Las Vegas, NV 89109. ☎ **888/ 2-VENICE** or 702/414-1000. www.venetian.com. 3,354 units. AC MINIBAR TV TEL. $125–$399 double. AE, CB, DC, DISC, JCB, MC, V. Free self- and valet parking.

The newest hotel spectacle (at this writing, at least), the Venetian falls squarely between an outright adult Disneyland experience and the luxury resort sensibility of the other recent hotels. With plenty of marble, soaring ceilings, and impressive pillars and archways, it's less kitsch than Caesars, but more theme park than Bellagio. The lobby (very much classy hotel—note also the arrival/departure lounges, which are so very un-Vegas in atmosphere and amount of sunlight), casino, and shops can all be accessed from outside through individual entrances, which helps avoid that irritating circuitous maneuvering required by most other locations.

The rooms are the largest and probably the most handsome in town, with a flair more European than Vegas. They are all "suites," with a good-sized bedroom giving way to steps down to a sunken living area, complete with pullout sofa bed. The marbled bathrooms are among our favorite in town, with glassed showers, deep soaking tubs (though your feet can easily kick the plug out), double sinks, fluffy towels, and lots of space—that does it for us every time. Peculiarly, there are no hair dryers.

But there is a certain amount of price gouging that unpleasantly reminds one of the real Venice. There is a charge for that in-room faxing and printing, while the minibar is automated, so if you so much as rearrange items inside you are charged for it. Don't even get us started on the plans (at press time) for outrageous fees to use the health club. We hope these are all things that will settle down in time, as there is so much here to like.

Dining/Diversions: There are many celebrity chefs and high-profile restaurants in residence at the Venetian including, **Star Canyon, Delmonico's Steakhouse, Pinot Brassiere, Valentino, Lutece, Postrio,** and **Zeffirino's.**

Amenities: 24-hour room service, in-room safe, in-room fax machine, three duel-line phones with modem access, shoe shine, dry cleaning/laundry, two TVs, concierge, beauty salon, spa and health club, 5-acre pool deck with five pools modeled after a Venetian garden with whirlpools, boutiques. Hearing-impaired devices (ranging from door knock lights to vibrating alarm clocks and telecaption decoders) are available upon request. Car rental, airport transportation, cellular phone rental, baby-sitting, health club and spa courtesy of the highly touted Canyon Ranch, and the **Grand Canal Shoppes.**

EXPENSIVE

✪ **Flamingo Hilton.** 3555 Las Vegas Blvd. S., between Sands Ave. and Flamingo Rd., Las Vegas, NV 89109. ☎ **800/732-2111** or 702/733-3111. Fax 702/733-3353. www.hilton.com. 3,999 units. A/C TV TEL. $69–$205 double; $250–$580 suite. Extra person $20. Children 17 and under stay free in parents' room. Inquire about packages and time-share suites. AE, CB, DC, DISC, JCB, MC, V. Free self- and valet parking.

The Flamingo has changed a great deal since Bugsy Siegel opened his 105-room oasis "in the middle of nowhere" in 1946. It was so luxurious for its time that even the janitors wore tuxedos. Jimmy Durante was the opening headliner, and the wealthy and famous flocked to the tropical paradise of swaying palms, lagoons, and waterfalls. While the Flamingo is a senior citizen on the Strip with a colorful history, a fresh, new look, enhanced by a recent $130 million renovation and expansion, has made Siegel's "real class joint" better than ever. Still, reaching the outside world (the Strip and Flamingo competitors) can be difficult; there is a lot of casino between you and the lobby, and then again between you and the street.

Rooms occupy six towers and are variously decorated. All accommodations offer in-room safes; TVs have in-house information and gaming instruction stations, a keno channel, video checkout, message retrieval, and account review. The pool area is especially lush and nice.

Dining/Diversions: Six restaurants, from a steakhouse, to Japanese to a deli.

Amenities: 24-hour room service, guest services desk, translation services (interpreters are available for more than 35 languages; gaming guides are available in six languages), casino, car-rental desk, tour and show desks, full-service beauty salon/barbershop, wedding chapel, four night-lit championship tennis courts with pro shop and practice alley (tennis clinics and lessons are available), shopping arcade, five swimming pools, health club and spa.

Harrah's Las Vegas. 3475 Las Vegas Blvd. S., between Flamingo and Spring Mountain rds., Las Vegas, NV 89109. ☎ **800/HARRAHS** or 702/369-5000. Fax 702/369-6014. www.harrahs.lv.com. 2,700 units. A/C TV TEL. $65–$195 standard "deluxe" double, $85–$250 standard "superior" double; $195–$1,000 suite. Extra person $15. Children 12 and under stay free in parents' room. AE, CB, DC, DISC, MC, V. Free self- and valet parking.

A recent radical face-lift has completely transformed Harrah's. It used to look like a Mississippi River showboat, but now it looks nothing like that. It's more elegant, with a European carnival theme. Overall, Harrah's has done a terrific job with its remodeling, creating a comfortable and fun environment while somehow eschewing both kitsch and the haughtiness that follows in the wake of other hotel conversions' more upscale images.

The rooms are also light and festive, with marble fixtures and light wood accents. All the rooms are larger than average; the points that emerge from both the old and the new tower wings translate inside into an extra triangle of space for a couch and table. In all rooms, TVs offer hotel information and keno channels, pay movies, Nintendo, and video account review and checkout.

Dining/Diversions: Restaurants include **The Range** steakhouse, **Asia,** and the **Garden Cafe.**

Amenities: 24-hour room service (including a special pizza and pasta menu), complimentary gaming lessons, casino, car-rental desk, tour and show desks, nice-sized video-game arcade, coin-op laundry, shops (see chapter 8 for details), unisex hair salon, health club and spa, an Olympic-sized swimming pool.

✪ **Mirage.** 3400 Las Vegas Blvd. S., between Flamingo Rd. and Sands Ave., Las Vegas, NV 89109. ☎ **800/627-6667** or 702/791-7444. Fax 702/791-7446. www.themirage.com. 3,323 units. A/C TV TEL. Sun–Thurs $79–$399 double, Fri–Sat and holidays $159–$399 double; $250–$3,000 suite. Extra person $30. AE, CB, DC, DISC, MC, V. Free self- and valet parking.

We really like this place. Actually, ask around; most visitors and locals agree. Even if they haven't stayed here, many consider it the most beautiful hotel in Vegas. From the moment you walk in and breathe the faintly tropically perfumed air (we think it's vanilla) and enter the lush rain forest, you just know that you are on vacation. It's a totally different experience from most Vegas hotels, where you step inside the door and are immediately the victim of a sensory assault.

Occupying 102 acres, the Mirage is fronted by more than a city block of cascading waterfalls and tropical foliage centering on a very active "volcano," which, after dark, erupts every 15 minutes, spewing fire 100 feet above the lagoons below. (In passing, that volcano cost $30 million, which is equal to the entire original construction cost for Caesars next door.) The lobby is dominated by a 53-foot, 20,000-gallon simulated coral reef aquarium stocked with more than 1,000 colorful tropical fish, including six sharks. This gives you something to look at while waiting (never for long) for check-in.

To get to the rooms, you must walk through a 90-foot domed atrium—a path meanders through palms, banana trees, waterfalls, and serene pools. The formerly tropical-themed rooms have been redone in varying neutrals, with liberal use of muted gold. A marble entryway, mirrors, vanity table, and canopy over the bed's headboard give even the standards a luxurious appearance. The bathrooms are marble and slightly on the small size, depending on the room. Oak armoires house 25-inch TVs, and phones are equipped with fax and computer jacks.

Off the casino is a habitat for Siegfried and Roy's white tigers, a plaster enclosure that allows for photo taking and "aaaahhhs." Out back is the pool, one of the nicest in Vegas; it has a quarter-mile shoreline, a tropical paradise of waterfalls, trees, water slides, and so forth. Behind the pool is the dolphin habitat and Siegfried and Roy's Secret Garden, which has a separate admission.

Dining/Diversions: A range of restaurants from the superb **Onda** and **Alex Stratta,** to the **Noodle Kitchen,** and **Kokomo's.**

Amenities: 24-hour room service, overnight shoe shine upon request, morning newspaper delivery, casino, car-rental desk, shops (Siegfried and Roy and Cirque du Soleil merchandise and others), unisex hairdresser and salon offering all beauty services, video arcade, business services center. A free tram travels between the Mirage and Treasure Island almost around the clock. The health club and spa is outstanding, as is the above-discussed pool area.

Rio Suites. 3700 W. Flamingo Rd., at I-15, Las Vegas, NV 89103. ☎ **800/ 752-9746** or 702/252-7777. Fax 702/252-0080. www.playrio.com. 2,582 units. A/C TV TEL. Sun–Thurs $95 suite, Fri–Sat $149 suite. Extra person $15. Inquire about golf packages. AE, CB, DC, MC, V. Free self- and valet parking.

The Rio Hotel confounded expectations by not only succeeding in an area somewhat removed from the Strip but by also thriving there. It recently completed an immediately popular $200 million addition: a 41-story tower and the Masquerade Village. Diverging from the rest of the tropically themed hotel, this latter simulates a European village, complete with shops, restaurants, and a bizarre live-action show in the sky. The addition is actually quite nice—not only is the architecture, in its faux way, aesthetically pleasing, but this part of the casino is much more airy, thanks to the very tall ceilings. Out back is a pool with a sandy beach, and two new pools in imaginative fish and shell shapes that seem inviting until you get up close and see how small they are. It could be especially disappointing after you have braved the long, cluttered walk (particularly from the new tower rooms) to get there.

The rooms are touted because of their size; every one is a "suite," which does not mean two separate rooms but rather one large one with a sectional, corner sofa, and coffee table at one end. The dressing areas are certainly larger than average and feature a number of extra amenities, such as refrigerators (unusual for a Vegas hotel room), coffeemakers, and small snacks. Windows, running the whole length of the room, are floor to ceiling, with a pretty impressive view.

Dining/Diversions: Restaurants include the exceptional **Fiore** and **Napa,** plus the **All American Bar and Grille, Antonio's, Mask** and **Mama Marie's Cuccini.**

Amenities: 24-hour room service, guest services desk, foreign currency exchange, shoe shine, complimentary shuttle bus to/from the MGM and the Forum Mall, casino, tour and show desks, unisex hair salon (all beauty services, including massage and facials), small video-game arcade, fitness room (stair machine, rowing machine, Lifecycle, four-station exercise machine), shops (gifts, clothing for the entire family, logo merchandise). Three whirlpool spas nestle amid rocks and foliage, there are two sand volleyball courts, and blue-and-white-striped cabanas (equipped with rafts and misting coolers) can be rented for $8 per hour or $25 per day.

✪ **Treasure Island at the Mirage.** 3300 Las Vegas Blvd. S., at Spring Mountain Rd., Las Vegas, NV 89177-0711. ☎ **800/944-7444** or 702/894-7111. Fax 702/894-7446. www.treasureislandlasvegas.com. 2,891 units. A/C TV TEL. From $69 double; from $109 suite. Extra person $30. Inquire about packages. AE, DC, DISC, JCB, MC, V. Free self- and valet parking.

They will deny it now if you ask them, but Treasure Island was originally conceived (more or less) as the family alternative to the more grown-up Mirage. Why else would you build a hotel that is essentially a blown-up version of Disneyland's Pirates of the Caribbean? But that's all behind them. Sure, the pirate theme remains with a vengeance, complete with plenty of skulls, crossbones, treasure chests, pirate ships' figureheads, Animatronic skeletons, and pirate nautical paraphernalia. But a $25 million face-lift has added more marble and gilded the bones, so to speak (actually, literally in some cases). It's still Pirates of the Caribbean, but with lots and lots of money thrown at it. Despite this, it still remains a top family choice and many kids are often running about, which some vacationers may not find desirable.

By the time you read this, the rooms will have been entirely redone, pretty much following the pattern of the Mirage, modified French Regency, a mélange of patterns, but the monochromatic color (many shades of gold) tones it down. There is a canopy over the head of the bed and a full mirrored wall. Armoires contain the TV, but in the King rooms the door that opens for TV viewing only goes to a 90° angle, blocking passage between bed and armoire. Good bathrooms feature a large soaking tub—a bather's delight.

Dining/Diversions: Restaurants include the **Buccaneer Bay Club, Madame Ching's, The Plank,** and the **Black Spot Grille.** The **Battle Bar,** offers a good view of the pirate battle, occurring several times nightly.

Amenities: 24-hour room service, limo rental, foreign currency exchange, shoe shine (in men's room in the lobby and casino), casino, tour and sightseeing desks, car-rental desk, travel agency, Mutiny Bay (an 18,000-square-foot, state-of-the-art video-game arcade and carnival midway; one highlight is a full-sized Mazda Miata motion-simulator ride), two wedding chapels, full-service unisex salon (days of beauty are an option), swimming pool, and a shopping arcade (for details, see chapter 8). A full-service spa and health club with a complement of machines, sauna, steam, whirlpool and massage, on-site trainers, TVs and stereos with headsets, and anything else you might need (including a full line of Sebastian grooming products in the women's locker rooms). A free tram travels between Treasure Island and the Mirage almost around the clock.

MODERATE

Imperial Palace. 3535 Las Vegas Blvd. S., between Sands Ave. and Flamingo Rd., Las Vegas, NV 89109. ☎ **800/634-6441** or 702/731-3311. Fax 702/735-8578. www.imperialpalace.com. 2,700 units. A/C TV TEL. $49–$99 double; $79–$149 "luv tub" suite, $159–$299 other suites. Extra person $15. Inquire about packages. AE, CB, DC, DISC, MC, V. Free self- and valet parking.

Though appearing even older than its 17 years, the Imperial Palace has much more going for it than a first impression might yield. The Strip location, right in the middle of the action, can't be beat. The standard rooms are just that, but they all have balconies, which is exceedingly rare in Vegas. The "luv tub" rooms are a great deal; for the price, you get a larger bedroom (with a mirror over the bed!) while the larger-than-usual bathroom features a 300-gallon sunken "luv tub" (with still more mirrors). A perfect Vegas hoot. Given the slightly larger size of the "luv tub" rooms, that $59 low-end fee plus the location make them one of the best bargains on the Strip.

Dining/Diversions: Several restaurants running the usual gamut.

Amenities: 24-hour room service, free gaming lessons, shoe shine in casino, casino, health club (machines, free weights, sauna, steam, massage, tanning, TV lounge), show and tour desks, car-rental desk, travel agency, unisex hairdresser, wedding chapel, shopping arcade. An Olympic-sized swimming pool is backed by a rock garden and waterfalls, and its palm-fringed sundeck area also has a whirlpool.

INEXPENSIVE

Vagabond Inn. 3265 Las Vegas Blvd. S., just south of Sands Ave., Las Vegas, NV 89109. ☎ **800/828-8032,** 800/522-1555, or 702/735-5102. Fax 702/735-0168. 126 units. A/C TV TEL. Sun–Thurs $42–$95 standard double, $65–$125 king room; Fri–Sat $52–$110 standard double, $72–$150 king room. Rates include continental breakfast. AE, CB, DC, DISC, MC, V. Free self-parking.

A central location just across the street from Treasure Island (a cool place from which to watch the pirate battle—drag out a lawn chair), plus clean, nicely decorated, basic motel rooms, make this a viable choice. One-third of the rooms have patios or balconies, and all offer cable TVs with pay-movie options. King rooms have wet bars and refrigerators. A wide selection of complimentary bath amenities is available at the front desk, and free coffee is served in the lobby around the clock, as is a daily continental breakfast of juice, fruit, and pastries. Facilities include coin-op washers and dryers. There's a swimming pool but no restaurant. A gratis airport shuttle and free local calls are pluses.

4 North Strip

VERY EXPENSIVE

✪ **Desert Inn Country Club Resort & Casino.** 3145 Las Vegas Blvd. S., between Spring Mountain Rd. and Convention Center Dr., Las Vegas, NV 89109. ☎ **800/634-6906** or 702/733-4444. Fax 702/733-4744. 702 units. A/C TV TEL. $175–$185 double; $215–$225 minisuite; $350–$555 suite. Extra person $35. Children under 12 stay free in parents' room. AE, CB, DC, DISC, JCB, MC, V. Free self- and valet parking.

The Desert Inn has long been the most glamorous and gracious of Vegas hotels; coming here means leaving the hectic Strip action behind. The Desert Inn considers itself more a resort than a hotel, and the property and prices reflect this. The property benefited from a

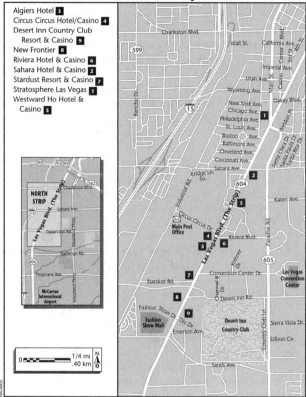

Algiers Hotel **3**
Circus Circus Hotel/Casino **4**
Desert Inn Country Club
  Resort & Casino **9**
New Frontier **8**
Riviera Hotel & Casino **6**
Sahara Hotel & Casino **2**
Stardust Resort & Casino **7**
Stratosphere Las Vegas **1**
Westward Ho Hotel &
  Casino **5**

recent renovation. The look now reflects a turn-of-the-century Palm Beach resort, with elegant, clean, and spare lines.

The newly redone rooms (in light golds and greens) feel spacious, with comfortable armchairs and matching hassocks. The fluffy bed coverings appear lusher than usual, and the mattresses are very firm. Rooms have views of either the Strip or the golf course (the latter really helps give the feel of a getaway), and some even have small balconies, though they are more for air currents than actual standing. Each room has a very big closet with an iron and ironing board. The bathrooms are perhaps the best in Vegas: beautiful and large, done in black and gray granite with double sinks, a separate enclosure for the toilet, and a glass shower separate from the tub. Amenities include a big basket of Neutrogena products, a phone, and a hair dryer.

Dining/Diversions: Several restaurants including the **Monte Carlo Room, Portofino,** and **Terrace Pointe.**

Amenities: 24-hour room service, concierge, shoe shine, golf course, five tennis courts, swimming pool (some suites have private swimming pools), health club and spa. Other facilities include a casino, tour and show desks, car-rental desk, beauty salon/barbershop, business center, shops, including golf and tennis pro shops.

EXPENSIVE

Riviera Hotel & Casino. 2901 Las Vegas Blvd. S., at Riviera Blvd., Las Vegas, NV 89109. ☎ **800/634-6753** or 702/734-5110. Fax 702/794-9451. http:// www.theriviera.com. 2,136 units. A/C TV TEL. $59–$95 double; $125–$500 suite. Extra person $20. Inquire about "Gambler's Spree" packages. AE, CB, DC, MC, V. Free self- and valet parking.

As a reaction to the ultimately futile attempt to restyle Vegas as a "family resort," the Riviera began to promote itself as an "alternative for grown-ups" and an "adult-oriented hotel." In addition to absolutely no attractions for kids, what this means is that they aren't shy about plastering posters of their flesh-intensive, naughty show *Crazy Girls* over most surfaces. Parents should probably take the hint and take their tykes elsewhere.

Rooms have recently been redone; gone are the dark tones and heavy appointments, in favor of muted florals, sandstone, and foam. It's less old-fashioned, but also has less character. Half the rooms offer pool views. Amenities include in-room safes and cable TVs with pay-movie options and in-house information stations.

Dining/Diversions: Several restaurants inlcuding **Kristofer's, Ristorante Italiano Kady's** and **Rik' Shaw.**

Amenities: 24-hour room service, shoe shine, casino (one of the world's largest), large arcade with carnival and video games, well-equipped health club (full complement of cardio and weight machines, free weights, steam, sauna, tanning, facials, salt/soap rubs, massage), Olympic-sized swimming pool and sundeck, wedding chapel, beauty salon/barbershop, comprehensive business services center, America West airlines desk, tour and show desks, car-rental desk, shops (see chapter 8 for details), two Har-Tru tennis courts lit for night play. A unique feature here: a wine-tasting booth operated by Nevada's only winery. Buyers, beware the booth by the Strip entrance to the casino that offers free or discounted tickets to many shows; it's a time-share deal and you must go look at property to get your reward.

MODERATE

New Frontier. 3120 Las Vegas Blvd. S., at Fashion Show Dr. ☎ **800/ 634-6966** or 702/794-8200. Fax 702/794-8401. 986 units. A/C TV TEL. Sun– Thurs $49 double, Fri–Sat $75 double; Sun–Thurs $85 atrium minisuite, Fri–Sat $115 atrium minisuite. AE, MC, V. Free outdoor parking.

For a long time, conscientious travelers avoided the Frontier, which was afflicted with a 6^1/$_2$-year-long labor strike. But it finally ended (over 50% of the workforce came back, which tells you something), and between that and new owners (the old ones fired Siegfried and Roy!), the venerable hotel is back. Staying here is fun simply because it is the oldest extant hotel on the Strip, dating back to 1942. (In Vegas terms, that's practically the Acropolis.) But that doesn't mean sacrificing all the fabulous comforts of new Las Vegas: In the works is one of those much vaunted total renovations that should take better advantage of the 41 acres of property (one of the largest sites in Vegas). As this is a process that will be going on throughout 1999, expect the place to look very different, though it will retain the country-western theme. Furthermore, the New Frontier will become a Radisson flagship property. Rooms and suites are large, comfortable, and done in tasteful colors, with coffeemakers and irons in every unit and windows that open. The atrium rooms, all minisuites, are some of the best-kept secrets in town thanks to that fresh air and the view of the atrium.

Dining/Diversions: Phil's Angus Steakhouse, Margarita's Mexican Cantina, and the **Cattleman's Buffet.**

Amenities: Room service 6am to 11pm, casino, outdoor pool, dry cleaning, beauty shop, arcade, cable TV.

Sahara Hotel & Casino. 2535 Las Vegas Blvd. S., at E. Sahara Ave., Las Vegas, NV 89109. ☎ **800/634-6666** or 702/737-2111. Fax 702/737-2027. 2,035 units. A/C TV TEL. $35–$55 standard double, $55–$85 deluxe double; $200–$600 suite. Extra person $10. Children under 14 stay free in parents' room. AE, CB, DC, DISC, MC, V. Free self- and valet parking.

One of the few venerable hotel casinos remaining in Vegas (it's come a long way since it opened in 1952 on the site of the old Club Bingo), the Sahara has just finished a major face-lift. Unfortunately, it hasn't created that nice of a hotel experience. Recent guests find the place, renovations notwithstanding, just a bit dreary and maybe even shabby. Again, this may simply be in comparison to the gleaming new kids in town, a fate suffered by most of the older hotels.

The room decor suffers from overkill, with stars and stripes assaulting the eyes and not looking terribly Moroccan (but then again, neither does Morocco). The boldly striped bedspreads on the otherwise comfortable beds are a particular mistake. The windows open, which is unusual for Vegas.

There is a handsome Olympic-sized pool, done in Moroccan mosaic tiles, and misters on the palm trees. Unfortunately, it is also right by the parking garage, which means you might be giving some casino-bound tourist an eyeful. It should be noted that the Sahara feels they are not as well equipped as other hotels for children and discourage you from bringing yours.

Dining/Diversions: The usual suspects in dining choices; steak/seafood, Mexican, buffet, and coffee shop.

Amenities: 24-hour room service, casino, beauty salon/barber-shop, car-rental desk, tour and show desks, shops, video-game arcade. The Sahara has a large swimming pool and sundeck with a pool shop and poolside bar in nearby thatch-roofed structures. A smaller pool shares the same courtyard setting.

Stardust Resort & Casino. 3000 Las Vegas Blvd. S., at Convention Center Dr., Las Vegas, NV 89109. ☎ **800/634-6757** or 702/732-6111. Fax 702/732-6257. www.stardustlv.com. 2,200 units. A/C TV TEL. $60–$1,000 Tower rooms and suites; $36–$200 Motor Inn rooms (2-person max). Extra person $10. Children 12 and under stay free in parents' room. AE, CB, DC, DISC, JCB, MC, V. Free self- and valet parking.

Opened in 1958, the Stardust is a longtime resident of the Strip, its 188-foot starry sign one of America's most recognized landmarks. Today, fronted by a fountain-splashed exterior plaza, the Stardust has kept pace with a growing city. In 1991, it added a 1,500-room tower and a 35,000-square-foot state-of-the-art meeting and conference center, part of a comprehensive $300 million expansion and renovation project. It's a likable hotel, but has no personality, despite being the only star of *Showgirls*. (It was probably chosen for its oh-so-Vegas lightbulb-intensive facade, which turns up in just about every Vegas establishing shot called for by commercials, TV, or movies.)

Rooms in the Towers are perfectly adequate, nice even, but frankly, completely forgettable. Also quite nice are Villa rooms in 2-story buildings surrounding a large swimming pool. Decorated in soft Southwestern pastels, they have private shaded patios overlooking the pool. The least expensive rooms are in the Stardust's Motor Inn—four 2-story white buildings with shuttered windows set far back on the property. In the past, they were rundown motel rooms but have been redecorated in more cheerful colors. A suite can be better, but it is a long walk to your hotel. Motor Inn guests can park at their doors. All

Stardust accommodations offer in-room safes, and TVs have Spectravision movie options and in-house information channels.

Dining/Diversions: Restaurants include **William B's, Tres Lobos, Ralph's Diner,** and a branch of **Tony Roma's.**

Amenities: 24-hour room service, shoe shine, free ice on every floor, casino, beauty salon/barbershop, video-game arcade, car-rental desk, show desk, shops (gifts, candy, clothing, jewelry, logo items, liquor). There are two large swimming pools, three whirlpool spas, and use of a health club and spa.

Stratosphere Las Vegas. 2000 Las Vegas Blvd. S., between St. Louis St. and Baltimore Ave., Las Vegas, NV 89104. ☎ **800/99-TOWER** or 702/380-7777. Fax 702/383-5334. www.grandcasinos.com. 1,500 units. A/C TV TEL. Sun–Thurs $39–$99 double, Fri–Sat $59–$139 double; $69–$400 suite. Extra person $15. Children 12 and under stay free in parents' room. Rates may be higher during special events. AE, CB, DC, DISC, JCB, MC, V. Free self- and valet parking.

A really neat idea, in that Vegas way, in a really bad location. At 1,149 feet, it's the tallest building west of the Mississippi. In theory, this should have provided yet another attraction for visitors; climb (okay, elevator) to the top and gaze at the stunning view. But despite being on the Strip, it's a healthy walk from anywhere—the nearest casino is the Sahara, which is 5 very long blocks away.

The rooms are furnished in Biedermeier-style cherrywood pieces with black lacquer accents. Enhanced by bright abstract paintings, they offer TVs with in-house information channels and pay-movie options, safes, phones with modem ports, and hair dryers and cosmetic mirrors in the bath. Ask for a high floor when you reserve to optimize your view.

When you go up to the top of the tower, indoor and outdoor observation decks offer the most stunning city views you will ever see, especially at night. For this price, this might be the place for you, but truth be told, this end of the Strip is getting ever more desolate—all the fun new action is some ways away—so you should probably consider it mostly as a place to lay your head.

Dining/Diversions: Two notable restaurants, among the many here, are the revolving **Top of the World,** and the **Montana Grille.**

Amenities: 24-hour room service, foreign currency exchange, casino, guest services desk, tour and show desk, video-game arcade, shopping arcade, three wedding chapels (offering incredible views from the 103rd floor), car-rental desk. An exercise facility, child care center, and vast resort-style pool and sundeck are in the works.

INEXPENSIVE

Algiers Hotel. 2845 Las Vegas Blvd. S., between Riviera Blvd. and Sahara Ave., Las Vegas, NV 89109. ☎ **800/732-3361** or 702/735-3311. Fax 702/792-2112. http://www.algiershotel.com. 106 units. A/C TV TEL. Sun–Thurs from $40 double, Fri–Sat and holidays from $55 double. Extra person $10. Children under 12 stay free in parents' room. AE, CB, DC, DISC, MC, V. Free self-parking at your room door.

A venerable denizen of the Strip, the Algiers opened in 1953. However, a recent multi-million-dollar renovation—including landscaping (note the lovely flower beds out back) and a new facade with a 60-foot sign—brought rooms and public areas up to date. There's no casino here, though you can play video poker in the bar. Neat 2-story, aqua-trimmed peach stucco buildings house nice-sized rooms (with dressing areas) that are clean and spiffy-looking. Free local calls are a plus. Facilities include a medium-sized pool and a palm-fringed sundeck.

✪ **Circus Circus Hotel/Casino.** 2880 Las Vegas Blvd. S., between Circus Circus Dr. and Convention Center Dr., Las Vegas, NV 89109. ☎ **800/444-CIRC,** 800/634-3450, or 702/734-0410. Fax 702/734-2268. www.circuscircuslasvegas.com. 3,744 units. A/C TV TEL. Sun–Thurs $39–$79 double, Fri–Sat $59–$99 double. AE, CB, DC, DISC, MC, V. Free self- and valet parking.

Perhaps the strongest evidence that things are changing in Las Vegas is the massive remodeling and renovation of this classic hotel and casino. The circus theme remains, but Jumbo the Clown has been replaced by commedia dell'arte harlequins. In other words, like everyone else, even the venerable Circus Circus, once the epitome of kitsch, is trying to be taken more seriously. But don't come expecting an adult atmosphere; the circus theme remains and the kid appeal along with it. The midway level features dozens of carnival games, a large arcade (more than 300 video and pinball games), trick mirrors, and ongoing circus acts under the big top from 11am to midnight daily. The world's largest permanent circus according to the *Guinness Book of World Records,* it features renowned trapeze artists, stunt cyclists, jugglers, magicians, acrobats, and high-wire daredevils.

The thousands of rooms here occupy sufficient acreage to warrant a free Disney World–style aerial shuttle (another kid pleaser) and minibuses connecting its many components. Tower rooms have brand-new, just slightly better-than-average furnishings, and offer safes and TVs with in-house information and gaming instruction stations. The Manor section comprises five white 3-story buildings out back, fronted by rows of cypresses. Manor guests can park at their doors, and a gate to the complex that can be opened only with a room key assures security. These rooms are usually among the least expensive in town, but we've said it before and we'll say it again: You get what you pay for. (However, as this was being written, the rooms were undergoing—at last—a needed renovation.)

All sections of this vast property have their own swimming pools; additional casinos serve the main tower and Skyrise buildings; and both towers provide covered parking garages.

Dining/Diversions: The old standbys, steak/seafood, coffee shop, Italian restaurant.

Amenities: 24-hour room service (continental breakfast and drinks only), shoe shine, three casinos, wedding chapel, tour and show desks, car-rental desk, unisex hairdresser, two swimming pools, two video-game arcades, shops (see chapter 8), Grand Slam Canyon Theme Park.

Adjacent to the hotel is **Circusland RV Park,** with 384 full-utility spaces and up to 50-amp hookups. It has its own 24-hour convenience store, swimming pools, saunas, whirlpools, kiddie playground, fenced pet runs, video-game arcade, and community room. The rate is $12 Sunday to Thursday, $16 Friday and Saturday, $18 holidays.

Westward Ho Hotel & Casino. 2900 Las Vegas Blvd. S., between Circus Circus Dr. and Convention Center Dr., Las Vegas, NV 89109. ☎ **800/634-6803** or 702/731-2900. 777 units. A/C TV TEL. $37–$56 double; $76 suite. Extra person $10. MC, V. Free parking at your room door.

Located next door to Circus Circus, the Westward Ho is fronted by a vast casino, with rooms in 2-story buildings that extend out back for several city blocks. In fact, the property is so large that a free bus shuttles regularly between the rooms and the casino 24 hours a day. There are three swimming pools and three whirlpool spas to serve all areas.

The rooms are clean and adequately furnished motel units. A good buy here: two-bedroom suites with $1^1/_2$ baths, living rooms with sofa beds, and refrigerators; they sleep up to six people.

There's a 24-hour restaurant in the casino under a stained-glass skylight dome. It serves a buffet breakfast, brunch and dinner, as well as an à la carte menu featuring traditional coffee-shop fare. Other facilities include a tour desk, free airport shuttle, a gift shop, a casino lounge where a three-piece country band entertains Monday to Saturday 7pm to 1am, and a deli in the casino serving sandwiches, ribs, and half-pound extra-long hot dogs.

5 East of the Strip

In this section we've covered hotels close by the Convention Center, along with those farther south on Paradise Road, Flamingo Road, and Tropicana Avenue.

VERY EXPENSIVE

Courtyard Marriott. 3275 Paradise Rd., between Convention Center Dr. and Desert Inn Rd., Las Vegas, NV 89109. ☎ **800/321-2211** or 702/791-3600. Fax 702/796-7981. www.marriott.com. 159 units. A/C TV TEL. Sun–Thurs $109 double, Fri–Sat $119 double; $119–$129 suite. Convention rates may be higher. AE, CB, DC, DISC, MC, V. Free parking at your room door.

The Courtyard is a welcome link in the Marriott chain. Although the services are limited, don't picture a no-frills establishment. This is a good-looking hotel, in a chain-hotel kind of way, with a pleasant, plant-filled lobby and very nice rooms indeed.

Like its public areas, the rooms, most with king-sized beds, still look spanking new. Decorated in shades of gray-blue, mauve, and burgundy, with sofas and handsome mahogany furnishings (including large desks), they offer TVs with multiple On-Command movie options. All rooms have balconies or patios.

Dining/Diversions: One dining room and one lounge.

Amenities: Room service 4 to 10pm, complimentary airport shuttle, small exercise room, medium-sized swimming pool with adjoining whirlpool, picnic tables and barbecue grills, coin-op washers/dryers.

✪ **Hard Rock Hotel & Casino.** 4455 Paradise Rd., at Harmon Ave., Las Vegas, NV 89109. ☎ **800/473-ROCK** or 702/693-5000. Fax 702/693-5010. www.hardrock.com. 670 units. A/C TV TEL. Sun–Thurs $75–$250 double, Fri–Sat $145–$300 double; from $250 suite. Extra person $25. Children 12 and under stay free in parents' room. AE, DC, MC, V. Free self- and valet parking.

The hip—from Hollywood and the music industry, among others—flock to the Hard Rock, drawn by the cool'n' rockin' ambience and the goodies offered by a boutique hotel. It's that Boomer-meets-Gen-X sensibility that finds tacky chic most hip, and that may explain the rooms, which are a big letdown. Though large and with fine rock photos on the walls, the spare furnishings in the older section are a little too close to '60's "no tell motel" for comfort. Suites are actually uglier than standard rooms, with a bath/shower combo crammed into a small chamber, with sinks outside in a dimly lit dressing area. Standard double rooms are quite large and come off somewhat more attractive, while their baths are less cramped. The

Accommodations East of the Strip

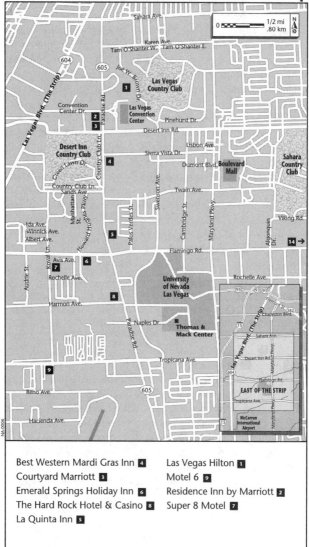

Best Western Mardi Gras Inn **4**   Las Vegas Hilton **1**
Courtyard Marriott **3**   Motel 6 **9**
Emerald Springs Holiday Inn **6**   Residence Inn by Marriott **2**
The Hard Rock Hotel & Casino **8**   Super 8 Motel **7**
La Quinta Inn **5**

rooms and suites in the new addition are much nicer by comparison, still a bit too '60's-futuristic hip to come off posh, but certainly less immediately drab and more comfortable. Bathrooms are a big step forward—bigger, brighter, shinier. On a high note, the beds have feather pillows, and mattresses are surprisingly comfortable. Uncharacteristically large 27-inch TVs offer pay-movie options and special music channels.

Dining/Diversions: The cuisine is the usual, while the restaurants offering it are a step up, including **AJ's Steakhouse, Nobu, Cantina Pink Taco, Mortoni's,** and, of course, the **Hard Rock Cafe.**

Amenities: 24-hour room service, concierge, casino, small video-game arcade, gift/sundry shop and immense Hard Rock retail store, show desk (for **The Joint** only; tickets to other shows can be arranged by the concierge), health club (offering a full complement of Cybex equipment, stair machines, treadmills, massage, and steam rooms), and a large and festive swimming pool area.

✪ **Las Vegas Hilton.** 3000 Paradise Rd., at Riviera Blvd., Las Vegas, NV 89109. ☎ **800/732-7117** or 702/732-7111. Fax 702/732-5790. www.lvhilton.com. 3,174 units, A/C TV TEL. $95–$279 double. Extra person $25. Children of any age stay free in parents' room. Inquire about attractively priced golf and other packages. CB, DC, DISC, ER, MC, V. Free self- and valet parking.

This is really quite a classy hotel, which is probably why so many business travelers prefer it. (That, and its location next to the Convention Center.) There are quite a few terrific restaurants, plus the largest hotel convention and meeting facilities in the world.

A serious renovation has added a number of new shops, plus **Star Trek: The Experience,** a themed attraction and accompanying space-themed casino. They want to start attracting more of a leisure crowd, but you do have to wonder how all these additions might change the otherwise high-rent atmosphere.

The newly remodeled rooms have partly marble floors and slightly larger marble bathtubs. Each has a small dressing area outside the bathroom. The rooms are nothing particularly special in terms of decor, but they are very comfortable. Some have views of the adjacent 18-hole golf course. They feature automatic checkout on the TV and a hotline number on the phone that sends you directly to housekeeping. All offer TVs (cached in handsome armoires) with HBO, On-Command pay-movie options, an in-house information channel, and video checkout capability.

Dining/Diversions: In addition to the excellent **Bistro Le Montrachet,** there is a **Benihana's,** plus several other dining options.

Amenities: 24-hour room service, foreign currency exchange, two casinos, car-rental desk, tour desk, travel agency, shops, small video-game arcade, business service center (faxing and express mail), multiservice beauty salon/barbershop, jogging trail, 18-hole golf course. Large swimming pool and recreation area, including tennis courts and a health club.

EXPENSIVE

La Quinta Inn. 3970 Paradise Rd., between Twain Ave. and Flamingo Rd., Las Vegas, NV 89109. ☎ **800/531-5900** or 702/796-9000. Fax 702/796-3537. www.laquinta.com. 251 units. A/C TV TEL. $85–$95 standard double, $89–$99 executive double; $115–$125 suite. Rates include continental breakfast; inquire about seasonal discounts. AE, CB, DC, DISC, MC, V. Free self-parking.

This is a tranquil alternative to Strip hubbub. The staff is terrific—friendly and incredibly helpful. The rooms are immaculate and attractive. Executive rooms feature one queen-sized bed, a small refrigerator, a wet bar, and a microwave oven. Double queens are larger, but have no kitchen facilities. And two-bedroom suites are not just spacious—they are really full apartments. They contain large living rooms (some with sofa beds), dining areas, and full kitchens. Ground-floor accommodations have patios, and all accommodations feature baths with oversized whirlpool tubs. TVs offer satellite channels and HBO.

Dining/Diversions: Complimentary continental breakfast (juice, bagels, cereal, muffins, fresh fruit, beverages) is served daily in the **Patio Café.**

Amenities: Car rentals/tours arranged at the front desk, coin-op washers/dryers, medium-sized swimming pool and adjoining whirlpool. A free 24-hour shuttle offers pickup and return to and from the airport and several Strip casino hotels.

✪ **Residence Inn by Marriott.** 3225 Paradise Rd., between Desert Inn Rd. and Convention Center Dr., Las Vegas, NV 89109. ☎ **800/331-3131** or 702/796-9300. www.marriott.com. 192 units. A/C TV TEL. $119 and up for studio; $149 and up for penthouse. Rates include continental breakfast. AE, CB, DC, DISC, MC, V. Free self-parking.

Staying here is like having your own apartment in Las Vegas. The property occupies 7 acres of perfectly manicured lawns, tropical foliage, and neat flower beds. It's a great choice for families and business travelers. Monday to Friday, they offer a free light dinner with beer, wine, and soda.

Accommodations, most with working fireplaces, are housed in condo-like, 2-story wood-and-stucco buildings, fronted by little gardens. TVs offer visitor information channels and VCRs (you can rent movies nearby), and all rooms have balconies or patios.

Dining/Diversions: A big continental buffet breakfast (fresh fruit, yogurt, cereals, muffins, bagels, pastries) is served each morning in the gatehouse. Weekday evenings from 5:30 to 7pm, complimentary buffets with beverages (beer, wine, coffee, soda), fresh popcorn, and daily varying fare (soup/salad/sandwiches, tacos, Chinese, barbecue, spaghetti, and so on) are also served.

Amenities: Local restaurants deliver food, and there's also a complimentary food-shopping service. Maids wash your dishes; car-rental desk, barbecue grills, coin-op washers/dryers, sports court (paddle tennis, volleyball, basketball). There's a good-sized swimming pool and whirlpool with a sundeck. Guests can use the health club next door at Courtyard Marriott (details above).

MODERATE

Best Western Mardi Gras Inn. 3500 Paradise Rd., between Sands Ave. and Desert Inn Rd., Las Vegas, NV 89109. ☎ **800/634-6501** or 702/731-2020. Fax 702/733-6994. http://www.mardigrasinn.com. 315 units. A/C TV TEL. $40–$125 double. Extra person $8. Children 18 and under stay free in parents' room. AE, CB, DC, DISC, JCB, MC, V. Free parking at your room door.

Opened in 1980, this well-run little casino hotel is a block from the Convention Center and close to major properties.

Accommodations are all spacious queen-bedded minisuites with sofa-bedded living room areas and eat-in kitchens, the latter equipped with wet bars, refrigerators, and coffeemakers. All are attractively decorated and offer TVs with HBO and pay-movie options. Staying here is like having your own little Las Vegas apartment.

Dining/Diversions: A pleasant restaurant/bar off the lobby serves typical coffee-shop fare.

Amenities: Free transportation to/from airport and major Strip hotels, small casino (64 slots/video poker machines), small video-game arcade, car-rental desk, tour and show desks, coin-op washers/dryers, unisex hairdresser, gift shop, RV parking. The inn has a large swimming pool with a duplex sundeck and whirlpool.

Emerald Springs Holiday Inn. 325 E. Flamingo Rd., between Koval Lane and Paradise Rd., Las Vegas, NV 89109. ☎ **800/732-7889** or 702/732-9100. Fax 702/731-9784. 150 units. A/C TV TEL. $69–$99 studio; $99–$129 whirlpool suite, $129–$175 hospitality suite. Extra person $15. Children 18 and under stay free in parents' room. AE, CB, DC, DISC, MC, V. Free self-parking.

Emerald Springs offers a friendly, low-key alternative to the usual glitz and glitter. Typical of the inn's hospitality is a bowl of apples for the taking at the front desk. And weeknights from 10:30pm to midnight you can "raid the icebox" at the **Veranda Cafe,** which offers complimentary cookies, peanut butter and jelly sandwiches, and coffee, tea, or milk. Although your surroundings here are serene, you're only 3 blocks from the heart of the Strip. Even the smallest accommodations (studios) offer small sofas, desks, and armchairs with hassocks. You also get two phones (desk and bedside), an in-room coffeemaker (with gratis coffee), and a wet bar with refrigerator.

Dining/Diversions: The **Veranda Cafe** will keep you from getting hungry.

Amenities: Concierge, complimentary limousine transportation to and from the airport and nearby casinos between 6:30am and 11pm (van service available 11pm to 6:30am), room service, business services, gratis newspapers available at the front desk, fitness room, nice-sized pool/sundeck and whirlpool in an attractively landscaped setting.

INEXPENSIVE

Motel 6. 195 E. Tropicana Ave., at Koval Lane, Las Vegas, NV 89109. ☎ **800/4-MOTEL-6** or 702/798-0728. Fax 702/798-5657. 602 units. A/C TV TEL. Sun–Thurs $35 single, Fri–Sat $58 single. Extra person $6. Children under 17 stay free in parents' room. AE, CB, DC, DISC, MC, V. Free parking at your room door.

Fronted by a big neon sign, Las Vegas's Motel 6 is the largest in the country, and it happens to be a great budget choice. Most Motel 6 properties are a little out of the way, but this one is quite close to major Strip casino hotels (the MGM is nearby). It has a big, pleasant lobby, and the rooms, in 2-story cream stucco buildings, are clean and attractively decorated. Some rooms have showers only; others, tub/shower baths. Local calls are free and your TV offers HBO.

Dining: Three restaurants (including a pleasant 24-hour family restaurant called **Carrows**) adjoin.

Amenities: A large, well-stocked gift shop, vending machines, a tour desk, two nice-sized swimming pools in enclosed courtyards, a whirlpool, and coin-op washers/dryers.

Super 8 Motel. 4250 Koval Lane, just south of Flamingo Rd., Las Vegas, NV 89109. ☎ **800/800-8000** or 702/794-0888. 290 units. A/C TV TEL. Sun–Thurs $41–$43 double, Fri–Sat $56–$58 double. Extra person $8. Children 12 and under stay free in parents' room. Pets $8 per night (1 pet only). AE, CB, DC, DISC, MC, V. Free self-parking.

Billing itself as "the world's largest Super 8 Motel," this friendly property occupies a vaguely Tudor-style stone-and-stucco building. Coffee is served gratis in a pleasant little lobby furnished with comfortable sofas and wing chairs. Rooms are clean and well maintained. Some have safes, and TVs offer free movie channels.

Dining/Diversions: The nautically themed **Ellis Island Restaurant,** open 24 hours, offers typical coffee-shop fare at reasonable prices.

Amenities: Limited room service via Ellis Island, free airport transfer, casino (actually located next door at Ellis Island; race book and 50 slot/poker/21 machines), small kidney-shaped pool/sundeck and adjoining whirlpool, car-rental desk, coin-op washers/dryers.

6 Downtown

EXPENSIVE

✪ **Golden Nugget.** 129 E. Fremont St., at Casino Center Blvd., Las Vegas, NV 89101. ☎ **800/634-3454** or 702/385-7111. Fax 702/386-8362. www.mirageresorts.com. 1,907 units. A/C TV TEL. $49–$299 double; $275–$500 suite. Extra person $20. AE, CB, DC, DISC, MC, V. Free self- and valet parking.

The Golden Nugget opened in 1946, the first building in Las Vegas constructed specifically for casino gambling. Steve Wynn took it over as his first major project in Vegas, in 1973. He gradually transformed the Old West/Victorian interiors (typical for Downtown) into something more high rent; marble and brass gleam, and the whole package seems considerably more resort-like and genuinely luxurious, especially for Downtown Vegas.

If the decor of the Mirage sounded appealing to you and you want to stay Downtown, come here, since the same people own them and the rooms look almost identical. In keeping with the name, the color scheme in the newly refurbished rooms is gold (rather than the beiges of the Mirage), but features they do share include the marble entryways, half-canopy beds, vanity tables with magnifying makeup mirrors, armoires, and marble bathrooms complete with hair dryers. In the North Tower, the rooms are slightly larger than in the South (and also slightly larger than at the Mirage).

Dining/Diversions: The **Carson Street Café, Stefano's, Lillie Langtry's,** and a **California Pizza Kitchen.**

Amenities: 24-hour room service, shoe shine, concierge, casino, car-rental desk, full-service unisex hair salon, shops (gifts, jewelry, designer fashions, sportswear, logo items), video-game arcade, swimming pool, and health club and spa.

Accommodations Downtown

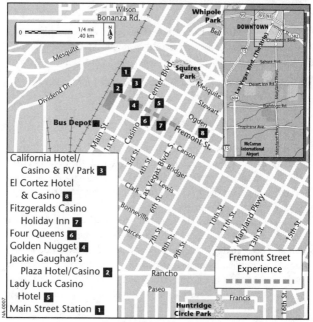

California Hotel/ Casino & RV Park **3**

El Cortez Hotel & Casino **8**

Fitzgeralds Casino Holiday Inn **7**

Four Queens **6**

Golden Nugget **4**

Jackie Gaughan's Plaza Hotel/Casino **2**

Lady Luck Casino Hotel **5**

Main Street Station **1**

MODERATE

✪ **Fitzgeralds Casino Holiday Inn.** 301 Fremont St., at 3rd St., Las Vegas, NV 89101. ☎ **800/274-LUCK** or 702/388-2400. Fax 702/388-2181. 652 units. A/C TV TEL. $40–$85 double; $60–$105 suite. Extra person $10. Children under 19 stay free in parents' room. AE, CB, DC, DISC, MC, V. Free self- and valet parking.

Fitzgeralds recently became a Holiday Inn franchise and has upgraded all their rooms to fit said chain's code. The result is attractive and has received an award for best redesign from the Governor's Conference. Fitzgeralds also has the only balcony in Downtown from which you can watch the Fremont Street Experience.

The look in the rooms is clean and comfortable, standard hotel room decor, done in shades of green (no, the leprechaun theme does not follow in here). Because this is the tallest building in Downtown (34 stories), you get excellent views: either snowcapped mountains, Downtown lights, or the Strip. Whirlpool tub rooms are $20 more and are slightly larger with wraparound windows. All offer safes and 25-inch TVs with pay-movie options.

Dining/Diversions: Food options include **Limerick's, Vincenzo's, Molly's Country Kitchen,** plus a McDonalds.

Amenities: 24-hour room service, complimentary gaming lessons, casino, tour and show desks, car-rental desk, gift shop, jewelry shop.

✪ **Four Queens.** 202 Fremont St., at Casino Center Blvd., Las Vegas, NV 89101. ☎ **800/634-6045** or 702/385-4011. Fax 702/387-5122. www.savenet.com/702/4queen.htm. 700 units. A/C TV TEL. $29–$179 double; $119–$350 suite. Extra person $15. AE, CB, DC, DISC, MC, V. Free self- and valet parking.

Opened in 1966 with a mere 120 rooms, the Four Queens (named for the owner's four daughters) has evolved over the decades into a major Downtown property occupying an entire city block. Their clientele is on the older side (50-plus), those who are not coming to Las Vegas for the first time.

Notably nice rooms, decorated in basic hotel-room style, are located in 19-story twin towers. Especially lovely are the North Tower rooms, decorated in a Southwestern motif and, in most cases, offering views of the Fremont Street Experience. South Tower rooms are done up in earth tones with dark-wood furnishings and wallpaper in small floral prints. All accommodations offer TVs with in-house information and pay-movie channels. Some rooms are equipped with small refrigerators and coffeemakers.

Dining/Diversions: There are four restaurants.

Amenities: 24-hour room service, gift shop, car-rental desk, tour and show desks, small video-game arcade, plus a basic workout room that is free.

INEXPENSIVE

California Hotel/Casino & RV Park. 12 Ogden Ave., at 1st St., Las Vegas, NV 89101. ☎ **800/634-6255** or 702/385-1222. Fax 702/388-2660. 855 units. A/C TV TEL. Sun–Thurs $50 double; Fri–Sat $60 double; holidays $70 double. Extra person $5. Children 12 and under stay free in parents' room. AE, CB, DC, DISC, MC, V. Free self- and valet parking.

This is a hotel with a unique personality. California-themed, it markets mostly in Hawaii, and since 85% of the guests are from the "Aloha State," it offers Hawaiian entrees in several of its restaurants and even has an on-premises store specializing in Hawaiian food-stuff.

The rooms, however, reflect neither California nor Hawaii. Decorated in contemporary-look burgundy/mauve or apricot/teal color schemes, they have mahogany furnishings and attractive marble baths. In-room safes are a plus, and TVs offer pay-per-view movies and keno channels.

Dining/Diversions: There are four restaurants.

Amenities: Room service (breakfast only), casino, car-rental desk, car wash, small rooftop pool, small video-game arcade, shops (gift shop, chocolates). A food store carries items popular with Hawaiians and there are several umbrella tables outside where these snacks can be eaten.

El Cortez Hotel & Casino. 600 Fremont St., between 6th and 7th sts., Las Vegas, NV 89101. ☎ **800/634-6703** or 702/385-5200. Fax 702/385-9765. http://www.elcortez.net. 428 units. A/C TV TEL. $32 double; $40 minisuite. Extra person $3. AE, DISC, MC, V. Free self- and valet parking.

This small hotel is popular with locals for its casual, "just-folks" Downtown atmosphere and its frequent big-prize lotteries (up to $50,000) based on Social Security numbers. The nicest accommodations are the enormous minisuites in the newer 14-story tower. Some are exceptionally large king-bedded rooms with sofas; others have separate sitting areas with sofas, armchairs, and tables, plus small dressing areas. The rooms in the original building are furnished more traditionally and with less flair, and they cost less. Local calls are just 25¢.

Dining/Diversions: Two restaurants.

Amenities: Small video-game arcade, beauty salon, gift shop, and barbershop.

Under the same ownership is **Ogden House,** just across the street, with rooms that go for just $18 a night.

Jackie Gaughan's Plaza Hotel/Casino. 1 Main St., at Fremont St., Las Vegas, NV 89101. ☎ **800/634-6575** or 702/386-2110. Fax 702/386-2378. 1,037 units. A/C TV TEL. $40–$120 double; $80–$150 suite. Extra person $8. Children under 12 stay free in parents' room. AE, DC, DISC, MC, V. Free self- and valet parking.

Built in 1971 on the site of the old Union Pacific Railroad Depot, the Plaza, a double-towered, 3-block-long property, permanently altered the Downtown skyline. Las Vegas's Amtrak station (currently unused) is right in the hotel, and the main Greyhound terminal adjoins it. Fremont Street literally ends right at the Plaza's front door, so you can't fault the location.

Accommodations are spacious and attractively decorated, with king rooms offering plush sofas. The suites in particular are huge, and the two-bedroom suite would be a terrific option for a large party of friends to share. Rooms in the North Tower look down on the Fremont Street Experience.

Dining/Diversions: The **Center Stage, Plaza Diner,** and **Back Stage,** should take care of most basic food needs.

Amenities: Guest services desk (also handles in-house shows), tour desk, casino, car-rental desk, shops, a wedding chapel, beauty salon/barbershop. There's a sports deck with a nice-sized swimming pool, a quarter-mile outdoor jogging track, and four Har-Tru tennis courts.

Lady Luck Casino Hotel. 206 N. 3rd St., at Ogden Ave., Las Vegas, NV 89101. ☎ **800/523-9582** or 702/477-3000. Fax 702/382-2346. www.ladyluck.com. 792 units. A/C TV TEL. $40–$155 double; Sun–Thurs $55–$75 junior suite, Fri–Sat $70–$105 junior suite. Extra person $8. AE, CB, DC, DISC, JCB, MC, V. Free self- and valet parking.

What the Lady Luck retains from its opening days in 1964, is a friendly atmosphere, one that has kept customers coming back for decades. Eighty percent of Lady Luck's clientele is repeat business. Tower rooms are decorated in a variety of attractive color schemes, mostly using muted Southwestern hues and handsome oak furnishings. It's all larger, brighter, and lighter than you might expect. All rooms are equipped with small refrigerators and TVs with pay-per-view movie options. Junior suites in the West Tower have parlor areas with sofas and armchairs, separate dressing areas, and baths with whirlpool tubs. The original Garden Rooms are a little smaller and less spiffy-looking in terms of decor; on the plus side, they're right by the pool, which is not heated, by the way (but there aren't a lot of pools in Downtown).

Dining/Diversions: Three restaurants.

Amenities: 24-hour room service, multilingual front desk, and complimentary airport shuttle, casino, tour, and show desks, car-rental desk, gift shop, unheated swimming pool and sundeck.

✪ **Main Street Station.** 200 N. Main St., between Fremont St. and I-95, Las Vegas, NV 89101. ☎ **800/465-0711** or 702/387-1896. Fax 702/386-4466. 452 units. A/C TV TEL. $45–$175 standard double. AE, CB, DC, DISC, MC, V. Free self- and valet parking.

Though not actually on Fremont Street, the Main Street Station is just 2 short blocks away, barely a 3-minute walk. Considering how terrific it is, this is hardly an inconvenience. Having taken over an abandoned hotel space, the Main Street Station reopened in November 1996 to become, in our opinion, one of the nicest hotels in Downtown and one of the best bargains in the city. The overall look is, admittedly as usual for Downtown, turn-of-the-century San Francisco. However, unlike everywhere else, the details here are outstanding, producing a beautiful hotel by any measure.

The long and narrow rooms are possibly the largest in Downtown. The ornate decorating downstairs does not extend up here. White-painted, wooded plantation shutters replace the usual curtains; each room has a very large gilt-framed mirror; the simple but not unattractive furniture is vaguely French provincial, done in medium-tone neutrals. It's all clean and in good taste. The bathrooms are small but well appointed. It should be noted that rooms on the north side overlook the freeway, and the railroad track is nearby. The soundproofing seems quite strong—we couldn't hear anything when inside, but then again, we are from Los Angeles. A few guests have complained about noise in these rooms, but the majority have had no problems. If you are concerned, request a room on the south side. Each room has Nintendo for a charge and movies for free.

Dining/Diversions: The restaurant offerings are particularly strong here, including the **Triple 7 Brew Pub,** the **Pullman Grille,** and the **Cascade Cafe.**

Amenities: Dry cleaning and laundry service, in-room massage, safety-deposit boxes, casino, gift shop, show desk, shopping and game-room arcade at California Hotel accessible via connecting walkway.

5

Dining

*A*mong the many images that people have of Las Vegas are cheap food deals, bargains so good the food is practically free. They think of the buffets—all a small country can eat—for only $3.99!

All that is true, but frankly, eating in Las Vegas is no longer something you don't have to worry about budgeting for. The buffets are certainly there—no good hotel would be without one—as are the cheap meal deals, but you get what you pay for. Some of the cheaper buffets, and even the more moderately priced ones, are mediocre at best, ghastly and inedible at worst. And we don't even want to think about those 69¢ beef stew specials.

However, there is some good, indeed, almost unheard-of news on the Vegas food scene. Virtually overnight, there has been an explosion of new restaurants that are of such high quality that Vegas can hold its head up alongside other big cities as a legitimate foodie destination.

Look at this partial list: Celebrity chefs Wolfgang Puck and Emeril Lagasse between them have half a dozen restaurants in town; deservedly famed chefs Julian Serrano and Jean Louis Palladin have set up shop in Bellagio's **Picasso** and the Rio's **Napa,** respectively; branches of L.A., New York, San Francisco, and Boston high-profile and highly regarded eateries such as **Pinot, Le Cirque, Aqua, Aureole, Olives, Star Canyon, Lutece, Border Grill,** and still others have all set up camp.

There are tricks to surviving dining in Vegas. If you can, make reservations in advance, particularly for the better restaurants. Eat as much as you can during off-hours, which admittedly are hard to find. But you know that noon to, say, 1:30 or 2pm is going to be prime for lunch, and 5:30 to 8:30pm (and just after the early shows get out) for dinner. Speaking of time, give yourself plenty of it, particularly if you have to catch a show.

1 Best Bets

- **Best All-Around:** Always feeling free to spend your money for you, we can safely say that dropping a small fortune on the

French cuisine at **Le Cirque** (☎ 702/693-8150), in Bellagio, the highly regarded New York City import, is a fine investment.

- **Biggest Thrill for Foodies:** The heralded chefs Jean-Louis Palladin and Julian Serrano are cooking in Vegas, at **Napa** (☎ 702/247-7961), in the Rio, and **Picasso** (☎ 702/693-7223), in Bellagio, demonstrating, along with several other fine new restaurants, that Vegas's rep for luckluster restaurants is no longer deserved.

- **Best Buffet:** For the Strip, it's the **Mirage Buffet** (☎ 702/791-7111). Not at all the cheapest in town, but the quality goes up accordingly. Downtown, the new **Main Street Station Garden Court,** 200 N. Main St. (☎ 702/387-1896), has an incredible buffet; all live-action stations, wood-fired brick-oven pizzas, fresh lovely salsas and guacamole in the Mexican section, and better-than-average desserts. No other Downtown establishment comes even close.

- **Best Sunday Champagne Brunch:** It's Midstrip's **Bally's** lavish **Sterling Sunday Brunch** (☎ 702/739-4111), where display tables embellished with floral arrangements and ice sculptures are laden with everything from mounds of fresh shrimp to sushi and sashimi, and fancy entrees include the likes of roast duckling with black-currant and blueberry sauce.

- **Best Graveyard Dinner Deal:** Downtown, **Binion's Horseshoe Coffee Shop,** 128 E. Fremont St., at Casino Center Blvd. (☎ 702/382-1600), offers a complete New York steak dinner served with potato, roll, and salad for just $3 from 10pm to 5:45am.

- **Best Cheap Breakfast:** Make your first stop of the day at the South Strip's **Cyclone Coffee Shop,** 3750 Las Vegas Blvd. S. (☎ 732/735-2400), at the Holiday Inn Casino Boardwalk, where a $1.29 breakfast includes two eggs, bacon or sausage, hash browns, and toast. It's served around the clock.

- **Best Restaurant Interiors:** The designers ran amok in **Mandalay Bay,** where a glass wine tower—requiring girls to be hauled up in harnesses—borrowed from the stage production of *Peter Pan* finishes off the moderne frills at **Aureole** (☎ 702/632-7401) and the post-Communist party decor at **Red Square** (☎ 702/632-7407) is topped by the fire and water walls at neighboring **rumjungle** (☎ 702/632-7777).

- **Best Spot for a Romantic Dinner:** At **Picasso,** you get to dine under the watchful gaze of a dozen or so works by the Grand Old

Man himself, while outside Bellagio water fountains dance and play in a fanciful and humorous manner. Pretty inspiring ambience, if you ask us.

- **Best Spot for a Celebration:** Let's face it, no one parties like the Red Party, so head to **Red Square** (☎ 702/632-7407) in Mandalay Bay, where you can have caviar and vodka in the ultimate capitalist revenge.
- **Best Free Show at Dinner:** At Treasure Island's **Buccaneer Bay Club** (☎ 702/894-7350) everyone rushes to the window when the ship battle begins.
- **Best View:** See all of Las Vegas from the revolving **Top of the World** (☎ 702/380-7711), at the Stratosphere, North Strip, 106 stories up.
- **Best Seafood:** The Asian-influenced dishes at **Aqua** (☎ 702/693-7223), in Bellagio, are the only fish dishes consistently worth eating in this desert town—fresh, light, beautifully and expertly flavored.
- **Best Italian:** For a Mediterranean angle, head to Todd English's **Onda** (☎ 702/791-7111, ext. 7354), in the Mirage, which is quietly but swiftly heading to the top of the "locals' favorite" list. For a Northern Italy meets Provence slant, **Fiore** (☎ 702/252-7702), in the Rio, enjoys a sterling reputation.
- **Best Deli:** The **Stage Deli** (☎ 702/893-4045), in Caesars, will give no cause for complaints.
- **Best Bistro:** Todd English recently won a James Beard Foundation award for Rising New Star. See why at a branch of his Boston-based restaurant, **Olives** (☎ 702/693-7223), in Bellagio.
- **Best Healthy/Veggie Conscious:** The **Enigma Cafe,** 918^{1}/$_{2}$ S. Fourth St. (☎ 702/386-0999), in the Gateway District, which makes it convenient for both the Strip and Downtown, offers a large selection of really cheap sandwiches, salads, and smoothies, in a pretty, relaxing setting.
- **Best New Orleans Cuisine: Emeril's New Orleans Fish House** (☎ 702/891-7374), in the MGM Grand, and his **Delmonico Steakhouse** (☎ 702/414-3737), in the Venetian, bring the celebrity chef's "Bam!" cuisine to the other side of the Mississippi, and we are glad.
- **Best Southwestern Cuisine:** The fact that it's the only notable Southwestern restaurant in town doesn't make the MGM Grand's **Coyote Cafe** (☎ 702/891-7349) any less impressive. Superstar Santa Fe chef Mark Miller brings contemporary

culinary panache to traditional Southwestern cookery, and the results are spicy and spectacular.

- **Best Red Meat: Lawry's The Prime Rib,** 4043 Howard Hughes
  Pkwy. (☎ **702/893-2223**), has such good prime rib, it's hard to
  ever imagine having any better, while **Prime** (☎ **702/693-7223**),
  in Bellagio, is thrilling red meat-eaters with even more cuts of
  cow.

2 South Strip

VERY EXPENSIVE

Aureole. Mandalay Bay, 3950 Las Vegas Blvd. S. ☎ **702/632-7401.** Reservations required. Fixed-price dinner $65. AE, DISC, MC, V. Daily 5–10:15pm.
NOUVELLE AMERICAN.

This branch of a New York City fave (it's pronounced *are-ree-all*)
run by Charlie Palmer is most noted locally for its glass wine tower.
Four stories of carefully chosen bottles (among other vineyard thrills
is the largest collection of Austrian wines outside of that country,
and well worth trying for a new wine experience) are plucked from
their perches by comely, cat-suited lasses who fly up and down via
pulleys. It's quite the show, and folks come in just to watch.

Should you come for the food? Perhaps. Certainly the Asian-
influenced fusion is solid, but more underwhelming than outstanding, and since it's currently a fixed price three-course meal, it may
simply not be worth the price.

۞ Coyote Cafe. MGM Grand, 3799 Las Vegas Blvd. S. ☎ **702/891-7349.**
Reservations recommended for the Grill Room, not accepted for the Cafe. Grill
Room main courses $15–$32. Cafe main courses $7.50–$17.50 (many are under $10). AE, CB, DC, DISC, JCB, MC, V. Grill Room daily 5:30–10pm. Cafe daily
7:30am–11pm. SOUTHWESTERN.

In a town where restaurant cuisine often seems stuck in a 1950s time
warp, Mark Miller's Coyote Cafe evokes howls of delight. His robust regional cuisine combines elements of traditional Mexican,
Native American, Creole, and Cajun cookery with cutting-edge
culinary trends.

The Grill Room menu changes monthly. If you're lucky, you
might find the heavenly "painted soup"—half garlicky black bean,
half beer-infused smoked Cheddar—"painted" with chipotle cream
and garnished with salsa fresca and de árbol chili powder. A reliable
main course is the salmon fillet crusted with ground pumpkin seeds
and corn tortillas topped with roasted chile/pumpkin-seed sauce and
presented on a bed of spinach-wrapped spaghetti squash studded

with pine nuts, corn kernels, scallions, and morsels of sun-dried tomato. The Cafe menu offers similar but somewhat lighter fare. Southwestern breakfasts ($6 to $9.50) range from huevos rancheros to blue-corn pancakes with toasted pine nuts, honey butter, and real maple syrup.

✪ **Emeril's New Orleans Fish House.** MGM Grand, 3799 Las Vegas Blvd. S. ☎ **702/891-7374.** Reservations required. Main courses $12–$18 at lunch, $18–$38 at dinner (more for lobster). AE, CB, DC, DISC, MC, V. Daily 11am–2:30pm and 5:30–10:30pm. CONTEMPORARY CREOLE.

Chef Emeril Lagasse, a ubiquitous presence on cable's Food Network, has brought his popular New Orleans restaurant to the MGM Grand, where it is tucked into an almost unseen corner of the hotel. The restaurant's quiet and comforting decor provides the stage for creative, exciting, "BAM!" food.

Although Lagasse caters to the tastes of everyone from poultry lovers to vegetarians, seafood is the specialty here, flown in from Louisiana or from anywhere that he finds the quality of the ingredients to be the very finest. We started off with the most recent edition of Lagasse's legendary savory "cheesecakes," the lobster cheesecake with tomato-tarragon coulis, topped with a dollop of succulent Louisiana choupique caviar. It's a heady, rich appetizer that may be completely unlike anything you've ever had. And try the barbecued shrimp, which come in a garlic-and-herb butter sauce that will have you mopping your plate with bread.

Our entrees did not fail to elicit a "Wow!" from everyone at the table. A Creole-seasoned seared ahi steak was stuffed with Hudson Valley foie gras and served in a bed of Lagasse's famous "smashed" potatoes, creamy and rich, with roasted shallots and a part-shallot reduction—absolutely luxurious. A medley of seafood, from caviar to shrimp to mussels and clams, came over pasta in a delicious and very spicy broth. And in a dish that bordered on the sinful, there was a marvelously seasoned filet mignon stuffed with a crawfish dressing and topped with bordelaise sauce with crawfish tails and sliced andouille sausage. Meat eaters will also be very happy with the utterly tender and flavorful filet of beef with tasso hollandaise sauce and homemade Worcestershire.

It would be difficult to recommend one particular dessert from the vast menu since they're all fabulous, but if it's your first visit, a slice of the banana cream pie with banana crust and caramel drizzle is one of the finest desserts you will ever have.

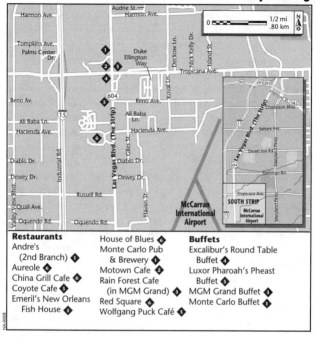

Restaurants
Andre's
  (2nd Branch) ❶
Aureole ❻
China Grill Cafe ❻
Coyote Cafe ❸
Emeril's New Orleans
  Fish House ❸

House of Blues ❻
Monte Carlo Pub
  & Brewery ❶
Motown Cafe ❷
Rain Forest Cafe
  (in MGM Grand) ❸
Red Square ❻
Wolfgang Puck Café ❸

Buffets
Excalibur's Round Table
  Buffet ❹
Luxor Pharoah's Pheast
  Buffet ❺
MGM Grand Buffet ❸
Monte Carlo Buffet ❶

EXPENSIVE

House of Blues. Mandalay Bay, 3950 Las Vegas Blvd. S. ☎ **702/632-7600.**
Main courses $8.95 at lunch, $10.95–$24.95 at dinner. AE, DISC, MC, V. Sun–
Thurs 8am–11pm, Fri–Sat 8am–midnight. SOUTHERN.

> Food and theme-wise the best of the theme restaurants, because the
> former is really pretty good (if a little more costly than it ought to
> be) and the latter's mock Delta/New Orleans look somehow works.
> The food is more nouvelle Southern than true Southern, and so
> alongside jambalaya and étouffée you get penne pasta with gouda
> and mushroom cream sauce. We are fond of their key lime pie with
> raspberry sauce. The bottle-cap bedecked bar has become a local
> late-night hangout, while the actual club is the best place in town
> to see rock bands. The gospel brunch might be worth checking out
> (food is good but too much of it), but be warned: It can be room-
> clearing loud, so bring earplugs.

✪ **Red Square.** Mandalay Bay, 3950 Las Vegas Blvd. S. ☎ **702/632-7407.**
Reservations recommended. Main courses $16.75–$31. AE, DC, MC, V. Sun–
Weds 5:30pm–2am, Thurs–Sat 5:30pm–4am. CONTINENTAL/RUSSIAN.

Let's go dancing on the grave of the USSR. The beheaded and pigeon-dropping adorned statue of Lenin outside Red Square only hints at the near profane delights inside. There you will find decayed posters that once glorified the Worker, cheek by jowl with a patch-work mix of remnants of Czarist trappings, as pillaged from toppled Bolsheviks and Stalinists. And then there's the ice-covered bar—all the better to keep your drinks nicely chilled—and how Czarist ex-cess is celebrated with an out-of-the-reach-of-the-proletariat, $2,500-a-month ice locker for storing vodka (sable robes—yes, really—are provided to keep visitors warm). It's all just one big post-Commu-nist party. (Sorry.)

Anyway, if you can lift your eyes from the theme-run-amuck, you might notice the food is quite good. Blow your expense account on some caviar (we found we liked nutty Osetra better than stronger Beluga), properly chilled in ice, served with the correct pearl spoon, accompanied by the right accoutrements. Or, more affordably, nosh on Siberian nachos—smoked salmon, citron caviar, and crème fraîche. Caesar salad comes as a whole head of Romaine and is quite good, though the dressing is a little tart—ask them to go lightly. The chef's special is a roquefort-crusted, tender filet mignon, with some soft caramelized garlic and a fine reduction sauce; it's a grand piece of meat. Try a silly themed drink: "Cuban Missile Crisis" is rain vodka, dark rum, sugar cane syrup, and lime juice. Dessert is not so clever, but is worth saving room for.

MODERATE

See also the listing for **Coyote Cafe** (p. 71), an expensive restaurant fronted by a more moderately priced cafe.

✪ **China Grill Cafe and Zen Sum.** Mandalay Bay, 3950 Las Vegas Blvd. S. ☎ **702/632-7405.** Reservations for 8 or more only. Main courses $8.50–$15.95. AE, DC, MC, V. Daily 11am–midnight. CHINESE.

This cheaper, cafe version of the China Grill is one of our favorite new restaurants in Vegas. Now, "cheaper" doesn't mean "budget," but it is a way to try the China Grill in a less pricey manner. And when they say "cafe," they don't mean French bistro; instead, it's Asian space age industrial, with lots of right angles, clean wood and metal, a dim sum bar that has robots serving platters from a con-veyor belt, and Zen evoked in various forms including overhead pro-jections of pithy sayings (though the atmosphere promotes anything but Zen-like calm). The dim sum menu is limited but interesting. Winners included lamb chile and mint potstickers with guava sauce

(sauce was subtle, but dumplings plump and meaty), and crispy beef and tomato dumplings with smoky chile firecracker sauce. Skip the bland turkey siu mai and dry spring rolls. You should also try a noodle dish—they should be ordinary, but can be quite fabulous. Stir-fried duck with shiitake and wokked noodles was simple but delicious. Food is served family style from big platters. Desserts are less stellar, but curious enough to be worth a try.

Motown Cafe. New York New York Hotel & Casino, 3790 Las Vegas Blvd. S. ☎ **702/740-6440.** Reservations not accepted. Main courses $7–$18. AE, DISC, JCB, MC, V. Sun–Thurs 7:30am–11:30pm, Fri–Sat 7:30am–2am. SOUTHWESTERN.

The menu at this tribute to Motown record label artists features light Southwestern cuisine (jambalaya, shrimp Creole) probably because no one could figure out what the indigenous cuisine of Detroit was. (This is in addition to the basic burgers and so forth.) They also offer a breakfast buffet. And as we all know, Motown music is just about the best there is for dancing, and the cafe stays open until 3am on weekdays and 4am on weekends for dancing.

Rain Forest Cafe. MGM Grand, 3799 Las Vegas Blvd. S. ☎ **702/891-8580.** Reservations not required. Main courses $9–$13 at breakfast, $10–$19 at dinner. AE, DC, DISC, JCB, MC, V. Mon–Thurs 8am–11pm, Fri–Sat 8am–midnight, Sun 8am–10pm. CALIFORNIA.

If you've always wanted to eat a meal in the Jungle Cruise ride at Disneyland, here's your chance. Decor-wise, this is possibly the best of the many theme restaurants in town. It's full of faux foliage, Animatronic animals (some of which are not indigenous to rain forests, but oh well), flowers, giant butterflies, and so forth. Water splashes, animals roar, music plays, thunderstorms hit periodically—it all adds up to one noisy experience, but not, sadly, a particularly educational one. The food is tasty and imaginative, if somewhat busy, and most dishes are variations on the usual pastas, sandwiches, and whatnot. The veggie burgers did earn serious raves from connoisseurs of same. Consider checking out the smoothies offered at the bar. Kids will love the sights and the children's menu. You won't love trying to steer them through the gift shop entrance.

✪ **Wolfgang Puck Café.** MGM Grand, 3799 Las Vegas Blvd. S. ☎ **702/895-9653.** Reservations not accepted. Main courses $9–$15. AE, DC, MC, V. Sun–Thurs 8am–11pm, Fri–Sat 8am–midnight. CALIFORNIA.

A brightly colored riot of mosaic tiles and other experiments in geometric design, the Wolfgang Puck Café stands out in the

MGM Grand. It's more or less Spago Lite: downscaled salads, pizzas, and pastas, all showing the Puck hand, and while perhaps a little more money than your average cafe, the food is comparably better, if sometimes not that special. However, it's all very fresh nouvelle cuisine, which makes a nice change of pace. The specialty pizzas are fun; constructed on crusts topped with fontina and mozzarella cheeses, they're brushed with pesto and layered with embellishments such as spicy jalapeño-marinated sautéed chicken, leeks, and cilantro. It's always a thrill to get a good salad in Vegas, and there are quite a few on this menu. Worth noting is the signature Chinois chicken salad tossed with crispy fried wontons, julienned carrots, cabbage, and green onions in a Chinese honey-mustard sauce. For something cheap, try the surprisingly large baby greens salad with the goat cheese toast—that and the very fine herb bread that comes gratis is $5, which fills you up in a fairly healthy way for not a lot of money. There does tend to be a line, particularly after *EFX* lets out just across the casino.

INEXPENSIVE

✪ **Monte Carlo Pub & Brewery.** Monte Carlo Resort & Casino, 3770 Las Vegas Blvd. S., between Flamingo Rd. and Tropicana Ave. ☎ **702/730-7777.** Reservations not accepted. Main courses $6–$8. AE, CB, DC, DISC, MC, V. Sun–Thurs 11am–1am, Fri–Sat 11am–3am. PUB FARE.

Lest you think we are big, fat foodie snobs who can't appreciate a meal unless it comes drenched in truffles and caviar, we hasten to direct you to this lively, working microbrewery and its hearty, not so high falutin' food. No fancy French frills, and best of all, no inflated prices. Combine the general high quality with generous portions—a nachos appetizer could probably feed eight (though it was not the best nachos appetizer ever)—and this may be a better deal than most buffets. It is, however, not the place for a quiet rendezvous, with about 40 TVs spread throughout (seems like a sports fan's dream) and music blaring.

Earning recent raves were the short ribs, in a fine barbecue sauce, cooked just right; the excellent chicken fingers and shrimp fried in beer appetizers; the garlic pizza with mounds of our favorite aromatic herb; the pizza topped with lamb, grilled eggplant, and goat cheese (well, maybe that has more frills than we promised); and the avocado and shrimp salads.

3   Mid-Strip

VERY EXPENSIVE

✪ **Aqua.** Bellagio, 3600 Las Vegas Blvd. S. ☎ **702/693-7223.** Reservations recommended. Main courses $29–$34 (lobster and whole foie gras higher). AE, DISC, MC, V. Daily 5:30–11pm. SEAFOOD.

Fish fans should certainly head quickly over to Aqua, a branch of a highly respected San Francisco restaurant, but even fish-phobes might reconsider their position when they try Aqua's slightly Asian-influenced pleasures. You can start your meal with a non-seafood choice like Hudson Valley foie gras, which comes with a warm apple Charlotte that tastes a bit like something you might eat at breakfast—though foie gras is hardly a breakfast meat. The mixed seasonal greens salad looks like a flower, and is a light, amiable mix of flavors.

For a main course, fish fans should go straight to the vaguely Japanese miso-glazed Chilean sea bass in a rich but not heavy shellfish consommé. More timid fish eaters might try the robust Hawaiian swordfish au poivre, though its side of pancetta-wrapped shrimp dumplings (think fancy bacon-wrapped shrimp) is not as successful. Also winning raves is the potato-crusted John Dory, and the lobster pot pie; the latter is cooked in a pot, then brought to table and disassembled with great ceremony, as 1¹/₂ pounds of lobster are laid out, a creamy sauce with veggies poured over it, and it is topped with the crust. Do try some of their dainty and clever desserts, particularly their signature root beer float—no, really, it's got root beer sorbet, sarsaparilla ice cream, a chocolate straw, and warm cookies right out of the oven.

Bacchanal. Caesars Palace, 3570 Las Vegas Blvd. S., just north of Flamingo Rd. ☎ **702/731-7731.** Reservations required. Fixed-price dinner $69.50, plus tax and gratuity. AE, CB, DC, DISC, MC, V. Tues–Sat 6–11pm with seatings at 6, 6:30, 9, and 9:30pm. CONTINENTAL.

This is the quintessential Vegas restaurant experience, where the food is considerably less important than the spectacle. A bacchanal is a devotee of the Roman god of wine, Bacchus. As a festival participant, a certain level of debauchery is required. You will be expected to accept a massage from a wine goddess (the toga-clad waitresses who dispense alcohol) or Hercules, be enticed by the belly dancers, and for pity's sake, eat and drink your fair share. Not for the introverted or inhibited. Giggling is allowed. Being aloof and above it all is not.

The six-course meal (entree, soup, salad, pasta, crudités, and dessert) is certainly plentiful and satisfactory—but you really don't come for the food. You come for the show, the royal service, the personalized greeting by Caesar and Cleopatra, the belly dancing, and of course, the wine goddesses, who keep your glass ever full. But be careful: There are stories of people who have slipped out to the bathroom—which requires a pass through the casino—after several glasses of wine and returned down $20,000. That may be more decadence than you can handle.

✪ **Buccaneer Bay Club.** Treasure Island, 3300 Las Vegas Blvd. S. ☎ **702/ 894-7350.** Reservations recommended. Main courses $20–$35. AE, CB, DC, DISC, JCB, MC, V. Daily 5–10:30pm. AMERICAN/CONTINENTAL.

This is a little-known gem (at least, outside of Treasure Island guests) that features a laudable menu more innovative than the standard found at other equivalent hotel restaurants. The whole thing overlooks the hotel's "bay" where a pirate battle is waged every 90 minutes. This probably isn't the best place to view it from (the windows are smallish, and you're behind the action), but the wait staff does notify you at show time and will hold your food service until it's through if you have chosen to watch. It's fun to watch everyone rush to the windows when they announce, "Pirates are on!"

Entrees range from poultry (chicken, duck, pheasant) to beef (filet mignon, prime rib, steak) to seafood (sea bass, lobster, salmon). A favorite here is the Pheasant Charles, which comes with pan-seared, thyme-roasted wild mushroom risotto and is served in a Merlot lingonberry sauce. There's also Colorado Buffalo Prime Rib, which is roasted and grilled over mesquite wood and served with creamy horseradish potatoes. If you've not tried buffalo before, do so now, as it will be one of the best pieces of cow-based meat you'll ever taste. Desserts include apple beignets, white chocolate cheesecake with raspberry sauce, and the house specialty apricot or harlequin (Grand Marnier, white and dark chocolate) minisoufflés.

Chinois. Caesars Palace, 3570 Las Vegas Blvd. S. ☎ **702/737-9700.** Reservations recommended. Main courses $11–$16.50 in the cafe, $19.75–$28 in the restaurant. AE, JCB, MC, V. Restaurant daily 5:30–10pm; cafe daily 11am–11pm. EURASIAN.

From Wolfgang Puck, the man who brought you Spago and gourmet frozen pizzas, comes another entry in the world of fine dining and innovative cuisine. It's more about presentation than truly

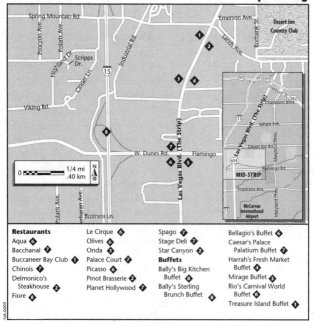

NA-0009

remarkable meals, but it's still good to have on the Vegas foodie scene.

The food—best described as nouvelle Asian—is served family style, which helps spread the rather high prices around some. There are specials every night, but you can count on Chinois "classics" every evening. Appetizers include Szechuan pancakes with stir-fried Peking duck, spring veggies, and wild mushrooms—everything combines into one new savory taste. We also recommend the lovely sautéed foie gras with rhubarb compote (it has a citrus zing to it) and a sauce made from port wine, figs, and spices. For entrees, keeping in a pricey vein, we are sorry to relate that the Shanghai lobster with a rich coconut curry sauce is marvelous. If you need to get talked out of it, however, the lobster can have some chewy bits. More budget-minded is the whole sizzling catfish, which along with a couple of appetizers will easily feed two people. The Cantonese duck with divine sesame crêpes is also superb, a light, nearly perfect rendering of that difficult fowl. Save room for the scrumptious chocolate mint gâteau dessert.

Delmonico Steakhouse. The Venetian, 3355 Las Vegas Blvd. S. ☎ **702/ 414-3737.** Reservations strongly recommended for dinner. Main courses $21–$36. AE, DC, DISC, MC, V. Daily 11:30am–2pm; Sun–Thurs 5:30–10:30pm, Fri–Sat 5:30–11pm. CREOLE/STEAK.

Watching the Food Network, you might well feel Emeril Lagasse is omnipresent. Slowly but surely, he's becoming as ubiquitous here in Vegas. This latest is a steak-house version of his hard-core classic Creole restaurant, and this ever-so-slight twist is just enough to make it a superior choice over the more disappointing New Orleans locale.

You can't go wrong with most appetizers, especially the superbly rich smoked mushrooms with homemade tasso over pasta—it's a meal in and of itself—any of the specials, or the gumbo, particularly if it's the hearty, near-homemade country selection. Do experiment at this stage, for you are better off later steering clear of complex entrees, no matter how intriguing they sound, for they are generally disappointing, in favor of more deceptively simple choices, which are more successful. The bone-in rib steak is rightly recommended (skip the gummy béarnaise sauce in favor of the fabulous homemade Worcester or the A.O.K. sauce). Sides are hit and miss—too salty creamed spinach being the latter while a sweet potato puree (a special, but maybe they will serve you a side if you ask sweetly) is most definitely the former. Too full for dessert? No, you aren't. Have a chocolate soufflé, a bananas foster cream pie, a chocolate Sheba (a sort of dense chocolate mousse), or the lemon ice-box pie, a chunk of curd that blasts tart lemon through your mouth.

✪ **Fiore.** Rio Suites, 3700 W. Flamingo Rd., at I-15. ☎ **702/252-7702.** Reservations recommended. Main courses $26–$48. AE, CB, DC, DISC, MC, V. Daily 5–11pm. ITALIAN/PROVENÇAL.

Fiore offers a deliciously simpatico setting for the brilliantly innovative cuisine of chef Kolachai Ngimsangaim. His seasonally changing menus complement the culinary elegance of northern Italy with the earthy exuberance of southern France. For an appetizer we had the sautéed herb-crusted prawns in a buttery mustard/anise sauce. This was followed by an entree of barbecued Atlantic salmon in honeyed hickory sauce, served with grilled polenta, portobello mushrooms, roasted Roma tomatoes, and grilled asparagus spears. Fiore's thoughtful list of more than 400 wines in several price ranges is international in scope and includes 45 premium by-the-glass selections. Consult knowledgeable sommelier Barrie Larvin for suggestions. Dine slowly, and consider including a cheese course—excellent cheeses are served with seasonal fruits. But do save room for dessert—perhaps a warm chocolate torte on crème anglaise embellished with raspberry stars and chocolate hearts. In addition to an extensive listing of cognacs, ports, and dessert wines, hand-rolled cigars elegantly presented in a mahogany humidor are a postprandial option on the terrace.

✪ **Le Cirque.** Bellagio, 3600 Las Vegas Blvd. S. ☎ 702/693-8150. Reservations required. Jacket and tie for gentlemen required. Main courses $29–$39. AE, DC, DISC, MC, V. Daily 5:30–11pm. FRENCH.

A branch of the much beloved New York City classic, this is the high profile, gourmet restaurant to blow your bankroll on. The subtlety of flavors demonstrates that this is truly sophisticated cuisine, rather than a place with just pretensions toward the same. The surprisingly small dining room (you may be virtually rubbing elbows with your neighbor) is decorated with murals of quaint bygone circus themes and a ceiling draped with gay fabric meant to evoke the Big Top. The busy decor does add to a cramped feeling, but the great care and solicitousness of the wait staff (surely the best in town) will surely soothe any rattled feelings. The menu changes seasonally, but here's what had us in raptures on a recent visit: appetizers of sea scallops layered with black truffle, wrapped in puff pastry, and a creamy foie gras du Tochon, marinated in sauterne and topped with more black truffle; main courses like properly aged filet topped with exquisite foie gras, and a vaguely Moroccan roasted honey-spiced glazed duck with figs (the caramelized onion on the side didn't quite work, but the figs most assuredly did). Desserts tickle your fancy as they cavort on the plate.

✪ **Onda.** Mirage, 3400 Las Vegas Blvd. S. ☎ 702/791-7111, ext. 7354. Reservations recommended. Main course $17.50–$31. AE, CB, DC, DISC, MC, V. Daily 5:30–11pm. ITALIAN.

Onda is anything but a run-of-the-mill hotel restaurant. Chef Todd English, whose Olives cafe over at Bellagio is also well worth your dining time, offers a Mediterranean slant on Italian cooking, coming up with a menu that is full of pleasant thrills, putting to shame most other attempts at Italian in town. Vegetables are flown in especially for Onda, so we encourage you toward menu choices that feature them. Begin with that basket of varied breads, making sure the gorgonzola-laced breadsticks are among them. Move on to antipasti with polenta, truffles, fresh mozzarella, onions, stuffed zucchini, roasted peppers, and goodness knows what else. Soup is good food, and in particular is the fine baby sweet spring pea puree with a dollop of mascarpone. A foil-wrapped veggie packet (slit at the table for you) includes porcini mushrooms good enough to make nonmushroom fans reconsider their previous conviction. Gnocchi in a pomonado sauce is light and wonderful. By now you don't need a heavy dessert, but the chocolate mousse cake is highly recommended if you can handle it, as is the sorbet sampler if you can't.

✪ **Palace Court.** Caesars Palace, 3570 Las Vegas Blvd. S., just north of Flamingo Rd. ☎ **702/731-7731.** Reservations required. Main courses $29–$55. AE, MC, V. Daily seatings 6–10pm FRENCH.

The Palace Court has long been considered one of the finest restaurants in town; when it went through a brief slump, foodies were disheartened, particularly since it's not cheap. It's still not cheap, but it is back up to its original standards and is worth the expense again.

It's hard to know where to begin with the lavish menu. The delicious tuna appetizer came with the perfect amount of ginger plus tender, paper-thin radishes—it is, however, not recommended for those on no- or low-salt diets. Sautéed fresh scallops, accompanied by baby asparagus, are perfect covered in a light and most mellow tarragon sauce that might have you licking your plate to get the last drop. Salade Riche is an array of leafy colors, some pungent strips of Swiss cheese, chunks of lobster, and a bit of delectable foie gras, all with a light dressing that does not drown out the salad flavors. If red snapper is offered on a special, skip it. Instead, go right to the rack of lamb with fresh goat cheese; "absolutely fabulous" was the comment that followed this amazing combo. Do consider a selection from the vast and beautifully chosen wine list.

Every dessert got a rave, especially the heavy, but not overly so, bittersweet chocolate cake; the crêpe souffle found even chocolate fans switching allegiances. The meal finishes up with jumbo chocolate-dipped strawberries and a plate of petit fours.

✪ **Picasso.** Bellagio, 3600 Las Vegas Blvd. S. ☎ **702/693-7111.** Reservations recommended. Fixed-price four-course dinner $70, five-course degustation $80. AE, CB, DC, DISC, MC, V. Sun–Tues and Thurs 6–10pm, Fri–Sat 6–11pm. FRENCH.

Steve Wynn spent months trying to talk Madrid-born chef Julian Serrano into coming to Bellagio. His dog-like tenacity paid off, and we should all thank him. This is an extraordinary dining experience, not the least of which is that while you eat, $30 million worth of Picassos gaze down over your shoulders. It's not like dining in a stuffy museum, however—the water fountains going off outside every 15 minutes (with staid diners rushing to the windows to check it out) pretty much take care of that.

Needless to say, Serrano's cooking is a work of art that can proudly stand next to masterpieces. The menu changes nightly and is always a choice between a four- or five-course fixed-price dinner or tasting menu. This may well be the best restaurant in Vegas, and given the sudden serious competition for such a title, that says a lot. The night we ate there, we were bowled over by roasted Maine lobster with a "trio" of corn—kernels, sauce, and a corn flan that was like eating slightly solid sunshine. Hudson Valley foie gras was crusted in truffles and went down most smoothly. A fillet of roasted sea bass came with a light saffron sauce and dots of cauliflower puree. And finally, lamb roti—perfectly done, tender, crusted with truffles, and an outstanding piece of lamb you had best heartily wish shows up the night you do. Portions are dainty, but so rich that you will have plenty to eat without groaning and feeling heavy when you leave. Desserts are powerful, yet prettily constructed. A molten chocolate cake leaves any other you may have tried in the dust, and comes with ice cream made with imported European chocolate. A crisp banana tart with coconut ice cream is a fine non-chocolate (foolish you) choice, while a passion fruit flan in a citrus soup sauce is perfect if you don't have much room left. Everything is delivered by an attentive staff who make you feel quite pampered.

○ **Spago.** Caesars Palace, 3500 Las Vegas Blvd. S. ☎ **702/369-6300.** Reservations recommended for the dining room; not accepted at the cafe. Dining room main courses $14–$31; cafe main courses $9.50–$23. AE, CB, DC, DISC, JCB, MC, V. Dining room Sun–Thurs 6–10pm, Fri–Sat 5:30–10:30pm. Cafe daily 11am–midnight. AMERICAN/ASIAN.

Spago is no longer the only foodie game in town, and you get the feeling it was so far ahead of the pack for so long that complacency has set in. Which is not to say it's not worth the expense—it just means that others have caught up with, and in some cases surpassed, it.

But it's still an experience going there—call it California casual elegance. The postindustrial interior is the very model of a modern major restaurant, while the exterior cafe on the Forum Shops is more relaxed and provides an opportunity for people-watching as fine as at any European sidewalk cafe.

The cafe menu features such familiar items as meat loaf and pizza, although glamorized versions—this isn't Country Kitchen, and so this pizza features smoked salmon. Not to mention crème fraîche. It sounds like an unholy hybrid of Italian and deli, but it's sublime. Other cafe specialties include Puck's signature Chinois chicken salad and a superb mesquite-fried salmon served with a tangy toss of soba noodles and cashews in a coconut-sesame-chile paste vinaigrette nuanced with lime juice and Szechuan mustard. The inside menu changes seasonally; examples of potential choices include scallops with a divine basil risotto, an appetizer of tuna sashimi in hot olive oil and sesame, or porcini mushrooms with a truffle sauce. The signature dish is a Chinese-style duck, moist but with a perfectly crispy skin. It's about as good as duck gets. It is served with a doughy steamed bun and Chinese vegetables. Desserts range from fresh fruit sorbets in surprising flavors (cantaloupe, honeydew), to a luscious brownie topped with homemade chocolate, whipped cream, and ice cream. The wine list is impressive, but the house wine was a disappointment and possibly not worth the cost.

EXPENSIVE

✪ **Pinot Brassiere.** The Venetian, 3355 Las Vegas Blvd. S. ☎ **702/735-8888.** Reservations recommended for dinner. Main courses $11.50–$16.95 at lunch, $18.50–$22.50 at dinner. AE, DISC, JCB, MC, V. Daily 11am–11pm. BISTRO.

This is the latest incarnation of a series of well regarded Los Angeles restaurants whose mothership, Patina, regularly tops "Best Of" lists for City of Angels foodies. While the more innovative cooking is going on at the latter, Pinot reliably delivers French and American favorites that are thoughtfully conceived and generally delicious. It's an excellent choice if you want a special meal that is neither stratospherically expensive nor too complex. Plus, this space is highly attractive, with various props culled from French auctions and flea markets forming the archetypal, clubby bistro feel.

Salads are possibly fresher and more generous than other similar starters in town (thank that California influence), and they can come paired with various toppings for *crostini* (toasted slices of French bread) such as herbed goat cheese. The signature dish, beloved by many, is a roasted chicken accompanied by heaping mounds of garlic fries, but if you wish to get a little more elaborate (and yet rather light), thin slices of smoked salmon with celery remoulade could be a way to go. Desserts are lovely, and ice cream is homemade—the chocolate alone should make you wish you'd never eaten at 31 Flavors, because it was wasted calories compared to this. *Note:* It is easy to graze through this menu and have a less costly meal here than at most other high-end places, and the constant operating hours mean you can also pop in for a nosh at times when other fine dining options are closed.

✪ **Star Canyon.** The Venetian, 3355 Las Vegas Blvd. S. ☎ **702/414-3772.** Reservations recommended for dinner. Main courses $10–$17 at lunch, $21–$30 at dinner. AE, MC, V. Daily 11:30am–2:30pm; Sun–Thurs 6–10pm, Fri–Sat 6–11pm. SOUTHWESTERN.

Texas-based chef Stephen Pyles is more or less credited with invent-ing Southwestern cuisine, and this new branch of his highly touted Dallas restaurant might just be the Best American Restaurant in Las Vegas. Not the place for intimate romantic encounters, this is de-cidedly the fun high-end restaurant in town, lively and playful, with a menu to match—it mixes haute and nouvelle with the down home, and the results are superlatively successful. Call it an alliance of frou-frou and yee-ha! For once, you can be assured that intrigu-ing blends of flavors and ingredients will all work together harmo-niously, making your tongue dance in glee, rather than your brow knit in confusion.

For this reason, we urge you to take some chances with appetizers—we'd go a bit more plain, though with equal satisfaction, with the main courses. A tamale pie's spicy crust is cooled by its filling of roast garlic custard, topped with crabmeat, while that gourmand's delight, seared foie gras, is most happily paired with a more humble corn cake, itself dressed up with pineapple salsa. Be sure to try the hearty, serious, chewy breads, which can come in flavors like pesto and chipolte. While you may justly feel tempted to make a meal of appetizers, don't. For then you would miss their signature dish, a bone-in ribeye, cowboy style (think Western spices), an utterly ten-der, flavorful dish (topped with a mile-high tower of crispy onions) that makes it hard to imagine a better piece of meat. Desserts are perhaps not quite as joy-producing, though the chocolate bread pud-ding is more like a heavy soufflé than a boring basic bread pudding.

MODERATE

See also the listing for **Spago** and **Chinois** (both above), expensive restaurants fronted by more moderately priced cafes.

✪ **Olives.** Bellagio, 3600 Las Vegas Blvd. S. ☎ **702/693-7223.** Reservations recommended for parties of 6 or more. Main courses $15–$19 at lunch, $20–$33.50 at dinner; flatbreads $10–$14.50. AE, DC, DISC, MC, V. Daily 11am–3pm and 5–11:30pm. ITALIAN/MEDITERRANEAN.

If there were an Olives cafe in our neighborhood, we would eat there regularly. The less expensive relative of the Mirage's Onda (as well as a branch of Todd English's originally Boston-based res-taurant), Olives is a strong choice for a light lunch that need not be as expensive as you might think. Try a flatbread—think pizza with an ultra-thin crust (like a slightly limp cracker), topped with delicious combinations like the highly recommended Moroccan spiced lamb, eggplant puree and feta cheese, or fig, prosciutto, and gorgonzola. They are rich and wonderful—split one between two people, along with that salad we just maligned, and you have an affordable and terrific lunch. Or try a pasta; we were steered toward the simple but marvelous spaggatini with roasted tomatoes, garlic, and Parmesan, and were glad. The constructed, but not too fussy, food gets more complicated and costly at night, adding an array of meats and chickens, plus pastas like butternut squash with brown butter and sage.

Planet Hollywood. Caesars Palace, 3500 Las Vegas Blvd. S. ☎ **702/ 791-STAR.** Reservations not accepted. Main courses $8–$20 (most under $13). AE, DC, MC, V. Sun–Thurs 11am–midnight, Fri–Sat 11am–1am. CALIFORNIA.

Arnold, Sly, Bruce, and Demi joined forces with some finance buddies to create a movie version of the Hard Rock. It was an instant success and a sure sign of the decline of Western civilization. Some of the objects displayed are worthless; others are sort of amusing— Barbara Eden's genie bottle, chariot wheels from *Ben Hur,* the side of beef Stallone sparred with in *Rocky,* the *Star Trek* control tower. Video monitors are everywhere, showing trailers for soon-to-be-released movies, themed video montages, and footage of Planet Hollywood grand openings around the world. Further reluctant credit is given for the more imaginative than average theme-restaurant menu: blackened shrimp served with Creole mustard sauce; linguine tossed with Thai shrimp, peanuts, and julienned vegetables in spicy sweet chile sauce; white chocolate bread pudding drenched in whisky sauce and topped with white chocolate ice cream.

✪ **Stage Deli.** Caesars Palace, 3500 Las Vegas Blvd. S. ☎ **702/893-4045.** Reservations accepted for large parties only. Main courses $10–$14, sandwiches $6–$14. AE, DC, DISC, JCB, MC, V. Sun–Thurs 7:30am–10:30pm, Fri–Sat 7:30am–midnight. DELI.

New York City's Stage Deli—a legendary hangout for comedians, athletes, and politicians—has been slapping pastrami on rye for more than half a century. Its Las Vegas branch retains the Stage's brightly lit, Big Apple essence. The deli is often not crowded. In addition to being handy for Caesars guests, if you are staying next door at the Mirage, it's easy to pop over, making it a satisfying breakfast alternative (to often overcrowded, overpriced, and not very good hotel breakfast joints in the area). The huge (we mean it) menu means finding something for even the pickiest of eaters.

Most of the fare—including fresh-baked pumpernickel and rye, meats, chewy bagels, lox, spicy deli mustard, and pickles—comes in daily from New York. The Stage dishes up authentic 5-inch-high sandwiches stuffed with pastrami, corned beef, brisket, or chopped liver. Maybe overstuffed is a better description. Unless you have a hearty appetite, are feeding two, or have a fridge in your room for leftovers, you might want to try the half sandwich and soup or salad combos.

4 North Strip

VERY EXPENSIVE

Morton's of Chicago. 3200 Las Vegas Blvd. S., in the Fashion Show Mall (take Spring Mountain Rd. off the Strip, make a right at Fashion Show Dr., and follow the signs). ☎ **702/893-0703.** Reservations recommended. Main courses $18–$30. AE, CB, DC, JCB, MC, V. Mon–Sat 5:30–11pm, Sun 5–10pm. STEAK/SEAFOOD.

This famous gourmet steak chain has a warm, clublike interior. Frequent power diners here include most hotel/casino owners as well as Strip entertainers Siegfried and Roy. Robert de Niro and Joe Pesci came in frequently during the filming of *Casino,* and, one night, Tony Curtis joined the wait staff in singing "Happy Birthday" to a guest.

Start off with an appetizer, perhaps a lump crabmeat cocktail with mustard-mayonnaise sauce. Entree choices include succulent prime Midwestern steaks prepared to your exact specifications, plus lemon oregano chicken, lamb chops, Sicilian veal, grilled swordfish, whole baked Maine lobster, and prime rib with creamed horseradish. Side orders such as flavorfully fresh al dente asparagus served with hollandaise or hash browns are highly recommended. Portions are bountiful; plan to share. A loaf of warm onion bread on every table is complimentary. Leave room for dessert, perhaps a Grand Marnier soufflé. There's an extensive wine list, and you may want to retreat to a sofa in the cozy mahogany-paneled bar/lounge for after-dinner drinks.

Phil's Angus Steakhouse. New Frontier, 3120 Las Vegas Blvd. S. ☎ **702/794-8233.** Reservations recommended. Main courses $17–$33 (lobster $50). AE, DISC, MC, V. Tues–Sat 5–11pm. STEAK/SEAFOOD.

Every hotel has a steak house, but only a few are worth singling out. This one is so good, we can't wait to eat here again, and even have the menu all planned out. The delicious lump crab cakes were interestingly combined with polenta and a spicy chile crème fraîche. That and the scotch salmon make excellent starters, as do the hearty, thick, and yet somehow light soups. You can pick your steaks from a platter. The petit filet melts in the mouth, with just the right beef flavor and a béarnaise sauce that was the proper accompaniment.

The porterhouse could literally be cut with a fork. Sides are ordered separately; the Yukon mashed potatoes with horseradish were quite tasty, and the sautéed spinach was perfectly done. For dessert, skip the tiramisù in favor of the crème caramel.

✪ **Top of the World.** Stratosphere Las Vegas, 2000 Las Vegas Blvd. S., between St. Louis St. and Baltimore Ave. ☎ **702/380-7711.** Reservations required. Main courses $21–$58. AE, CB, DC, DISC, JCB, MC, V. Sun–Thurs 5–11pm, Fri–Sat 5pm–midnight. AMERICAN/CONTINENTAL.

Okay, revolving restaurants are the very definition of kitsch. But you know what? We like 'em. And when you've got views like these, well, there is a difference between having good taste and being made of stone.

Because you are 869 feet in the air, Vegas is stretched out before you in a glittering palette. Who knew this town could be so beautiful? This proves the Stratosphere is good for something. The Top of the World restaurant may not have the best food in Vegas (though some things are actually pretty good), but it has hands down the best view. (It takes about an hour for one revolution.) You will be so busy admiring the Strip, noticing that Vegas goes on much further than you thought, wondering which casino that particular cluster of lights is, and trying to spot your hotel, that you won't even notice what you are eating. It's one of the most romantic spots in town to dine. And that's why we gave it the star.

But it's expensive, and the entrees, at least, are not worth the cost. Having anticipated that customers might want to fill up tables just ordering a small snack, there is a $15 per person minimum. Here's what you do: Order only the generous-size appetizers and desserts. You won't be disappointed, and you can easily make the minimum. The desserts are stellar, with the standout being the expensive ($9) but easily shared by two (it's huge and rich) Chocolate Stratosphere Tower. Yep, a chocolate replica of the very building you are sitting in; the top part is filled with a terrific chocolate mousse, and the whole thing gets covered in chocolate sauce, poured by your waiter with great ceremony. It's a gimmick, but chocolate lovers will be thrilled.

EXPENSIVE

Chin's. 3200 Las Vegas Blvd. S., in the Fashion Show Mall (turn at the Frontier sign). ☎ **702/733-8899.** Reservations recommended. Main courses $10–$12 at lunch, $10–$29.50 at dinner. AE, DC, MC, V. Mon–Sat 11:30am–9:30pm, Sun noon–9:30pm. CHINESE.

Chin's has been a Vegas fixture for 20 years and is consistently voted by locals in the *Las Vegas Review* as their favorite Chinese restaurant. It is certainly a surprise for anyone who knows Chinese food solely through take-out or strip malls. The simple, stark decor produces an ambience of low-key elegance. The prices will surprise you, too. This is not $1 Chinese food. But as owner Mr. Chin points out, Chinese food takes so much time to prepare (all that chopping, dicing, splicing, and what not) and to present in the traditionally stylish way (no steam trays here) that it's a wonder anyone would ever charge just a couple dollars for a dish.

However, anyone with broad experience with Chinese food won't find anything terribly surprising here. Experiments with more radical dishes failed (too-timid tourists?), and so the menu is on the safe side. Standouts include the sweetly cloying strawberry chicken (think lemon chicken but with a different fruit; Chin's created this twist on a familiar dish, and other local restaurants have copied it); an appetizer of sinful deep-fried shrimp puffs (stuffed with minced shrimp and mildly curried cream cheese); splendid spring rolls; and barbecued pork-fried rice that strikes that tricky, careful balance between dry and greasy.

MODERATE

Cafe Heidelberg German Deli and Restaurant. 610 E. Sahara. ☎ **702/731-5310.** Reservations highly recommended for Friday and Saturday nights. Main courses under $10 at lunch, $9.95–$16 at dinner. DISC, MC, V. Mon–Sat 10am–9pm, Sun 11am–8pm. GERMAN.

A once ponderous and dated German restaurant has been transformed into a German cafe already well packed (admittedly, with only six booths, not hard to do) with locals. Certainly, it's not a Vegas type of place, and since it's close enough to the Strip, it's a good place for refuge. Recommended is the sausage sampler platter, so you can finally learn the difference between knockwurst and bratwurst, and the schnitzel sandwich of delicious breaded veal. Wash it down with a vast choice of imported beer. This is also a full-service deli and German market and so would be a good place to pick up a picnic for sightseeing out of the city.

Dive! 3200 Las Vegas Blvd. S., in the Fashion Show Mall. ☎ **702/369-DIVE.** Main courses $7–$14. AE, CB, DC, DISC, MC. V. Sun–Thurs 11:30am–10pm, Fri–Sat 11:30am–11pm. AMERICAN.

Notable for being one of the few theme restaurants not devoted to memorabilia, Dive! is partly the brainchild of Steven Spielberg and movie exec Jeffrey Katzenberg. The outside is admittedly quite fun: yellow submarine crashing through a 30-foot wall of water that cascades into an oversized pool erupting with depth-charge blasts. Its gunmetal-gray interior replicates the hull of a submarine with vaulted cylindrical ceilings, porthole-shaped (albeit neon-accented, since this is Vegas) windows, exposed conduits that burst with steam, sonar screens, and working periscopes. Every hour a high-tech show projected on a 16-cube video wall (and 48 additional monitors throughout the restaurant) simulates a fantasy submarine dive. And overhead, a luxury ocean liner, a manta ray research vessel, exotic fish, a fighting shark, and model subs circumnavigate the room on a computerized track. It's all whimsical and imaginative. Surprise—they serve submarine sandwiches (among other choices).

Kids should love it and adults will find it slightly less annoying than, say, Chuck E. Cheese (and with somewhat more sophisticated food).

INEXPENSIVE

Capriotti's. 324 W. Sahara Ave (and Las Vegas Blvd. S.). ☎ **702/474-0229.** All sandwiches under $10. No credit cards. Mon–Sat 10am–7pm. SANDWICHES.

Don't be fooled by the sizes listed at the no-frills, mom-and-pop Capriotti's sandwich shop. The so-called "small" should actually be called "too big." Plan to share. They roast their own beef and turkeys on the premises, and providing the help gets the stuff out of the ovens in time, it's mighty tasty and special (but otherwise, the meat can be too dry). Interesting combinations and tastes are the standard here, and the result is a very good sandwich indeed. The standout sandwich is the "Bobby," which combines a virtual Thanksgiving dinner—turkey, dressing, cranberry sauce—on a French roll, for a taste sensation so marvelous you wonder why no one thought of it before. The shop is convenient to Downtown and is right off the Strip, but those farther away should note they will deliver with a $10 minimum.

Dona Maria Tamales. 910 Las Vegas Blvd. S., corner of Charleston Blvd. ☎ **702/382-6538.** Main courses $5.45–$8 at breakfast, $6–$13 at lunch or dinner. AE, CB, MC, V. Sun–Thurs 8am–10pm, Fri–Sat 8am–11pm. MEXICAN.

Decorated with Tijuana-style Mayan quiltwork and calendars, this is your quintessential Mexican diner, convenient to both the north end of the Strip and Downtown. They use lots of lard, lots of cheese, and lots of sauce. As a result, the food is really good—and really fattening. That just makes it all the better. Locals apparently agree; even at lunchtime the place is crowded.

You will start off with homemade chips and a spicy salsa served in a mortar. Meals are so large that it shouldn't be a problem getting full just ordering off the sides, which can make this even more of a budget option. Naturally, the specialty is the fantastic tamales, which come in red, green, cheese, or sweet. They also serve up excellent enchiladas, chile rellenos, burritos, and fajitas. All dinners include rice, beans, tortillas, and soup or salad. Sauces are heavy but oh so good.

✪ **Liberty Cafe at the Blue Castle Pharmacy.** 1700 S. Las Vegas Blvd. ☎ **702/383-0101.** Reservations not accepted. Nothing over $6.50. No credit cards. 24 hours. DINER.

You can go to any number of retro soda fountain replicas (such as Johnny Rockets) and theme restaurants that pretend to be cheap diners, but why bother when the (admittedly, decidedly unflashy) real thing is just past the end of the Strip? The soda fountain/lunch counter at the Blue Castle Pharmacy was Las Vegas's first 24-hour restaurant, and it has been going strong for 60 years. Plunk down at the counter, and watch the cooks go nuts trying to keep up with the orders. The menu is basic comfort food: standard grill items (meat loaf, ground round steak, chops), fluffy cream pies, and classic breakfasts served "anytime"—try the biscuits and cream gravy at 3am. But the best bet is a one-third-pound burger and "thick creamy shake," both the way they were meant to be and about as good as they get. At around $5, this is half what you would pay for a comparable meal at the Hard Rock Cafe. And as waitress Beverly says, "This is really real." Places like this are a vanishing species—it's worth the short walk from the Stratosphere.

Rincon Criollo. 1145 Las Vegas Blvd. S. ☎ **702/388-1906.** Reservations not accepted. Main courses $6.50–$10, paella (for 3) $20. AE, DISC, MC, V. Tues–Sun 11am–10pm. CUBAN.

Located beyond the wedding chapels on Las Vegas Boulevard, Rincon Criollo has all the right details for a good, cheap ethnic joint: full of locals and empty of frills. It's not the best Cuban food ever, but it gets the job done. The main courses (featuring Cuban pork and chicken specialties) are hit and miss; try the marinated pork leg or, better still, ask your server for a recommendation. Paella is offered, but only for parties of three or more (and starts at $20). The side-course *chorizo* (a spicy sausage) is excellent, and the Cuban sandwich (roast pork, ham, and cheese on bread, which is then pressed and flattened out) is huge and tasty. For only $3.50, the latter makes a fine change-of-pace meal.

5 East of the Strip

In this section we cover restaurants close by the Convention Center, along with those farther south on Paradise Road, Flamingo Road, and Tropicana Avenue.

VERY EXPENSIVE

Bistro Le Montrachet. Las Vegas Hilton, 3000 Paradise Rd. ☎ **702/732-5755.** Reservations recommended. Main courses $23–$46. AE, CB, DC, DISC, JCB, MC, V. Thurs–Tues 5–10:30pm. FRENCH.

Not all the culinary stars in Vegas are on the Strip or have a high-profile name. This elegant little room (gleaming with highly sheened wood, and with most diners seated in intimate booths) is a jewel well

Dining East of the Strip

Allie's ❺
Bistro Le Montrachet ❷
Celebrity Deli ❾
Einstein Bros. Bagels ⑫
Gordon Biersch ❻
Hard Rock Cafe ❽
Lawry's The Prime Rib ❼
Mediterranean Café & Market ⑩

Pamplemousse ❶
Ricardo's ⑭
Toto's ⑬
Z Tejas Grill ❸

Buffets

Las Vegas Hilton Buffet of
  Champions ❹
Sam's Town, The Great Buffet ⑪

93

worth your while. Service is perfect, without being cloying, and dishes are exquisitely presented. In-house smoked salmon (neither too smoky nor raw tasting, but just right) is thinly sliced with great ceremony at the table and served with paper-thin Bermuda onions and toast points. Foie gras is seared to almost caramelizing, drizzled with a lovely madeira wine sauce, and then curiously skewered with a spring of tarragon into spinach mashed potatoes stacked in a column. There is a wonderful lobster bisque made from their own lobster base, heavy cream, cognac, and cayenne pepper. Be careful—it's very heavy and far too good not to finish, so you could easily fill up on the soup alone. Snapper, normally a dull fish, here fulfills its potential with an ultra-light batter, and a bay shrimp and scallion cream sauce. It melts in your mouth. "Out of this world," vow those who have tried the medallions of New Zealand farm-raised (and so thus not gamey) venison, which is curiously and successfully breaded with finely chopped and seared blackened mushrooms. By dessert, you will probably be too full for anything but their delightful lemon soufflé with a creamy lemon custard at the bottom. They choose excellent wines, but don't skip the outstanding, rich roast house coffee.

EXPENSIVE

✪ **Lawry's The Prime Rib.** 4043 Howard Hughes Pkwy., at Flamingo Rd., between Paradise Rd. and Koval Lane. ☎ **702/893-2223.** Reservations recommended. Main courses $20–$30. AE, DC, DISC, JCB, MC, V. Sun–Thurs 5–10pm, Fri–Sat 5–11pm. STEAK/SEAFOOD.

If you love prime rib, come here. If you could take or leave prime rib, Lawry's will turn you into a believer. Because Lawry's does one thing, and it does it better than anyone else. Lawry's first opened in Los Angeles in 1938 and still remains a popular tradition. Over the years, they have added three branches, the most recent landing in Las Vegas at the beginning of 1997. Yes, you can get prime rib all over town for under $5. But that's a tuna fish sandwich to Lawry's caviar (if one mixes food metaphors).

Eating at Lawry's is a ceremony, with all the parts played the same for the last 60 years. Waitresses in brown-and-white English maid uniforms, complete with starched white cap, take your order—for side dishes, that is. The real decision, what cut of rib you are going to have, comes later. Actually, that's the only part of the tradition that has changed. Lawry's has added fresh fish (halibut, salmon, or swordfish, depending on the evening) to its menu. Anyway, you tell the waitress what side dishes you might want (sublime creamed spinach, baked potato) for an extra price. Later, she returns with a

👫 Family-Friendly Restaurants

Buffets Cheap meals for the whole family. The kids can choose what they like, and there are sometimes make-your-own sundae machines.

Dive! (*see p. 90*) Housed in a submarine and featuring a zany high-tech show every hour projected on a video wall, this is the most fun family-oriented spot of all.

Rain Forest Cafe (*see p. 75*) This is like eating in the Jungle Book Ride at Disneyland. Animals howl, thunder wails, everywhere there is something to marvel at, there is a decent kids' menu, and they might even learn a little bit about ecology and the environment.

Hard Rock Cafe (*see p. 97*) Kids adore this restaurant, which throbs with excitement and is filled with rock memorabilia.

Planet Hollywood (*see p. 86*) This popular chain houses a veritable museum of movie memorabilia, and the action on numerous video monitors keeps kids from getting bored.

Pink Pony This bubble-gum pink circus-motif 24-hour coffee shop at Circus Circus will appeal to kids. And Mom and Dad can linger over coffee while the kids race upstairs to watch circus acts and play carnival games.

Sherwood Forest Cafe Kids love to climb on the lavender dragons fronting this 24-hour coffee shop at Excalibur, and they also enjoy numerous child-oriented activities while you're on the premises.

spinning salad bowl (think of salad preparation as a Busby Berkeley musical number). The bowl, resting on crushed ice, spins as she pours Lawry's special dressing in a stream from high over her head. Tomatoes garnish. Applause follows. Eventually, giant metal carving carts come to your table, bearing the meat. You name your cut (the regular Lawry's, the extra-large Diamond Jim Brady, only for serious carnivores, and the wimpy thin English cut), rare, medium, well. It comes with terrific Yorkshire pudding, nicely browned and not soggy, and some creamed horseradish that is combined with fluffy whipped cream, simultaneously sweet and tart.

Flavorful, tender, perfectly cooked, lightly seasoned, this will be the best prime rib you will ever have. Okay, maybe that's going too far, but the rest is accurate, honest. It just has to be tasted to be believed. You can finish off with a rich dessert (English trifle is highly recommended), but it almost seems pointless. Incidentally, the other Lawry's are decorated English-manor style, but the Vegas branch has instead tried to re-create a 1930s restaurant, with art deco touches all around and big-band music on the sound system.

Pamplemousse. 400 E. Sahara Ave., between Santa Paula and Santa Rita drives, just east of Paradise Rd. ☎ **702/733-2066.** Reservations required. Main courses $17.50–$26. AE, CB, DC, DISC, MC, V. Seatings daily at 6–10pm. FRENCH.

Evoking a cozy French countryside inn, Pamplemousse is a catacomb of low-ceilinged rooms and intimate dining nooks with rough-hewn beams. It's all very charming and un-Vegasy.

The meal always begins with a large complimentary basket of crudités (about 10 different crisp, fresh vegetables), a big bowl of olives, and, a nice country touch, a basket of hard-boiled eggs. From there, you might proceed to an appetizer of lightly floured bay scallops sautéed in buttery grapefruit sauce, followed by an entree of crispy duck breast and banana in a sauce of orange honey, dark rum, and crème de banane. Filet mignon, New York steak, and rack of lamb are always featured. For dessert, perhaps there'll be homemade dark chocolate ice cream with pralines in a sabayon sauce. An extensive, well-rounded wine list complements the menu.

MODERATE

✪ **Allie's American Grille.** Marriott Suites, 325 Convention Center Dr. ☎ **702/650-2000.** Main courses $8.25–$15, sandwiches $6–$9.25. AE, CB, DC, DISC, MC, V. Mon–Fri 6:30am–10:30pm, Sat–Sun 7am–10pm. SOUTHWESTERN.

Don't miss this little treasure. Tucked away on the other side of the bar in the Marriott Suites, Allie's is a coffee shop at breakfast time, but for lunch and dinner it turns into a cafe with a delightful menu best described as nouveau Southwestern. Check out the chicken portobello quesadilla appetizer, or the Pacific Rim yellowfin tuna salad—tuna on crispy Asian vegetables. The salmon BLT is a seared salmon steak over an inch thick with delicious maple pepper bacon, Grey Poupon sauce, and lovely leafy lettuce on a toasted brioche. Served with french fries and a cilantro coleslaw, it was a delicious, inventive take on an old favorite. The salmon was fresh and all the flavors combined perfectly. The rigatoni primavera had fresh spinach, asparagus, and tomatoes in a light, creamy sauce. There is a lovely dessert menu featuring a genuine root-beer float.

Gordon-Biersch Brewing Company. 3987 Paradise Rd., just north of Flamingo Rd. ☎ **702/312-5247.** Main courses $11–$16. AE, DISC, MC, V. Sun–Thurs 11:30am–10pm, Fri–Sat 11:30am–11pm; bar open until 2am. CALIFORNIA.

This is a traditional brew pub (exposed piping and ducts, but the place is still comfortable and casual), but it's worth going to for a nosh as well. The menu is pub fare meets California cuisine (kids will probably find the food too complicated), and naturally, there are a lot of beers (German-styled lagers) to choose from. Appetizers include satays, potstickers, calamari, baby-back ribs, delicious beer-battered onion rings, and amazing garlic-encrusted fries. A wood-burning pizza oven turns out California-type toppings—eggplant, shrimp, and so forth. For lunch, there are various pastas, stir-fries, sandwiches, and salads. The dinner menu eliminates the sandwiches and adds rosemary chicken, steaks, fish items, and, just in case you forgot it was a brew pub–type joint, beer everything: beer-glazed ham, beer meat loaf, beer barbecued glazed ribs.

Hard Rock Cafe. 4475 Paradise Rd., at Harmon Ave. ☎ **702/733-7625.** Main courses $7–$18. AE, DC, DISC, JCB, MC, V. Sun–Thurs 11am–11:30pm, Fri–Sat 11am–midnight. AMERICAN.

The original Hard Rock Cafe opened in London as a meeting place for American expatriates and homesick exchange students dying for a good burger. T-shirts then simply said "Hard Rock Cafe," with no identifying city. No need for one. Now that Hard Rocks are everywhere (can it be long before there is one in Tibet?), the cachet is gone.

But this is the only Hard Rock (at least until 2001) attached to a hotel and a truly extraordinary casino, so let's cut this branch some slack. Allegedly, some stars do eat here; it's not out of the question, because if a big rock act is playing in town, they will be playing at the Hard Rock. In the meantime, the menu offers some good salads in addition to the burgers. An inexpensive children's menu is a plus for families. Don't be frightened by the line outside—it's usually not for the restaurant but the on-premises Hard Rock merchandise store. The Hard Rock Hotel & Casino is next door (see chapter 4).

Ricardo's. 2380 Tropicana Ave., at Eastern Ave. (northwest corner). ☎ **702/798-4515.** Reservations recommended. Main courses $7.50–$13; lunch buffet $7.25; children's plates $3–$4, including milk or soft drink with complimentary refills. AE, CB, DC, DISC, MC, V. Sun–Thurs 11am–10pm, Fri–Sat 11am–11pm. MEXICAN.

This hacienda-style restaurant is a great favorite with locals. Start off with an appetizer of deep-fried battered chicken wings served with melted Cheddar (ask for jalapeños if you like your cheese sauce hotter). Nachos smothered with cheese and guacamole are also very good here. For an entree, you can't go wrong with chicken, beef, or pork fajitas served sizzling on a hot skillet atop sautéed onions, mushrooms, and peppers; they come with rice and beans, tortillas, a selection of salsas, guacamole, and tomato wedges with cilantro. All the usual taco/enchilada/tamale combinations are also listed. A delicious dessert is *helado* Las Vegas: ice cream rolled in corn flakes and cinnamon, deep-fried, and served with honey and whipped cream. Be sure to order a pitcher of Ricardo's great margaritas. The same menu is available all day, but a buffet is offered at lunch. The kids' menu on a placemat with games and puzzles features both Mexican and American fare.

Z Tejas Grill. 3824 Paradise Rd., between Twain Ave. and Corporate Dr. ☎ **702/732-1660.** Reservations recommended. Main courses $7.25–$12 at lunch, $8.75–$17 at dinner. AE, CB, DC, DISC, JCB, MC, V. Daily 11am–11pm. TEX-MEX.

This Austin, Texas–based restaurant's rather odd name came about because its original chef, a Frenchman, kept referring to it as "zee" Tejas Grill. Featuring self-proclaimed "South by Southwestern" cuisine, it recently got a handsome makeover, lining the interior with stream-lined warm woods and black accents. There is a vine-covered patio for outdoor dining, rare for Vegas, with misters for summer and a fireplace and heaters for winter. For some reason, traffic noise does not permeate from the nearby street. You might also consider downing some large and excellent margaritas at the newly enlarged, very lively bar, particularly on weeknights, when happy hour (4–7pm) finds all starters half price. Given the size of said starters, this would be a very cheap meal option. In particular, we like the generously portioned grilled fish tacos, which come wrapped in fresh tortillas, stuffed with all kinds of veggies and served with a spicy Japanese sauce. Not your usual drippy, fattening tacos. Less of a bargain, but mighty tasty, is the tender and piquant black sesame tuna, with a black peppercorn vinaigrette and a soy mustard sauce. There is a larger version of this found under the entrees, called "Voodoo Tuna"—it's not quite as good. A better choice would be the spicy grilled Jamaican jerk chicken, nuanced with lime and served with peanut sauce and rum-spiked coconut-banana ketchup; it comes with two side dishes—when we were there, garlic mashed potatoes and a corn casserole soufflé.

INEXPENSIVE

Celebrity Deli. 4055 S. Maryland Pkwy., at Flamingo Rd. ☎ **702/733-7827.** Reservations not accepted. Main courses $7–$12. Mon–Sat 9am–8pm, Sun 9am–4pm. AE, MC, V. DELI.

A basic, solid New York deli, lacking the mammoth portions of the Stage Deli (though perhaps that's a good thing) but lacking also the occasionally mammoth prices of same. It also does not require navigating the Strip and the Caesars Forum Shops (which means it's more convenient for those staying at accommodations east of the Strip), and, in many ways, it's more authentic. As mentioned, these are not the monster portions of modern-day chain delis, but you won't go hungry. Don't look for anything vegetarian here; instead, you got your pastrami on rye, your matzo ball soup, chopped liver, tongue, meat loaf, lox and bagel, etc. Desserts are a bit sparse for a deli, but you can't go wrong with the black-and-white cookies. Go ahead—have a nosh.

Einstein Bros. Bagels. 4624 S. Maryland Pkwy., between Harmon and Tropicana aves., in the University Gardens Shopping Center. ☎ **702/795-7800.** All items under $6. MC, V. Mon–Sat 6am–8pm (until 5pm in summer), Sun 7am–5pm. BAGELS.

You may not like digging into an enormous buffet first thing in the morning, and continental breakfast in a hotel is usually a rip-off. A welcome alternative is a fresh-baked bagel, of which there are 15 varieties here—everything from onion to wild blueberry. Cream cheeses also come in many flavors, anything from sun-dried tomato to vegetable and jalapeño. Einstein's is a pleasant place for the morning meal, with both indoor seating and outdoor tables cooled by misters. Service is friendly, and four special-blend coffees are available each day.

✪ Mediterranean Café & Market. 4147 S. Maryland Pkwy., at Flamingo Rd., in the Tiffany Square strip mall. ☎ **702/731-6030.** Reservations not accepted. Main courses $8–$16 (all sandwiches under $5). AE, DISC, MC, V. Mon–Sat 11am–9pm. MEDITERRANEAN.

It is an immeasurable thrill to find this totally authentic, mom-and-pop Middle Eastern restaurant in Las Vegas, where high-quality ethnic eateries are scarce. Everything here is homemade and delicious. You might order up a gyro (slivers of rotisseried beef and lamb enfolded into a pita with lettuce and tomato). Other good choices are a filo pie layered with spinach and feta cheese, served with hummus; skewers of grilled chicken and vegetable kabobs with lavash bread and hummus; and a combination platter of hummus, tabbouleh, stuffed grape leaves, and falafel. All entrees come with pita bread and salad. Try a side order of *bourrani* (creamy yogurt dip mixed with steamed spinach, sautéed garlic, and slivered almonds). Finish up with baklava and rich Turkish coffee. Wine and beer are available. You can also come by in the morning for Middle Eastern breakfasts. A Mediterranean market adjoins.

Toto's. 2055 E. Tropicana Ave. ☎ **702/895-7923.** Reservations not required. Main courses $6.25–$14.25. AE, DISC, MC, V. Daily 11am–11pm. MEXICAN.

A family-style Mexican restaurant favored by locals, with enormous portions and quick service, this is good value for your money. Perhaps even more so; with all that food, you could probably split portions and still be satisfied. There are no surprises on the menu, though there are quite a few seafood dishes. Everything is quite tasty and they don't skimp on the cheese. The nongreasy chips come with fresh salsa, and the nachos are terrific. Chicken tamales got a thumbs-up, while the veggie burrito was happily received by non–meat eaters; though not especially healthy, all the ingredients were fresh, with huge slices of zucchini and roasted bell peppers. The operative word here is *huge;* the burritos are almost the size of your arm. The generous portions continue with dessert—a piece of flan was practically pie-sized. The Sunday margarita brunch is quite fun, and the drinks are large (naturally) and yummy.

6 West Las Vegas

EXPENSIVE

Garlic Cafe. 3650 S. Decatur Blvd., at Spring Mountain Rd. ☎ **702/ 368-4000.** Reservations recommended. Main courses $9.25–$28. AE, DISC, MC, V. Mon–Sat 11am–2pm; daily 5–10pm. INTERNATIONAL.

If you don't like garlic, there is no reason to read further. If you do like garlic, head toward the Garlic Cafe right now. Garlic is the food of the gods, and Warren, the owner/chef/creator of this cafe, understands that. Unlike similar ventures (the Stinking Rose in San Francisco, for example), this is a more international menu. Warren found that garlic was a unifying theme around the world, so here are dishes from Thailand, Jamaica, Japan, Hungary, and so on. You can decide on the level of garlic in your dish. Their garlic scale usually runs from 1 to 5 (each level is one head of garlic, so a "5" equals five whole heads), and they will go as high as you want. The current record holder is up to 60. The waiters will help you decide what level is best for any given dish; certain ones (like the duck) would get overwhelmed by too much of our favorite seasoning.

Everyone gets a roast *skordalia* (partly puréed garlic) and bagel-chip appetizer, but you can order still others; the choices differ nightly but will always include a perfectly roasted head of garlic. The entree portions are huge (which makes up for the somewhat high prices), and they are very nicely presented. Not to mention imaginatively—okay, incredibly eccentrically—named. Like the Salmon in Garfunkel Crust (a fillet of salmon in a garlic-basil cracker crust with béarnaise sauce) or Grandpa Murray in a Hurry "Don't Worry!" Chicken Curry. If you're nice, maybe they will let you take the menu home so that you don't have to try to remember what you ate. Finish it off with some garlic ice cream. It's not as weird as it sounds—a very good vanilla with just a hint of garlic that somehow works in a sweet-and-sour kind of way. The real fun comes with the chocolate-covered (roasted) garlic clove.

MODERATE

Cathay House. 5300 W. Spring Mountain Rd., in Spring Valley. ☎ **702/876-3838.** Reservations recommended. Main courses $6.75–$19. AE, CB, DC, DISC, JCB, MC, V. Daily 11am–10:30pm. CHINESE.

Las Vegas actually has a Chinatown—a very large strip mall (naturally) on Spring Mountain Road near Wynn. There are several Asian restaurants there, but ask locals who look like they know, and they will send you instead farther up Spring Mountain Road to the Cathay House (on the opposite side of the street). It's about a 7-minute drive from Treasure Island.

Ordering dim sum, if you haven't experienced it, is sort of like being at a Chinese sushi bar, in that you order many individual, tasty little dishes. Of course, dim sum itself is nothing like sushi. Rather, it's a range of potstickers, pan-fried dumplings, *baos* (soft, doughy buns filled with meat like barbecued pork), translucent rice noodles wrapped around shrimp, sticky rice in lotus leaves, chicken feet, and so forth. Some of it's steamed, some is fried—for that extra good grease! You can make your own dipping sauce by combining soy sauce, vinegar, and hot pepper oil. The Chinese eat this for breakfast; the rest of us probably can't handle it until a bit later in the day. The wait staff pushes steam carts filled with little dishes; point, and they will attempt to tell you what each one is. Better, just blindly order a bunch and dig in. Each dish ranges from approximately $1 to $3; each server makes a note of what you just received, and the total is tallied at the end. (For some reason, it almost always works out to about $9 a person.) Dim sum is usually available only until midafternoon.

Viva Mercados. 6182 W. Flamingo, at Jones. ☎ **702/871-8826.** Reservations for large parties only. Main courses $8–$17. AE, DISC, MC, V. Sun–Thurs 11am–10pm, Fri–Sat 11am–11pm. MEXICAN.

Ask any local about Mexican food in Vegas and almost certainly they will point to Viva Mercados as the best in town. That recommendation, plus the restaurant's health-conscious attitude, makes this worth the roughly 10-minute drive from the Strip.

Given all those warnings lately about Mexican food and its heart attack–inducing properties, Viva Mercados's approach to food is nothing to be sniffed at. No dish is prepared with or cooked in any kind of animal fat. Nope, the lard so dear to Mexican cooking is not found here. The oil used is an artery-friendly canola. Additionally, this makes the place particularly appealing to vegetarians, who will also be pleased by the regular veggie specials. Everything is quite fresh, and they do particularly amazing things with seafood. Try the Maresco Vallarta, which is orange roughy, shrimp, and scallops cooked in a coconut tomato sauce, with capers and olives. They have all sorts of noteworthy shrimp dishes, and 11 different salsas, ranked 1 to 10 for degree of spice. (Ask for advice, first.) The staff is friendly (try to chat with owner Bobby Mercado) and the portions hearty.

INEXPENSIVE

✪ **Enigma Cafe.** 918¹/₂ S. Fourth St., at Charleston Blvd. ☎ **702/386-0999.** Reservations not accepted. No items over $6. Mon 7am–3pm, Tues–Fri 7am–midnight, Sat–Sun 9am–midnight. No credit cards. CALIFORNIA/MEDITERRANEAN.

Finding the Enigma Cafe is almost as good as finding a breeze on a really hot Vegas day. Or maybe it's more like suddenly finding yourself transported out of Vegas and into California. Owners Julie and Len have taken two 1930s-era cottages and turned them into a cafe/coffeehouse/art space that, during the day, is a restful garden patio setting At night the space blooms with candles, live music, and poetry readings.

The menu is a huge relief: healthful, interesting sandwiches ("Mossy Melt" is tuna salad "revved up with" horseradish and havarti, toasted open-face) and familiar ones (ham and Swiss, but well garnished), salads (again with a range from the ordinary green variety to "Dr. Bombay's" curried chicken breast with veggies), hummus burritos, and the "Tippy Elvis Supreme" (named after a local polka band/art project), which is peanut butter and bananas (what else?). You can get a side platter of hummus, feta cheese, veggies, and pita, or have a thick fruit smoothie. And that doesn't even begin to cover their wide range of coffee drinks. Best of all, it's cheap. Considering the soothing effect it has on your mind, spirit, wallet, and stomach, Enigma is like a vacation from your vacation. This is actually very close to both the Strip and Downtown, particularly the latter, where good (and healthful) food is hard to find.

7 Downtown

VERY EXPENSIVE

☻ Andre's. 401 S. 6th St., at Lewis St., 2 blocks south of Fremont St. ☎ **702/ 385-5016.** Reservations required. Main courses $20–$33. AE, CB, DC, MC, V. Daily from 6pm; closing hours vary. FRENCH.

Andre's has long been the bastion of gourmet dining in Vegas, but with all those new big boys crowding the Strip, it runs the risk of getting overlooked. It shouldn't. Besides, it still dominates Downtown. In a small, converted 1930s house you find an elegant French Provincial atmosphere, overseen by owner-chef Andre, who brings over 40 years of experience to the table. Much of the wait staff is also French, but not the sort who give the French a bad name. They will happily lavish attention on you and guide you through the menu. Food presentation is exquisite, and choices change seasonally. On a recent visit, an appetizer of Northwest smoked salmon mille feulle with cucumber salad and sevruga caviar was especially enjoyed, as was a main course of grilled provini veal tornados with chive sauce accompanied by a mushroom and foie gras crêpe. You get the idea. Desserts are similarly lovely, an exotic array of rich delights. An extensive wine list (more than 900 labels) is international in scope and includes many rare vintages; consult the sommelier.

Note: An additional branch of Andre's has opened in the **Monte Carlo Hotel & Casino,** 3775 Las Vegas Blvd. S. (☎ **702/ 798-7151**).

EXPENSIVE

Limerick's. Fitzgeralds Casino Holiday Inn, 301 Fremont St., at 3rd St. ☎ **702/388-2400.** Reservations recommended. Main courses $14–$21. AE, DISC, MC, V. Daily 5:30–10:30pm. STEAK/SEAFOOD.

An extensive renovation in 1996 turned a down-at-the-heels joint into a posh steak house. Decorated in the classic Olde English gentlemen's club style, Limerick's is meant to be an oasis of gracious dining away from hectic casino life, and the overall effect is comforting and moderately womblike, particularly in the cozy booths at the back. Unfortunately, casino "ca-chings" still creep in, but it's not overly bothersome. The menu is classic, upscale steak house: beef, chops, some lobster, and chicken. The portions are Vegas-sized (the small prime rib was 14 ounces), so bring an appetite, or take your leftovers back to the room to feed the kids for a couple days. The filet mignon was tender enough to cut with a fork, while the lamb chops came with a pecan mustard glaze. Patrons who don't eat red meat might want to try the apricot chicken. Appetizers are mostly seafood, though there is a fine-sounding baked Brie with strawberry preserves. "Chef's choice" desserts change nightly, and the wine list is good and extensive.

✪ **Second Street Grill.** Fremont Hotel, 200 E. Fremont St. ☎ **702/385-3232.** Main courses $17–$23. Reservations recommended. AE, DC, DISC, MC, V. Sun, Mon, and Thurs 5–10pm, Fri–Sat 5–11pm. INTERNATIONAL.

One of the better-kept secrets of Las Vegas, this is a Downtown jewel. A lovely bit of romantic, cozy class tucked away inside the Fremont Hotel, with excellent food to boot. There is hardly a misstep on the menu, from taste to beautiful presentation. To call this Hawaiian-influenced would be accurate, but don't think of the "Polynesian" craze of the '60s and '70s (in other words, forget flaming whatevers, and sickly sweet-and-sour sauce). This is more like what you would find in a top-flight restaurant on the Big Island. You begin with warm sourdough bread accompanied by a garlic, eggplant, and olive oil dipping sauce. For starters, try the unusual lemon chicken potstickers and the duck confit. Entrees include lobster, ahi tuna, and filet mignon, but the whole fish (opaka paka on a recent visit), served in a bowl with a giant tea-leaf lid, is the best bet. It comes with sautéed mushrooms that will melt in your mouth. Other notable side dishes include some fabulous pesto mashed potatoes. Tiramisù fans should be pleased with the Grill's version of that ubiquitous dessert; it's light on the alcohol and more like an airy tiramisù cheesecake. But don't skip the Chocolate Explosion: a piece of chocolate cake topped with chocolate mousse, covered with a rich chocolate shell.

INEXPENSIVE

✪ **Binion's Horseshoe Coffee Shop.** Binion's Horseshoe, 128 E. Fremont St., at Casino Center Blvd. ☎ **702/382-1600.** Reservations not accepted. Main courses $4.25–$15 (most under $8). AE, CB, DC, DISC, MC, V. Daily 24 hours. AMERICAN.

Down a flight of steps from the casino floor, this no humble hotel coffee shop has a magnificent, pressed copper ceiling, rich oak paneling, walls hung with original oil paintings you'll wish you owned,

Dining Downtown

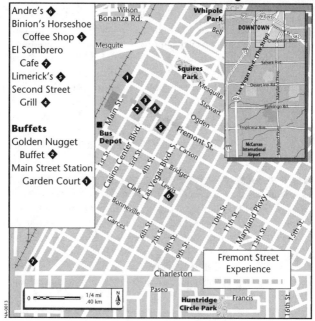

Andre's ◆
Binion's Horseshoe
   Coffee Shop ❸
El Sombrero
   Cafe ◆
Limerick's ◆
Second Street
   Grill ◆

Buffets
Golden Nugget
   Buffet ◆
Main Street Station
   Garden Court ◆

and displays of antiques, turn-of-the-century magazine covers, and black-and-white photographs of the Old West.

The menu lists all the traditional Las Vegas coffee-shop items: sandwiches, burgers, southern-fried chicken, steak and seafood entrees, along with breakfast fare. And you can't beat Binion's specials: two eggs with an immense slab of grilled ham, home fries, toast, and tea or coffee ($3 from 6am to 2pm); a 10-ounce New York steak dinner with baked potato, salad, and roll and butter ($4 from 10pm to 5:45am); a 7-ounce New York steak with eggs, home fries, and toast ($3 from 10pm to 5:45am); a 10-ounce prime-rib dinner, including soup or salad, potato, and vegetables ($5.25 from 5 to 9:45pm)—$6.25 for a 16-ounce T-bone steak instead of prime rib. All bar drinks are available, and there's peanut butter cream pie for dessert.

✪ **El Sombrero Cafe.** 807 S. Main St. ☎ **702/382-9234.** Everything under $10. AE, MC, V. Mon–Sat 11am–10pm. MEXICAN.

This kind of hole-in-the-wall Mexican joint can be found all over California, but not always so readily elsewhere. That it's also the kind of family-run (since 1950) place increasingly forced out of Vegas by giant hotel conglomerates makes it even more worth your time—it's becoming harder and harder, particularly in Downtown, to find budget options that present you with food that is more than just mere fuel. Mexican food fans in particular should seek this friendly place out, though it's not in an attractive part of town. Portions are generous, better than average, and unexpectedly spicy. They also cater to special requests—changing the beef burrito to a chicken one (an option that comes highly recommended), for example, without batting an eyelash. The enchilada and taco combo also won raves.

8   Buffets & Sunday Brunches

Lavish, low-priced buffets are a Las Vegas tradition, designed to lure you to the gaming tables, and to make you feel that you got such a bargain for your meal you can afford to drop more money. They're a gimmick, and we love them. Something about filling up on too much prime rib and shrimp just says "Vegas" to us. Of course, there is quite a range, from some perfunctory steam table displays and salad bars heavy on iceberg lettuce, to unbelievably opulent spreads with caviar and free-flowing champagne. Some are quite beautifully presented, as well. Some of the food is awful, some of it merely works as fuel, and some of it is memorable.

No trip to Las Vegas is complete without trying one or two buffets. Of the dozens, the most noteworthy are described below. Mind you, almost all buffets have some things in common. Unless otherwise noted, every one listed below will have a carving station, a salad bar (quality differs), and hot main courses and side dishes. We will try only to point out when a buffet has something original or notable.

Note: Buffet meals are extremely popular, and reservations are usually not taken (we've indicated when they are accepted, and in all those cases, they are highly recommended). Arrive early (before opening) or late to avoid a long line, especially on weekends.

SOUTH STRIP
MODERATE
Mandalay Bay's Bay Side Buffet. 3950 Las Vegas Blvd. S. ☎ **702/ 632-7402.** Breakfast $8.50, lunch $9.50, dinner $13.50, Sunday brunch $14.50. AE, CB, DC, DISC, MC, V. Daily 7am–10pm.

This is a particularly pretty, not overly large, buffet. Actual windows, floor to ceiling, no less, overlooking the beach part of the elaborate pool area, make it less stuffy and eliminate that closed-in feeling so many of the other buffets in town have. The buffet itself is adequately arranged but features nothing particularly special, though there are some nice cold salads, hearty meats, and a larger and better-than-average dessert bar (they make their own desserts and it shows).

INEXPENSIVE

✪ **Excalibur's Round Table Buffet.** 3850 Las Vegas Blvd. S. ☎ **702/ 597-7777.** Breakfast $5, lunch $6, dinner $8. AE, CB, DC, DISC, MC, V. Daily 7am–10pm.

This strikes the perfect balance of cheap prices, mandatory, tacky decor, and adequate food. This is what you want in a cheap Vegas buffet. But on a recent trip they didn't have mashed potatoes or macaroni salad, which are essential for an archetypal buffet. The plates are large, so you don't have to make as many trips to the buffet tables.

✪ **Luxor's Pharaoh's Pheast Buffet.** 3900 Las Vegas Blvd. S. ☎ **702/ 262-4000.** Breakfast $6, lunch $7.50, dinner $10. AE, DC, DISC, MC, V. Daily 6:30am–11pm.

Located on the lower level, where the Luxor showroom used to be, this huge new buffet looks like it was set in the middle of an archaeological dig, complete with wood braces holding up the ceiling, pot shards, papyrus, and servers dressed in khaki dig outfits. It's a unique and fun decor—be sure to avoid tripping on the mummies and their sarcophagi sticking half up out of the ground. The food is better than most cheap buffets, including a Mexican station with some genuinely spicy food, Chinese stir-fry, and different Italian pastas. Desserts were disappointing. A beer and wine cart makes the rounds. Word has probably gotten out, unfortunately, because the lines are always enormous.

MGM Grand Buffet. 3799 Las Vegas Blvd. S. ☎ **702/891-7777.** Brunch $6, dinner $8; reduced prices for children under 10, free for children under 4. AE, DC, DISC, MC, V. Daily 7am–2:30pm and 4–10pm.

This rather average buffet does feature a fresh Belgian waffle station at breakfast. Dinner also has all-you-can-eat shrimp and an all-you-can-eat shrimp and prime-rib option. Also available: low-fat, sugar-free desserts! And at all meals you get a full pot of coffee on your table.

Monte Carlo Buffet. 3770 Las Vegas Blvd. S. ☎ **702/730-7777.** Breakfast $6.75, lunch $6.99, dinner $9.75, Sunday brunch $10.95. AE, CB, DC, DISC, MC, V. Daily 7am–10pm.

A "courtyard" under a painted sky, the Monte Carlo's buffet room has a Moroccan market theme, with murals of Arab scenes, Moorish archways, oriental carpets, and walls hung with photographs of, and artifacts from, Morocco. Dinner includes a rotisserie (for chicken and pork loin, or London broil), a Chinese food station, a taco/fajita bar, a baked potato bar, numerous salads, and more than a dozen desserts, plus frozen yogurt and ice-cream machines. Lunches are similar. At breakfast, the expected fare is supplemented by an omelet station, and choices include crêpes, blintzes, and corned beef hash. Fresh-baked New York–style bagels are a plus.

MID-STRIP
VERY EXPENSIVE

✪ **Bally's Sterling Sunday Brunch.** 3645 Las Vegas Blvd. S. ☎ **702/ 739-4111.** Reservations recommended. Brunch $49.95. AE, CB, DC, JCB, MC, V. Sunday 9:30am–2:30pm.

This brunch is served in the clubby elegant precincts of Bally's Steakhouse. Flower arrangements and ice sculptures grace lavish buffet spreads tended by white-hatted chefs. There's a waffle and omelet station, a sushi and sashimi bar, and a brimming dessert table. You might choose smoked fish with bagels and cream cheese, or help yourself from a mound of fresh shrimp. Entrees vary weekly. On one visit, the possibilities included rolled chicken stuffed with pistachios and porcini mushrooms, beef tenderloin, steak Diane, seared salmon with beet butter sauce and fried leeks, roast duckling with black currant and blueberry sauce, penne Florentine with pine nuts, and smoked chicken in vodka sauce. Of course, there are deli and breakfast meats, vegetables and scrumptious salads, cheeses, raw bar offerings, seasonal fruits and berries, and side dishes such as stuffed potatoes with caviar and sour cream. Champagne flows freely.

MODERATE

Caesars Palace Palatium Buffet. 3570 Las Vegas Blvd. S. ☎ **702/ 731-7110.** Breakfast $7.35, lunch $9.25, dinner $14.95, Friday seafood dinner $23.35 (includes one lobster); Sat–Sun brunch $14.95 adults (includes unlimited champagne), $7 children 4 to 12, free for children under 3. AE, CB, DC, DISC, MC, V. Daily 7:30am–10pm.

Named for the 2nd-century meeting place of Rome's academy of chefs, this is a rather busy, stuffy room with slightly better than run-of-the-mill buffet quality. Selections at lunch and dinner include elaborate salad bars and fresh-baked breads while the evening meal includes a cold seafood station. Weekend brunches are quite lavish, with omelet stations (in addition to egg dishes), breakfast meats, fresh-squeezed juices, potatoes prepared in various ways, pastas, rice casseroles, carved meats, cold shrimp, smoked salmon, and a waffle and ice-cream sundae bar, in addition to two dessert islands spotlighting cakes and pastries. Now *that's* a buffet!

Harrah's Fresh Market Buffet. 3475 Las Vegas Blvd. S. ☎ **702/369-5000.** Breakfast $7.99, lunch $8.99, dinner $12.99, Sat–Sun champagne brunch $12.99. AE, CB, DC, DISC, MC, V. Mon–Fri 7am–10pm, Sat–Sun 10am–10pm.

The theme here is farmer's market, which means lots of big sculptures of fresh fruits and vegetables, if not the actual fresh fruits and vegetables. Following the new trend of various food stations, as opposed to one long buffet, you will find seafood, pasta, Mexican, Asian, and American specialties ranging from meat loaf to Cajun entrees. Above-average food combined with an extremely friendly staff makes this a better buffet choice.

✪ **Mirage Buffet.** 3400 Las Vegas Blvd. S. ☎ **702/791-7111.** Breakfast $8.50, lunch $9.50, dinner $13.50; Sun brunch $14.50; reduced prices for children 4 to 10, free for children under 4. AE, CB, DC, DISC, MC, V. Mon–Sat 7–10:45am, 11am–2:45pm, and 5:30–10pm; Sun 11:30am–9:30pm.

The Mirage offers lavish spreads in a lovely garden-themed setting with palm trees, a plant-filled stone fountain, and seating under verdigris eaves and domes embellished with flowers. You pay somewhat more here than at other buffets, but you certainly get what you pay for. The salad bars alone are enormous, filled with at least 25 different choices such as Thai beef, seafood, salad Niçoise, tabbouleh, Chinese chicken, Creole rice, and tortellini. At brunch, champagne flows freely, and a scrumptious array of smoked fish is added to the board, along with such items as fruit-filled crêpes and blintzes. And every meal features a spectacular dessert table (the bread pudding in bourbon sauce is noteworthy). For healthful eating there are many light items to choose from, including sugar- and fat-free puddings. And on Sunday a nonalcoholic sparkling cider is a possible champagne alternative.

INEXPENSIVE

✪ **Rio's Carnival World Buffet.** 3700 W. Flamingo Rd. ☎ **702/252-7777.** Breakfast $7.95, lunch $9.95, dinner $12.95. AE, CB, DC, MC, V. Daily 8am–10:30am and 11am–11pm.

The buffet here is located in a festively decorated room with variegated wide, sequined ribbons looped overhead and seating amid planters of lush, faux tropical blooms. Chairs and booths are upholstered in bright hues—green, purple, red, orange, and turquoise. This is an excellent buffet with cheerfully decorative food booths set up like stations in an upscale food court. A barbecued chicken and ribs station offers side dishes of baked beans and mashed potatoes. Other stations offer stir-fry (chicken, beef, pork, and vegetables), Mexican taco fixings and accompaniments, Chinese fare, a Japanese sushi and teppanyaki grill, a Brazilian mixed grill, Italian pasta and antipasto, and fish-and-chips. There's even a diner setup for hot dogs, burgers, fries, and milk shakes. All this is in addition to the usual offerings of most Las Vegas buffets. A stunning array of oven-fresh cakes, pies, and pastries (including sugar-free and low-fat desserts) is arranged in a palm-fringed circular display area, and there's also a make-your-own sundae bar. A full cash bar is another Rio plus. Everything is fresh and beautifully prepared and presented.

Treasure Island Buffet. 3300 Las Vegas Blvd. S. ☎ **702/894-7111.** Breakfast $6.99, lunch $7.50, dinner $9.99, Sun brunch $9.99. AE, DC, DISC, JCB, MC, V. Mon–Sat 7–10:45am and 11am–3:45pm; daily 4–10:30pm; Sun 7:30am–3:30pm.

The buffet is served in two internationally themed rooms. The American room, under a central rough-hewn beamed canopy hung with the flags of the 13 colonies, re-creates New Orleans during the era of Jean Lafitte. And the Italian room, modeled after a Tuscan villa overlooking a bustling piazza, has strings of festival lights overhead and food displays under a striped awning. Both rooms are filled with authentic antiques and artifacts typical of their locales and time periods. And both also serve identical fare, including extensive American breakfasts. Dinners offer a Chinese food station, peel-and-eat shrimp, a salad bar, potato and rice side dishes, cheeses and cold cuts, fresh fruits and vegetables, breads, and a large choice of desserts. Lunch is similar, and Sunday brunch includes unlimited champagne.

NORTH STRIP
INEXPENSIVE

Circus Circus Buffet. 2880 Las Vegas Blvd. S. ☎ **702/734-0410.** Breakfast $4.49, lunch $5.49, dinner $6.99, Sat–Sun brunch $5.49. AE, CB, DC, DISC, MC, V. Mon–Fri 7–11:30am, noon–4pm, and 4:30–10pm; Sat–Sun 7am–4pm and 4:30–11pm.

Here's a choice: just about the cheapest buffet on the Strip, versus the worst buffet food in town. Here you'll find 50 items of typical cafeteria fare, and none of them all that good. Kids love it; some adults find it inedible. If food is strictly fuel for you, you can't go wrong here. Otherwise, trundle off to another buffet.

EAST OF THE STRIP
MODERATE

Las Vegas Hilton Buffet of Champions. 3000 Paradise Rd. ☎ **702/ 732-5111.** Breakfast $8, lunch $9, dinner $13, weekend brunch $12 (includes unlimited champagne); half price for children age 12 and under. CB, DC, DISC, ER, MC, V. Daily 8am–2:30pm and 5–10pm.

As the name implies, the room, located near the casino entrance to the race and sports SuperBook, is sports-themed. Cream walls are adorned with attractive murals and photographs of hockey, football, boxing, and horse racing, and there are bookshelves stocked with sporting literature. All in all, it's one of the better-looking buffet rooms in town. And the fare is fresh and delicious with special mention going to the prime rib, and the outstanding cream puffs and superior rice pudding (it's hard to find good desserts at Vegas buffets). Dinner additionally features all-you-can-eat crab and shrimp. Friday night seafood selection is particularly large and palatable.

INEXPENSIVE

✪ **Sam's Town, The Great Buffet.** 5111 Boulder Hwy. ☎ **702/456-7777.** Breakfast $4, lunch $7, dinner $9 (Fri seafood buffet $13); Sun brunch $8; all buffets half price for children 6 and under. AE, CB, DC, DISC, MC, V. Daily 8am– 3pm and 4–9pm.

Friendly service and good food have made Sam's Town's buffets extremely popular. About 70% of their clientele are local folks, not tourists. The buffet room is as homey as your living room, with fruit-motif carpeting, gaslight-style brass chandeliers, and planters of foliage creating intimate dining niches. Dinner includes a Chinese stir-fry station, a burger grill, and a wide array of side dishes and fresh fruits and vegetables. For dessert, numerous pies and cakes are supplemented by frozen yogurt with homemade fudge, homemade candies, caramel apples, and fruit cobbler. Cajun seafood entrees are featured on Tuesday night. But best of all are the Friday seafood buffets, offering paella, deep-fried oysters, crawfish étouffée, Cajun red snapper, steamed Dungeness crab with drawn butter, shrimp scampi with pasta, raw oysters, peel-and-eat shrimp, and much more. Sunday champagne brunch offers extensive breakfast and lunch fare, including blintzes, Mexican breakfast tortes, a carving station, Southern and Cajun specialties, and unlimited champagne.

DOWNTOWN
MODERATE

✪ **Golden Nugget Buffet.** 129 E. Fremont St. ☎ **702/385-7111.** Breakfast $5.75, lunch $7.50, dinner $10.25, Sun brunch $11. AE, CB, DC, DISC, MC, V. Mon–Sat 7am–3pm and 4–10pm, Sun 8am–10pm.

This buffet has often been voted number one in Las Vegas. Not only is the food fresh and delicious, but it's served in an opulent dining room with marble-topped serving tables amid planters of greenery and potted palms. Most of the seating is in plush booths. The buffet tables are also laden with an extensive salad bar (about 50 items), fresh fruit, and marvelous desserts including Zelma Wynn's (Steve's mother) famous bread pudding. Every night fresh seafood is featured. Most lavish is the all-day Sunday champagne brunch, which adds such dishes as eggs Benedict, blintzes, pancakes, creamed herring, and smoked fish with bagels and cream cheese. *Note:* This stunning buffet room is also the setting for a $3 late-night meal of steak and eggs with home fries and biscuits with gravy; it's served 11pm to 4am.

INEXPENSIVE

✪ **Main Street Station Garden Court.** 200 N. Main St. ☎ **702/387-1896.** Breakfast $5, lunch $7, dinner $9; Fri seafood buffet $13; Sat and Sun champagne brunch $8; free for children 3 and under. AE, CB, DC, DISC, MC, V. Mon–Fri 7am–10:30am, 11am–3pm, and 4–10pm; Sat–Sun 7am–3pm and 4–10pm.

Set in what is truly one of the prettiest buffet spaces in town (and certainly in Downtown), with very high ceilings and tall windows bringing in much-needed natural light, the Main Street Station Garden Court buffet is one of the best in town, much less in Downtown. Featuring nine live-action stations (meaning you can watch your food being prepared), including a wood-fired brick-oven pizza (delicious), many fresh salsas at the Mexican station, a barbecue rotisserie, fresh sausage at the carving station, Chinese, Hawaiian, and Southern specialties (soul food and the like), and so many more we lost count. On Friday night, they have all this plus nearly infinite varieties of seafood all the way up to lobster. We ate ourselves into a stupor and didn't regret it.

6

What to See & Do in Las Vegas

*Y*ou aren't going to lack for things to do in Las Vegas. More than likely, you have come here for the gambling, which should keep you pretty busy (we say that with some understatement). But you can't sit at a slot machine forever. (Or maybe you can.) In any event, it shouldn't be too hard to find ways to fill your time between poker hands.

Just walking on the Strip and gazing at the gaudy, garish, absurd wonder of it all can occupy quite a lot of time. This is the number-one activity we recommend in Vegas; at night, it is a mind-boggling sight like no other. And, of course, there are shows and plenty of other nighttime entertainment. But if you need something else to do, or if you are trying to amuse yourself while the rest of your party gambles away, this chapter will guide you. Don't forget to check out the free attractions, such as Bellagio's water fountain ballet, Mirage's volcano and white tiger exhibit, Treasure Island's pirate battle, and the new masquerade show at the Rio.

You could also consider using a spa at a major hotel; they are too pricey (as high as $25 a day) to fill in for your daily gym visit, but spending a couple of hours working out, sweating out Vegas toxins in the steam room, and generally pampering yourself will leave you feeling relaxed, refreshed, and ready to go all night again.

There are also plenty of out-of-town sightseeing options, like **Hoover Dam** (a major tourist destination).

1 Las Vegas Attractions

Bellagio Gallery of Fine Art. Bellagio, 3600 Las Vegas Blvd. S. ☎ **888/488-7111.** Admission $12 (includes audio tour). Tickets must be reserved in advance. Hotel guests can reserve tickets 90 days in advance, nonguests 7 days. Daily 9am–midnight.

Okay, we admit it; we were the first to scoff at the idea of Steve Wynn putting his art collection on display—and charging for it! How many people will come to Vegas, we sniffed, and not only go see a bunch of paintings, but will pay for the privilege? Tons, apparently. The gallery has had lines out the door since it opened, and it's virtually impossible to get in without an advance reservation. For the life of us, we can't figure out how Wynn knew this would be so, but we humbly bow to his business savvy yet again.

Having said that, while it is greatly encouraging that Vegas is responding so well to culture, it should be pointed out that this is not a museum. It is a private collection of works by many of the big-name modern artists of the last 100 years, ranging from Impressionism to Pop Art. Certainly the list is like a roll call for the Modern Art Hall of Fame: Picasso, van Gogh, Cézanne, Degas, Gauguin, Manet, Monet, Matisse, Renoir, Pollack, Miró, and de Kooning. And if none are precisely masterpieces, they are for the most part highly regarded works by masters. But this is officially a gallery, and so unlike in a museum, everything is for sale, and consequently any given piece of art has the potential to suddenly disappear (already the inventory has changed due to sales).

✪ **Caesars Magical Empire.** Caesars Palace, 3570 Las Vegas Blvd. S. ☎ **800/445-4544** or 702/731-7333. Reservations required. Admission (including a 3-course meal and wine, tax, and gratuities) $75.50 adults, half price for children 5–10. Tues–Sat 4:30–10:30pm. Children must be at least 5 years of age.

Caesars spent a lot of money constructing this facility, and it shows. It's an impressive place of tunnels, grottoes, revolving rooms, theaters, and so forth, with a surprise around every corner. Upon arrival, you are assigned to a group of no more than 24, which is escorted through catacombs by Centurion guards to a private dining room. There you are treated to an intimate magic show by your own private magician. Assisted by some very funny wait staff, there is usually a little story played out as you eat your dinner. Up-close magic is performed between courses. Afterward, you are taken through the rest of the Cavern (beware the Forbidden Crypt of Ramses if you have anything even remotely resembling motion sickness—they ask only if you have "balance problems"); you'll end up in a 7-story dome, with massive Egyptian columns and sculptures, where you can see several other magic shows ranging in size. Here, you can experience **Lumineria,** a 5-minute show combining smoke, dancing fire, and high-tech lighting effects (cover your eyes before the finale—it's nearly blinding), or chat with some skeletons (Habeas and Corpus) on the walls and, best of all, request songs from "Invisibella," the player-piano ghost with a nearly unlimited repertoire and a great sense of humor. All throughout are additional spots

Las Vegas Attractions

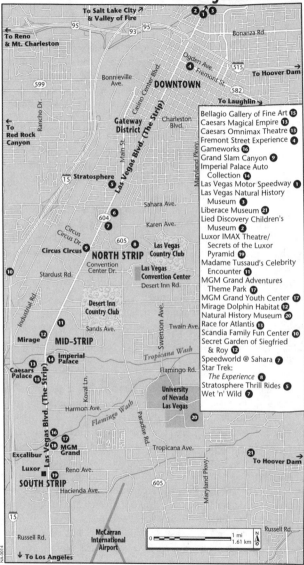

Bellagio Gallery of Fine Art **15**
Caesars Magical Empire **13**
Caesars Omnimax Theatre **13**
Fremont Street Experience **4**
Gameworks **16**
Grand Slam Canyon **9**
Imperial Palace Auto
  Collection **14**
Las Vegas Motor Speedway **1**
Las Vegas Natural History
  Museum **3**
Liberace Museum **21**
Lied Discovery Children's
  Museum **2**
Luxor IMAX Theatre/
  Secrets of the Luxor
  Pyramid **19**
Madame Tussaud's Celebrity
  Encounter **11**
MGM Grand Adventures
  Theme Park **17**
MGM Grand Youth Center **17**
Mirage Dolphin Habitat **12**
Natural History Museum **20**
Race for Atlantis **13**
Scandia Family Fun Center **10**
Secret Garden of Siegfried
  & Roy **12**
Speedworld @ Sahara **7**
Star Trek:
  The Experience **8**
Stratosphere Thrill Rides **5**
Wet 'n' Wild **7**

with some kind of trick to them; be sure to ask the bartenders for advice.

Allow yourself at least 3 hours to see everything once. Considering how much show, spectacle, food, and just plain entertainment you get, this is one of the best values in the city. By the way, currently, Caesars is holding free tours of the space from 11am to 3pm, so you might want to come by and get a sneak peak and behind-the-scenes look.

Caesars OMNIMAX Theatre. Caesars Palace, 3570 Las Vegas Blvd. S. ☎ **800/634-6698** or 702/731-7901. Admission $7 adults; $5 seniors, children 2–12, hotel guests, and military personnel. Show times vary. You must purchase tickets at the box office (open daily 8am–10pm) on the day of the performance.

If you've never seen one of these 3-D-like films, you're in for a treat. The OMNIMAX Theatre here is housed in a geodesic dome, a space-age environment with 368 seats that recline 27°, affording a panoramic view of the curved 57-foot screen. The movies, projected via 70mm film (which is 10 times the frame size of ordinary 35mm film), offer an awesome visual display enhanced by a state-of-the-art sound system (89 speakers engulf the audience in sound). Depending on the film being shown, viewers might soar over the Rocky Mountains, plummet down steep waterfalls, ride the rapids, travel into outer space, or perch at the rim of an erupting volcano. Shows change frequently, but whatever you see will be stupendous.

✪ **Fremont Street Experience.** Fremont St., between Main St. and Las Vegas Blvd. in Downtown Las Vegas. www.vegasexperience.com. Free admission. Shows nightly.

For some years, Downtown Vegas has been losing ground to the Strip. But thanks to a $70 million revitalization project, that is starting to change. Fremont Street, the heart of "Glitter Gulch," has been closed off and turned into a pedestrian mall. The Fremont Street Experience is a 5-block open-air pedestrian mall, a landscaped strip of outdoor cafes, vendor carts, and colorful kiosks purveying food and merchandise. Overhead is a 90-foot-high steel-mesh "celestial vault"; at night, it is the **Sky Parade,** a high-tech light-and-laser show (the canopy is equipped with more than 2.1 million lights) enhanced by a concert hall–quality sound system, which takes place four times nightly. But there's music between shows as well. Not only does the canopy provide shade, it cools the area through a misting system in summer and warms you with radiant heaters in winter. The difference this makes cannot be overemphasized; what was once a ghost town of tacky, rapidly aging buildings, in an area with more undesirables than not, is now a bustling (at least at night), friendly, safe place (they have private security guards who hustle said undesirables away). It's a place where you can stroll, eat, or even dance to the music under the lights.

✪ **Gameworks.** 3769 Las Vegas Blvd. S., in the Showcase Mall. ☎ **702/ 432-GAME.** Sun–Thurs. 10am–1am, Fri–Sat 10am–2am.

What do you get when Steven Spielberg and his Dreamworks team get in on the video-game arcade action—grown-up state-of-the-art fun. High-tech movie magic has taken over all sorts of traditional arcade games and turned them interactive, from a virtual reality batting cage, to a Jurassic Park game that lets you hunt dinosaurs. There are motion simulator rides galore, and even actual motion activities like rock climbing. But classic games, from Pacman to pool tables, are here too, though sometimes with surprising twists such as air hockey, where sometimes multiple pucks will shoot out at once. All this doesn't come exactly cheap; you purchase a block of time ($20 for an hour, though if you get there at opening you get 2 hours for $20), which goes on a debit card that you then insert into the various machines to activate them. But you do get value for your money, which makes this a viable alternative to casinos, particularly if you have children (though it's clearly geared toward a college age and older demographic). The latter probably should be 10 years old and up—any younger, and parents will need to stand over them, rather than go off and have considerable fun on their own.

Imperial Palace Auto Collection. Imperial Palace Hotel, 3535 Las Vegas Blvd. S. ☎ **702/731-3311.** Admission $7 adults, $3 seniors and children under 12, free for children under 5 and AAA members. Daily 9:30am–11:30pm.

If you're not a "car person," don't assume you won't be interested in this premier collection of antique, classic, and special-interest vehicles. There's more here than just cars and trucks. Check out the graceful lines and handsome sculpture of one of the 43 Model J Dusenbergs (the largest collection in the world valued at over $50 million). The craftsmanship and attention to detail make these cars, and others here, true works of art.

There's also a great deal of history. Take a walk down President's Row where you can see JFK's 1962 "bubbletop" Lincoln Continental, Lyndon Johnson's 1964 Cadillac, Eisenhower's 1952 Chrysler Imperial 20-foot-long parade car, Truman's 1950 Lincoln Cosmopolitan with gold-plated interior, FDR's unrestored 1936 V-16 Cadillac, and Herbert Hoover's 1929 Cadillac.

Las Vegas Motor Speedway. 7000 Las Vegas Blvd. N., directly across from Nellis Air Force base (take I-15 north to Speedway exit 54). ☎ **702/644-4443** for ticket information. Tickets $10–$75 (higher prices for major events).

This 107,000-seat facility, the first new superspeedway to be built in the Southwest in over 2 decades, opened with a 500K Indy Racing League event. A $100 million state-of-the-art motor-sports entertainment complex, it includes a $1^{1}/_{2}$-mile superspeedway, a $2^{1}/_{2}$-mile FIA-approved road course, paved and dirt short-track ovals, and a 4,000-foot drag strip. Also on the property are facilities for Go-Kart, Legends Car, Sand Drag, and Motorcross competition. The new speedway is accessible via shuttle buses to and from the Imperial Palace hotel, though some of the other major hotels have their own shuttles to the Speedway.

✪ **Liberace Museum.** 1775 E. Tropicana Ave., at Spencer St. ☎ **702/798-5595.** Admission $6.95 adults, $4.95 seniors over 60 and students, free for children under 12. Mon–Sat 10am–5pm, Sun 1–5pm.

You can keep your Louvres and Vaticans and Smithsonians; this is a museum. Housed, like everything else in Vegas, in a strip mall, this is a shrine to the glory and excess that was the art project known as Liberace. You've got your costumes (bejeweled), your many cars (bejeweled), your many pianos (bejeweled), and many jewels (also bejeweled). It just shows what can be bought with lots of money and no taste. Unless you have a severely underdeveloped appreciation for camp or take your museum-going very seriously, you shouldn't miss it. The museum is $2^{1}/_{2}$ miles east of the Strip on your right.

Luxor IMAX Theater/In Search of the Obelisk. Luxor Las Vegas, 3900 Las Vegas Blvd. S. ☎ **702/262-4000.** Admission $7.95 for IMAX 2-D, $8.95 for 3-D; $6 for In Search of the Obelisk. Sun–Thurs 9am–11pm, Fri–Sat 9am–1am. Show times vary depending on the length of the film.

This is a state-of-the-art theater that projects films on a 7-story screen. There are two different films running: one in standard two dimensions, the other 3-D. The glasses for the latter are really cool headsets that include built-in speakers, bringing certain sounds right into your head. The movies change periodically but always include some extraordinary special effects. If you have a fear of heights, make sure to ask for a seat on one of the lower levels.

In Search of the Obelisk is a motion-simulator ride in which technology is used to create an action adventure involving a chase sequence inside a pyramid. You have an option to take a different route if you have motion sickness, which means you won't get the best special effects. Otherwise, it's a standard thrill ride with interesting touches.

Madame Tussaud's Celebrity Encounter. 3355 Las Vegas Blvd. S. ☎ **702/ 990-3530.** Admission $12.50 adults, $10 children 4-12; $10.75 seniors and Nevada residents. 10am–10pm daily.

Madame Tussaud's waxworks exhibition has been the top London attraction for nearly 2 centuries, so even if you aren't a fan of wax museums, this, its sole branch on this side of the Atlantic, is probably worth a drop in. Figures here are as state of the art as wax replicas can get, painstakingly constructed to perfectly match the original person. There is no Chamber of Horrors, but the exhibit makes up for it by having all the waxworks free-standing, allowing guests to get up close and personal. Go ahead, lay your cheek next to Elvis' or Sinatra's and have your photo taken. The emphasis is on film, television, music, and sports celebrities, who are housed in five themed rooms. There's also a behind-the-scenes look at the lengthy process involved in creating just one of these figures.

Race for Atlantis IMAX 3-D Ride. Caesars, 3500 Las Vegas Blvd. S. Admission $9.50 adults, $6.75 children under 12. Sun–Thurs 10am–11pm, Fri–Sat 10am–midnight.

Following the trend in virtual reality theme-park rides, Caesars Palace joined forces with IMAX to create the Race for Atlantis. If you've never been on a virtual reality ride, you will enjoy it, but the production values pale compared to *Star Trek: The Experience* (but then again, that's also twice as expensive). Not for the weak of stomach.

Secret Garden of Siegfried and Roy & ✪ Mirage Dolphin Habitat. Mirage Hotel, 3400 Las Vegas Blvd. S. ☎ **702/791-7111.** Admission $10, free for children under 10. Secret Garden open Mon, Tues, Thurs, Fri 11am–5pm, Sat–Sun 10am–5pm. Dolphin Habitat open Mon–Fri 11am–7pm, Sat–Sun 10am–7pm. Dolphin exhibit open only on Wed, when the Secret Garden is closed; admission $5. Hours subject to change.

Siegfried and Roy's famous white tigers have long had a free exhibit in the Mirage. They still do, but now they have an additional space, a gorgeous area behind the dolphin exhibit. Here, the white tigers are joined by white lions, Bengal tigers, an Asian elephant, a panther, and a snow leopard. (Many of these are bred by Siegfried and Roy and are also in their nightly show.) It's really just a glorified zoo, featuring only the big-ticket animals; however, it is a very pretty place, with plenty of foliage and some bits of Indian- and Asian-themed architecture. Zoo purists will be horrified at the smallish spaces the animals occupy, but all are rotated between here and their more lavish digs at the illusionist team's home. What this does allow you to do is get very up close with a tiger, which is quite a thrill—those paws are massive indeed. Visitors are given little

portable phonelike objects on which they can play a series of pro-
grams, listening to Roy and Mirage owner Steve Wynn discuss
conservation or the attributes of each animal and deliver anecdotes.

The Dolphin Habitat is more satisfying. It was designed to
provide a healthy and nurturing environment and to educate the
public about marine mammals and their role in the ecosystem. Specialists worldwide were consulted in creating the habitat, which was
designed to serve as a model of a quality, secured environment. The
pool is more than eight times larger than government regulations
require, and its 2.5 million gallons of man-made seawater are cycled
and cleaned once every 2 hours. It must be working, as the adult
dolphins here are breeding regularly. The Mirage displays only dolphins already in captivity—no dolphins will be taken from the wild.
You can watch the dolphins frolic both above and below ground
through viewing windows, in three different pools. (There is nothing quite like the kick you get from seeing a baby dolphin play.) The
knowledgeable staff, who surely have the best job in Vegas, will answer questions. If they aren't already, ask them to play ball with the
dolphins; they toss large beach balls into the pools, and the dolphins
hit them out with their noses, leaping out of the water cackling with
dolphin glee. You catch the ball, getting nicely wet, and toss it back
to them. If you have never played ball with a dolphin, shove that
happy child next to you out of the way and go for it. There is also
a video of a resident dolphin (Duchess) giving birth (to Squirt) un-
derwater. You can stay as long as you like, which might just be
hours.

Speedworld at Sahara. Sahara Hotel & Casino, 2535 Las Vegas Blvd. S.
☎ **702/737-2111.** Indy-car simulator $8 (you must be at least 48 in. tall to
ride), 3-D simulator $3. Open daily at 10am; closing hours vary seasonally but
usually 10pm.

As auto racing is the fastest-growing spectator sport in America,
Speedworld is sure to be a popular stop. Consisting of two parts, the
first is an 8-minute virtual reality ride featuring a three-quarter-sized
replica of an Indianapolis race car.

A separate 3-D motion theater sets you up, complete with
goggles, to view a film that puts you right inside another race car,
for yet another stomach-churning (more so than the virtual reality
portion) ride. Speed junkies and race-car buffs will be in heaven
here, though those with tender stomachs should consider shopping
at the well-stocked theme gift shop instead.

Star Trek: The Experience. Las Vegas Hilton, 3000 Paradise Rd. ☎ **888/
GO-BOLDLY.** www.startrekexp.com. Admission $14.95. Daily 11am–11pm.

It goes without saying that Trekkers (note use of correct term) will be delighted with this. On the other hand, normal, sensible fans, and those who couldn't care less about *Star Trek,* may find themselves saying, "I spent $14.95 and 2 hours in line for this?"

A fancy entry in the latest Vegas attractions fad, the motion-simulator ride, you can't fault the setup and interior design; after a walk through a space-themed casino (check out those light-beam-activated slot machines!), your long wait in line will be somewhat entertaining, thanks to memorabilia (displayed as if this were the stuff of fact, not fiction) and TVs showing various *Trek* clips. As you make your way to the ride proper, you encounter actors dressed in Trek-gear, who let you know that you've crossed the line into the Trek future. There is a story line, but we won't spoil it for you; suffice to say it involves evil doings by the Borgs, time travel, and if all doesn't work out, the very history of *Star Trek* could be affected. Do expect to be beamed aboard the *Enterprise* (that's really kind of cool), and know that if you have a sensitive stomach, you can skip the actual motion-simulator part, a wild and sometimes headache-inducing chase through space. In addition to the expected lengthy wait (on average, 20 minutes; best shot at a slight lull would be between noon and 1pm on weekdays), the quality of your experience can vary depending on the quality of those Trek-garbed actors, whose line delivery can be awfully stilted. On the way out, through the shops selling everything Trek and space-oriented, don't miss the TV showing a "news report" about some of the very things you just experienced.

Stratosphere Thrill Rides. Stratosphere, 2000 Las Vegas Blvd. S. ☎ **702/ 380-7777.** Admission for Big Shot $6; for Roller Coaster $5; $3 per re-ride, plus $6 to ascend the tower (if you dine in the buffet room or Top of the World, there's no charge to go up to the tower). Sun–Thurs 10am–1am, Fri–Sat 10am–2am. Minimum height requirement for both rides is 48 in.

Atop the 1,149-foot Stratosphere Tower are two marvelous thrill rides. The **Let It Ride High Roller** (the world's highest roller coaster) was recently revamped to go at even faster speeds as it zooms around a hilly track that is seemingly suspended in midair. Even more fun is the **Big Shot,** a breathtaking free-fall ride that thrusts you 160 feet in the air along a 228-foot spire at the top of the tower, then plummets back down again. Sitting in an open car, you seem to be dangling in space over Las Vegas. We have one relative, a thrill-ride enthusiast, who said he never felt more scared than when he rode the Big Shot. After surviving, he promptly put his kids on it; they loved it. *Note:* The rides are shut down in inclement weather and high winds.

2   Getting Married

This is one of the most popular things to do in Las Vegas. Why? It's very easy to get married here. Too easy. See that total stranger standing next to you? Grab him or her, head down to the **Clark Country Marriage License Bureau,** 200 S. 3rd St., at Briger Avenue (☎ **702/455-3156;** open Monday to Sunday 8am to midnight, 24 hours legal holidays), to get your license, find a wedding chapel (not hard since there are about 50 of them in town; they line the north end of the Strip—Las Vegas Boulevard South—and most hotels have one), and tie the knot. Just like that. No blood test, no waiting period—heck, not even an awkward dating period.

You can pick a chapel just by driving down the Strip, but we've listed four of our favorites. You can also call **Las Vegas Weddings and Rooms** (☎ **800/488-MATE**), a one-stop shop for wedding services. They'll find a chapel or outdoor garden that suits your taste (not to mention such only-in-Vegas venues as the former mansions of Elvis Presley and Liberace), book you into a hotel for the honeymoon, arrange the ceremony, and provide flowers, a photographer (or videographer), wedding cake, limo, car rental, music, champagne, balloons, and a garter for the bride. Basically they can arrange anything you like. Theme weddings are a specialty. They even have a New Age minister on call who can perform a Native American ceremony. And yes, you can get married by an Elvis impersonator. Let Las Vegas Weddings arrange your honeymoon stay—sightseeing tours, show tickets, and meals, as well.

✪ **Cupid's Wedding Chapel.** 827 Las Vegas Blvd. S. ☎ **800/543-2933** or 702/598-4444. http://www.cupidswedding.com. Sun–Thurs 10am–10pm, Fri–Sat 10am–1am.

"The little chapel with the big heart." Well, they just might be. The manager explains that, unlike other chapels on the Strip, they schedule weddings an hour apart. This gives them time for the full production number; they pride themselves on offering "a traditional church wedding at a chapel price." "I am a die-hard romantic," said the manager, "I want huggin', kissin', and I don't care if they faint—a wedding is a place for romance." You just know she cries at each and every service they perform.

✪ **Divine Madness.** 111 Las Vegas Blvd. S. (half a block south of Fremont). ☎ **800/717-4734** or 702/384-5660.

Oh, yeah, now *this* is how to do a Vegas wedding. "From innocent lace to erotic leather," they offer the chance to create your own fantasy wedding. You want to dress up like spacemen? They can do that. Kings and queens? No problem. Scarlett O'Hara? Kid stuff. They've got all the costumes on hand, including well-chosen accessories, and while said outfits may not look that spiffy in person, they will look fabulous in the photographs—and the photographs, after all, are why you have a wedding like this in the first place. The staff is as fun as they ought to be, comfortable, casual, and busy, and the whole thing is infectious, so watch out—you might well find yourself getting married as a cartoon character.

San Francisco Sally's Victorian Chapel. 1304 Las Vegas Blvd. S. ☎ **800/ 658-8677** or 702/385-7777. http://www.zip2.com/klas-tv/sfsally. Sun–Thurs 10am–4pm, Fri–Sat 10am–8pm.

An extremely tiny wedding chapel bursting at the seams with Victorian frills (fringed lamps, swags of lace curtains). They basically offer "an Olde Tyme Parlor Wedding." This is perfect if you want a very intimate wedding—like you, your intended, and someone to officiate. It literally can't hold more than six people. The women who run it refer to themselves as "a bunch of mother hens"; they're delightful and will pamper you to within an inch of your life.

✪ **A Special Memory Wedding Chapel.** 800 S. Fourth St., at Gass. ☎ **800/9-MARRYU** or 702/384-2211. www.aspecialmemory.com. Sun–Thurs 8am–10pm, Fri–Sat 8am–midnight.

This is a terrific new wedding chapel, particularly when compared to the rather tired facades of the classics on the Strip. This is absolutely the place to go if you want a traditional, big-production wedding; you won't feel in the least bit tacky. It's a New England church–style building, complete with steeple. The interior looks like a proper church (well, a plain one—don't think ornate gothic cathedral). It is all very clean and new and seats about 87 comfortably. Should all this just be too darn nice and proper for you, they also offer a drive-up window (where they do about 300 weddings a month!). It costs you $25—just ring the buzzer for service. They have a photo studio on site and will do a small cake, cold cuts, and champagne receptions. There is a gazebo for outside weddings, and they sell T-shirts!

3 Especially for Kids

Like much of the rest of the world, you may be under the impression that Las Vegas has evolved from an adults-only fantasyland into a vacation destination suitable for the entire family. The only explanation for this myth is that Las Vegas was referred to as "Disneyland for adults" by so many and for so long that the town became momentarily confused and decided it actually was Disneyland. Some of the gargantuan hotels then spent small fortunes on redecorating in an attempt to lure families with vast quantities of junk food and a lot of hype. They now vehemently deny that any such notion ever crossed their collective minds, and, no, they don't know how that roller coaster got into the parking lot.

To put things simply, Las Vegas makes money—lots and lots of money—by promoting gambling, drinking, and sex. These are all fine pursuits if you happen to be an adult, but if you haven't reached the magical age of 21, you really don't count in this town. In any case, the casinos and even the Strip itself are simply too stimulating, noisy, and smoky for young kids.

Older progeny may have a tolerance for crowds and the incessant pinging of the slot machines, but they will be thoroughly annoyed with you when casino security chastises them if they so much as stop to tie their shoe laces anywhere near the gaming tables.

Nevertheless, you may have a perfectly legitimate reason for bringing your children to Las Vegas (like Grandma was busy, or you were just stopping through on your way from somewhere else), so here are some places to take the children both on and off the Strip.

Circus Circus (see p. 54) has ongoing circus acts throughout the day, a vast video game and pinball arcade, and dozens of carnival games on its mezzanine level. Behind the hotel is Grand Slam Canyon, detailed below. **Excalibur** (see p. 35) also offers video and carnival games, plus thrill cinemas and free shows (jugglers, puppets, etc.). At **Caesars Palace,** the Magical Empire (for kids 12 and older only, see p. 114), Race for Atlantis IMAX ride, and OMNIMAX movies (see p. 116) are a thrill for everyone in the family; a video-game arcade adjoins the OMNIMAX Theatre. Animated talking statues in the **Forum Shops** are also a kick, while kids should also be wowed by clamoring around inside the giant moving Trojan horse outside FAO Schwarz, in the shops, and marveling at the Atlantis fountain show. *Star Trek: The Experience* (see p. 120) deserves to draw families to the **Las Vegas Hilton,** but it may be a bit much for younger children. The ship battle in front of **Treasure Island** (see p. 47) is sure to please, as will the erupting volcano and the Secret Garden of Siegfried and Roy and Dolphin Habitat at the **Mirage** (see p. 111); while you're here, see the tigers and the sharks. Ditto the various attractions at **Luxor Las Vegas** (the IMAX Theater, p. 118; and Secrets of the

Luxor Pyramid, p. 120) and Speedworld (p. 120) at the **Sahara.** Children 10 and up will love the many options for play (from high tech to low tech, from video wonders to actual physical activity) offered at Gameworks, as will their parents.

Appropriate shows for kids include *Tournament of Kings* at **Excalibur** (see p. 35), *Siegfried and Roy* at the **Mirage** (see p. 183), *Lance Burton* at the **Monte Carlo** (see p. 182), *EFX* at the **MGM Grand** (see p. 178), and Cirque du Soleil's *Mystère* at **Treasure Island** (see p. 176). As a general rule, early shows are less racy than late-night shows.

Adventuredome. 2880 Las Vegas Blvd. S., behind Circus Circus Hotel. ☎ **702/794-3939.** Free admission; pay per ride. AE, DC, DISC, MC, V. Park hours vary; call ahead.

This isn't a half-bad place to spend a hot afternoon, especially now that Circus Circus, the casino/hotel that built this indoor amusement park, has undergone a face-lift. The glass dome that towers overhead lets in natural light, a solace to those of us who look peaked under the glow of the artificial kind. A double-loop roller coaster careens around the simulated Grand Canyon, and there's the requisite water flume, a laser tag area, and a modest number of other rides for kids of all ages. A dinosaur-bone excavation area will provide a good time for preschoolers, and a place to rest for the supervising adults. Video games and an arcade are separate from the attractions, cutting down just a tad on the noise level. Jugglers and magicians provide impromptu entertainment. Our only caveat is don't leave kids here alone; they could easily get lost.

Las Vegas Natural History Museum. 900 Las Vegas Blvd. N., at Washington. ☎ **702/384-3466.** Admission $5 adults; $4 seniors, students, and military; $2.50 children 4–12; free for children under 4. Daily 9am–4pm.

Conveniently located across the street from the Lied Discovery Children's Museum (described below), this humble temple of taxidermy harkens back to elementary school field trips circa 1965, when stuffed elk and brown bears forever protecting their kill were as close as most of us got to exotic animals. Worn around the edges but very sweet and relaxed, the museum is enlivened by a hands-on activity room and two life-sized dinosaurs that roar at one another intermittently. A small boy was observed leaping toward his dad upon watching this display, so you might want to warn any sensitive little ones that the big tyrannosaurs aren't going anywhere. Surprisingly, the gift shop here is particularly well stocked with neat items you won't mind too terribly buying for the kids.

Lied Discovery Children's Museum. 833 Las Vegas Blvd. N., a half block south of Washington, across the street from Cashman Field. ☎ **702/ 382-5437.** Admission $5 adults, $4 seniors and children 2–17. DISC, MC, V. Tues–Sun 10am–5pm.

A hands-on science museum designed for curious kids, the bright, airy, 2-story Lied makes an ideal outing for toddlers and young children. With lots of interactive exhibits to examine, including a miniature grocery store, a bubble tube for encasing oneself inside a soap bubble, a radio station, and music and drawing areas, you'll soon forget your video poker losses. Clever, thought-inducing exhibits are everywhere. Learn how it feels to be handicapped by playing basketball from a wheelchair. Feed a wooden "sandwich" to a cut-out of a snake and to a human cut-out, and see how much nutrition each receives. See how much sunscreen their giant stuffed mascot needs to keep from burning. On weekend afternoons from 1 to 3pm, free drop-in art classes are offered, giving you a bit of time to ramble around the gift store or read the fine print on the exhibit placards. The Lied also shares space with a city library branch, so after the kids run around you can calm them back down with a story or two.

MGM Grand Adventures. Behind the MGM Grand Hotel, 3799 Las Vegas Blvd. S. ☎ **800/929-1111.** Admission $10 adults, free for children 42 inches and under. Sky Screamer: 1 person $35, 2 people $30 each, 3 people $25 each (includes general park admission). Open daily. Hours and cost vary seasonally.

This theme park, slapped together without a great deal of thought on a former parking lot, looks as if some Hollywood set designers dropped off a variety of hokey movie facades and then, unburdened, cheerfully rode off into the sunset. The attractions, such as a clothes-soaking log flume and kiddie bumper cars, are sparsely scattered among a great many food and T-shirt emporiums. It leaves one with the impression that fun has a lot to do with the contents of one's pocketbook and/or stomach. For some peculiar reason, the park sports three tiny boxing arenas where you and a friend can suit up like samurai and duke it out. This is also home of the Sky Screamer, a combination bungee jump/swing that will thrill kids old enough (and daring enough) to give it a try. (They must be at least 10 years old and 42 inches to ride the Screamer.) There is a separate charge for this ride on top of park admission. It's also fun just to sit on a bench and watch people on this contraption.

Scandia Family Fun Center. 2900 Sirius Ave., at Rancho Dr. just south of Sahara Ave. ☎ **702/364-0070.** Free admission, but there's a fee for each game or activity. Super Saver Pass $11 (includes 1 round of miniature golf, 2 rides, and 5 game tokens); Unlimited Wristband Package $16 (includes unlimited bumper boat and car rides, unlimited miniature golf, and 10 tokens for batting cages or arcade games). Mar–Oct– daily 24 hours; Nov–Feb Sun–Thurs 10am–11pm, Fri–Sat 24 hours.

This family amusement center located just a few blocks off the Strip is still the most viable alternative for those who need to amuse children not quite old enough for Gameworks, or for those on a tighter budget. Certainly it's where local families come for outings, and they keep the batting cages hopping ($1.25 for 25 pitches). The arcade is a bit warm and stinky, and other parts (including miniature car racing and bumper boats, $4 per ride, small children ride free with an adult) are a bit worn, but the miniature golf course (three 18-hole courses, $5.50 per game, free for children under 6) is quite cute. Still, we do have to wonder about those round-the-clock weekend hours; we certainly hope those playing miniature golf at 4am are not parents occupied by children.

Wet 'n' Wild. 2601 Las Vegas Blvd. S., just south of Sahara Ave. ☎ **702/871-7811.** www.wetnwild.com. Admission $24 adults, $12 seniors over 55, $18 children under 10, free for children under 3. Early May–Sept 30 daily 10am–6 or 8pm (sometimes later). Season and hours vary somewhat from year to year, so call ahead.

When temperatures soar, head for this 26-acre water park right in the heart of the Strip and cool off while jumping waves, careening down steep flumes, and running rapids. Many Las Vegas packages include a free admission (sometimes partial-day).

4 Playing Golf

There are dozens of local courses, including very challenging ones—the **Sheraton Desert Inn Country** has hosted many PGA tournaments. Beginner and intermediate golfers might prefer the other courses listed. *Note:* Greens fees vary radically depending on time of day and year.

Angel Park Golf Club. 100 S. Rampart Blvd., between Charleston Blvd. and Westcliff St. ☎ **888/446/5358** or 702/254-4653. Greens fees $45–$125.

This 36-hole par-70/71 public course was designed by Arnold Palmer. Players call this a great escape from the casinos, and claiming no matter how many times they play it, they never get tired of it. In addition to the 18-hole Palm and Mountain courses, which are both very challenging, Angel Park offers a night-lit Cloud 9 Course (12 holes for daylight play, 9 at night), where each hole is patterned after a famous par-3.

Yardage: Palm Course 6,438 championship, 5,721 regular, 4,565 ladies; Mountain Course 6,783 championship, 6,272 regular, 5,143 ladies.

Facilities: pro shop, night-lit driving range, 18-hole putting course, restaurant, snack bar, cocktail bar, beverage cart.

Craig Ranch Golf Club. 628 W. Craig Rd., between Losee Rd. and Martin Luther King Blvd. ☎ **702/642-9700.** Greens fees $17 walking, $25 in golf cart.

This is an 18-hole, par-70 public course.

Yardage: 6,001 regular, 5,221 ladies.

Facilities: driving range, pro shop, PGA teaching pro, putting green, snack bar.

Desert Inn Golf Club. 3145 Las Vegas Blvd. S. ☎ **702/733-4290.** Greens fees $160 for guests, $225 for nonguests.

The Desert Inn course gets the nod from champions. It's an 18-hole, par-72 resort course, the most famous and demanding in Las Vegas. *Golf Digest* calls it one of America's top resort courses and what Las Vegas golf is all about. The very high fees may make it out of your reach. The driving range is open to Desert Inn and Caesars guests only; anyone can play the course, but nonguests pay a higher fee.

Yardage: 7,150 championship, 6,715 regular, 5,800 ladies.

Facilities: driving range, putting green, pro shop, restaurant. You can reserve 90 days in advance for Sunday to Thursday, 2 days in advance for Friday and Saturday.

Desert Rose Golf Club. 5483 Clubhouse Dr., 3 blocks west of Nellis Blvd., off Sahara Ave. ☎ **702/431-4653.** Greens fees $50–$75.

This is an 18-hole, par-71 public course.

Yardage: 6,511 championship, 6,135 regular, 5,458 ladies.

Facilities: driving range, putting and chipping greens, PGA teaching pro, pro shop, restaurant, cocktail lounge.

Las Vegas National Golf Club. 1911 Desert Inn Rd., between Maryland Pkwy. and Eastern Ave. ☎ **702/796-0016.** Greens fees $50–$175.

This is an 18-hole (about 8 with water on them), par-72 public course, and a classic layout. If you play from the back tees, it can really be a challenge. The 1996 Las Vegas Invitational, won by Tiger Woods, was held here. Discounted tee times available. Reservations up to 60 days in advance; $5 to $7 fee applies.

Yardage: 6,815 championship, 6,418 regular, 5,741 ladies.

Facilities: pro shop, golf school, driving range, restaurant, cocktail lounge.

5 Staying Active

You need not be a slot-hypnotized slug when you come to Vegas. The city and surrounding areas offer plenty of opportunities for active sports. In addition to many highly rated golf courses (described above), just about every hotel has a large swimming pool and health club, and tennis courts abound. All types of water sports are offered at Lake Mead National Recreation Area, there's rafting on the Colorado, horseback riding at Mount Charleston and Bonnie Springs, great hiking in the canyons, and much, much more. Do plan to get out of those smoke-filled casinos and into the fresh air once in a while. It's good for your health and your finances.

Note: When choosing a hotel, check out its recreational facilities, all listed in chapter 4.

TENNIS Tennis buffs should choose one of the many hotels in town that have tennis courts.

Bally's (☎ 702/739-4598) has eight night-lit hard courts. Fees per hour range from $10 to $15 for guests, $15 to $20 for nonguests. Facilities include a pro shop. Hours vary seasonally. Reservations are advised.

The **Flamingo Hilton** (☎ 702/733-3444) has four outdoor hard courts (all lit for night play) and a pro shop. It is open to the public daily 7am to 7pm. Rates are $20 per hour for nonguests, $12 for guests. Lessons are available. Reservations are required.

The **Desert Inn** (☎ 702/733-4557) has five outdoor hard courts (all lit for night play) and a pro shop. They are open to the public. Hours are daybreak to 10pm. Rates are $10 per person for a daily pass (you book for an hour but can stay longer if no one is waiting); they are free for guests. Reservations are necessary.

In addition to hotels, the **University of Nevada–Las Vegas (UNLV),** Harmon Avenue just east of Swenson Street (☎ 702/895-0844), has a dozen courts (all lit for night play) that are open weekdays 6am to 9:45pm, weekends 8am to 9pm. Rates are $5 per person per day on weekdays; $10 weekends. You should call before going to find out if a court is available.

6 A Trip to Hoover Dam

30 miles SE of Las Vegas

This is one of the most popular excursions from Las Vegas, visited by 2,000 to 3,000 people daily. Why should you join them? Because it's an engineering and architectural marvel and it changed the Southwest forever. Without it, you wouldn't even be going to Vegas.

GETTING THERE   By Car   Go east on Flamingo or Tropicana to U.S. 515 south, which automatically turns into 93 south and takes you right to the dam. This will involve a rather dramatic drive, as you go through Boulder City, come over a rise, and Lake Mead suddenly appears spread out before you. It's a beautiful sight. At about this point, the road narrows down to two lanes and traffic can slow considerably. On busy tourist days, this means the drive can take an hour or more.

Go past the turnoff to Lake Mead. As you near the dam, you'll see a 5-story parking structure tucked into the canyon wall on your left. Park here ($2 charge) and take the elevators or stairs to the walkway leading to the new Visitor Center.

If you would rather go on an **organized tour, Gray Line** (☎ **702/ 384-1234**) offers several Hoover Dam packages, all of them including admission and a tour of the dam. When you're in Las Vegas, look for discount coupons in numerous free publications available at hotels. The 4¹/₂-hour **Hoover Dam Shuttle Tour** departs daily at 7:45am, 9:45am, and 11am and includes pickup and drop-off and a stop at the Ethel M Chocolate Factory; the price is $29.50 for adults, $22.50 for children 2 to 9. Most elaborate is the **Grand Hoover Dam and Lake Mead Cruise Tour,** departing daily at 9:45am, which includes a 90-minute paddlewheeler cruise on Lake Mead with a light lunch available for an extra cost, plus admission to Hoover Dam; $45 for adults, $39 for children 2 to 9. You can inquire at your hotel sightseeing desk about other bus tours.

✪ HOOVER DAM

There would be no Las Vegas as we know it without Hoover Dam. Certainly not the neon and glitz. In fact, the growth of the entire Southwest can be tied directly to the electricity that came from the dam.

Until Hoover Dam was built, much of the southwestern United States was plagued by two natural problems: parched, sandy terrain that lacked irrigation for most of the year, and extensive flooding in spring and early summer when the mighty Colorado River, fed by melting snow from its source in the Rocky Mountains, overflowed its banks and destroyed crops, lives, and property. On the positive side, raging unchecked over eons, the river's turbulent, rushing waters carved the Grand Canyon.

In 1928, prodded by the seven states through which the river runs during the course of its 1,400-mile journey to the Gulf of California, Congress authorized construction of a dam at Boulder Canyon (later moved to Black Canyon). The Senate's declaration of intention was that "A mighty river, now a source of destruction, is to be curbed and put to work in the interests of society." Construction began in 1931. Because of its vast scope, and the unprecedented problems posed in its realization, the project generated significant advances in many areas of machinery production, engineering, and construction. An army of more than 5,200 laborers was assembled, and work proceeded 24 hours a day. Completed in 1936, 2 years ahead of schedule and $15 million under budget (let's see James Cameron top that!), the dam stopped the annual floods and conserved water for irrigation, industrial, and domestic use. Equally important, it became one of the world's major electrical generating plants, providing low-cost, pollution-free hydroelectric power to a score of surrounding communities. Hoover Dam's $165 million cost has been repaid with interest by the sale of inexpensive power to a number of California cities and the states of Arizona and Nevada. The dam is a government project that paid for itself—a feat almost as awe-inspiring as its engineering.

The dam itself is a massive curved wall, 660 feet thick at the bottom and tapering to 45 feet where the road crosses it at the top. It towers 726.4 feet above bedrock (about the height of a 60-story skyscraper) and acts as a plug between the canyon walls to hold back up to 9.2 trillion gallons of water in Lake Mead—the reservoir created by its construction. Four concrete intake towers on the lake side drop the water down about 600 feet to drive turbines and create power, after which the water spills out into the river and continues south. All the architecture is on a grand scale, and the design has beautiful art deco elements, unusual in an engineering project. Note, for instance, the monumental 30-foot bronze sculpture, *Winged Figures of the Republic,* flanking a 142-foot flagpole at the Nevada entrance. According to its creator, Oskar Hansen, the sculpture symbolizes "the immutable calm of intellectual resolution, and the enormous power of trained physical strength, equally enthroned in placid triumph of scientific achievement."

The dam has become a major sightseeing attraction along with Lake Mead, America's largest artificial reservoir and a major Nevada recreation area.

TOURING THE DAM

The very nice **Hoover Dam Visitor Center,** a vast 3-level circular concrete structure with a rooftop overlook, opened in 1995. You'll enter the Reception Lobby, where you can buy tickets, peruse informational exhibits, photographs, and memorabilia, and view three 12-minute video presentations (respectively, about the importance of water to life, the events leading up to the construction of Hoover Dam, and the construction itself as well as the many benefits it confers). Exhibits on the Plaza Level include interactive displays on the environment, habitation, and development of the Southwest, the people who built the dam, and related topics. Yet another floor up, galleries on the Overlook Level demonstrate, via sculpted bronze panels, the benefits of Hoover Dam and Lake Mead to the states of Arizona, Nevada, and California. The Overlook Level additionally provides an unobstructed view of Lake Mead, the dam, the power plant, the Colorado River, and Black Canyon. (There are multiple photo opportunities throughout this trip.) You can visit an exhibit center across the street where a 10-minute presentation in a small theater focuses on a topographical map of the 1,400-mile Colorado River. It also has a cafeteria. Notice, by the way, how the rest rooms in the center only have electric dryers, no paper towels. A tribute?

Thirty-minute tours of the dam depart from the Reception Lobby every 15 minutes or so daily, except Christmas. The Visitor Center opens at 8:30am, and the first tour departs soon after. The last tour leaves at 6pm, and the center closes at 6:30pm. Admission is $8 for adults, $7 for senior citizens, and $2 for children 6 to 16, free for children under 6. More extensive, and expensive, hard-hat tours are offered every half hour between 9:30am and 3:30pm; "Survive the tour and you keep the hard hat!" Although it's not compulsory, it's not a bad idea to call in advance for the tour (☎ **702/294-3522**). Both tours, by the way, are "not recommended for claustrophobics or those persons with defibrillators."

The tour begins with a 561-foot elevator descent into the dam's interior, where an access tunnel leads to the Nevada wing of the power plant. (You only cross to Arizona on the hard-hat tour.) In the three stops on the regular tour, you see the massive turbines that generate the electricity using the water flow, go outside on the downriver side of the dam looking up at the towering structure (which is pretty awesome), and then go into one of the tunnels that contains a steel water diversion pipe that feeds the turbines. (It's one of the largest steel water pipes ever made—its interior could accommodate two lanes of automobile traffic.)

7

About Casino Gambling

What? You didn't come to Las Vegas for the Liberace Museum? We are shocked. *Shocked.*

Yes, there are gambling opportunities in Vegas. We've noticed this. You will, too. The tip-off will be the slot machines in the airport as soon as you step off the plane. Or the slot machines in the convenience stores as soon as you drive across the state line. Let's not kid ourselves, gambling is what Vegas is about. The bright lights, the shows, the showgirls, the food—it's all there just to lure you in and make you open your wallet. (The free drinks certainly help ease the latter as well.)

You can disappoint them if you want, but what would be the point? *This is Las Vegas.* You don't have to be a high roller. You would not believe how much fun you can have with a nickel slot machine. You won't get rich, but neither will most of those guys playing the $5 slots, either. Of course, that's not going to stop anyone from trying. Almost everyone plays in Vegas with the hopes of winning The Big One. That only a few ever do doesn't stop them from trying again and again and again. That's how the casinos make their money, by the way.

Remember also that there is no system that is sure to help you win. We all have our own system and our own ideas. Reading books and listening to others at the tables will help you pick up some tips, but if there were a surefire way to win, the casinos would have taken care of it (and we will leave you to imagine just what that might entail). Try to have the courage to walk away when your bankroll is up, not down. Remember, your children's college fund is just that, and not a gambling budget supplement.

The first part of this chapter tells you the basics of betting. Knowing how to play the games not only improves your odds but makes playing more enjoyable. In addition to the instructions below, you'll find dozens of books on how to gamble at all casino hotel gift shops, and many casinos offer free gaming lessons on the premises. The second part of this chapter describes all the major casinos in town. Remember that gambling is supposed to be entertainment; picking a gaming table where the other players are laughing, slapping each other on the back, and generally enjoying themselves tends to make for considerable more fun than a table where everyone is sitting around in stony silence, morosely staring at their cards. Unless you really need to concentrate, pick a table where everyone seems to be enjoying themselves, and you will too, even if you don't win. Maybe.

1   The Games

BACCARAT

The ancient game of baccarat, or *chemin de fer,* is played with eight decks of cards. Firm rules apply, and there is no skill involved other than deciding whether to bet on the bank or the player. Any beginner can play, but check the betting minimum before you sit down, as this tends to be a high-stakes game. The cards are shuffled by the croupier and then placed in a box that is called the "shoe."

Players may wager on "bank" or "player" at any time. Two cards are dealt from the shoe and given to the player who has the largest

---

Baccarat Rules

PLAYER'S HAND

Having	
0-1-2-3-4-5	Must draw a third card.
6-7	Must stand.
8-9	Natural. Banker cannot draw.

BANKER'S HAND

Having	Draws	Does Not Draw
	When giving Player 3rd card of:	When giving Player 3rd card of:
3	1-2-3-4-5-6-7-9-10	8
4	2-3-4-5-6-7	1-8-9-10
5	4-5-6-7	1-2-3-8-9-10
6	6-7	1-2-3-4-5-8-9-10
7	*Must stand.*	
8-9	Natural. Player cannot draw.	

If the player takes no third card, the banker must stand on 6. No one draws against a natural 8 or 9.

wager against the bank, and two cards are dealt to the croupier acting as banker. If the rule calls for a third card (see rules on chart
shown, above), the player or banker, or both, must take the third
card. In the event of a tie, the hand is dealt over.

The object of the game is to come as close as possible to the number 9. To score the hands, the cards of each hand are totaled and the
last digit is used. All cards have face value. For example: 10 plus 5
equals 15 (score is 5); 10 plus 4 plus 9 equals 23 (score is 3); 4 plus
3 plus 3 equals 10 (score is 0); and 4 plus 3 plus 2 equals 9 (score
is 9). The closest hand to 9 wins.

Each player has a chance to deal the cards. The shoe passes to the
player on the right each time the bank loses. If the player wishes, he
or she may pass the shoe at any time.

Note: When you bet on the bank and the bank wins, you are
charged a 5% commission. This must be paid at the start of a new
game or when you leave the table.

BIG SIX

Big Six provides pleasant recreation and involves no study or effort.
The wheel has 56 positions on it, 54 of them marked by bills from
$1 to $20 denominations. The other two spots are jokers, and each
pays 40 to 1 if the wheel stops in that position.

All other stops pay at face value. Those marked with $20 bills pay
20 to 1; the $5 bills pay 5 to 1; and so forth.

BLACKJACK

The dealer starts the game by dealing each player two cards. In some
casinos they're dealt to the player faceup, in others facedown, but the
dealer always gets one card up and one card down. Everybody plays
against the dealer. The object is to get a total that is higher than that
of the dealer without exceeding 21. All face cards count as 10; all
other number cards except aces count as their number value. An ace
may be counted as 1 or 11, whichever you choose it to be.

Starting at his or her left, the dealer gives additional cards to the
players who wish to draw (be "hit") or none to a player who wishes
to "stand" or "hold." If your count is nearer to 21 than the dealer's,
you win. If it's under the dealer's, you lose. Ties are a push and nobody wins. After all the players are satisfied with their counts, the
dealer exposes his or her facedown card. If his or her two cards total 16 or less, the dealer must "hit" (draw an additional card) until
reaching 17 or over. If the dealer's total goes over 21, he or she must

pay all the players whose hands have not gone "bust." It is important to note here that the blackjack dealer has no choice as to whether he or she should stay or draw. A dealer's decisions are predetermined and known to all the players at the table.

HOW TO PLAY   Here are eight "rules" for blackjack.

1. Place the amount of chips that you want to bet on the betting space on your table.
2. Look at the first two cards the dealer starts you with. If your hand adds up to the total you prefer, place your cards *under your bet money,* indicating that you don't wish any additional cards. If you elect to draw an additional card, you tell the dealer to "hit" you by making a sweeping motion with your cards, or point to your open hand (watch your fellow players).
3. If your count goes over 21, you go "bust" and lose, even if the dealer also goes "bust" afterward. Unless hands are dealt faceup, *you then turn your hand faceup on the table.*
4. If you make 21 in your first two cards (any picture card or 10 with an ace), you've got blackjack. *You expose your winning hand immediately,* and you collect 1¹/₂ times your bet, unless the dealer has blackjack, too, in which case it's a push and nobody wins.
5. If you find a "pair" in your first two cards (say, two 8s or two aces), you may "split" the pair into two hands and treat each card as the first card dealt in two separate hands. *Turn the pair faceup on the table,* place the original bet on one of these cards, then place an equal amount on the other card. *Split aces are limited to a one-card draw on each.*
6. You may double your original bet and make a one-card draw after receiving your initial two cards. *Turn your hand faceup* and you'll receive one more card facedown.
7. Anytime the dealer deals himself or herself an ace for the "up" card, you may insure your hand against the possibility that the hole card is a 10 or face card, which would give him or her an automatic blackjack. To insure, you place an amount up to one half of your bet on the "insurance" line. If the dealer does have a blackjack, you do not lose, even though he or she has your hand beat, and you keep your bet and your insurance money. If the dealer does not have a blackjack, he or she takes your insurance money and play continues in the normal fashion.
8. *Remember:* The dealer *must* stand on 17 or more and must hit a hand of 16 or less.

PROFESSIONAL TIPS   Advice of the experts in playing blackjack is as follows.

1. *Do not* ask for an extra card if you have a count of 17, 18, 19, 20, or 21 in your cards, no matter what the dealer has showing in his or her "up" card.
2. *Do not* ask for an extra card when you have 12, 13, 14, 15, 16, or more if the dealer has a 2, 3, 4, 5, or 6 showing in his or her "up" card.
3. *Do ask* for an extra card or more when you have a count of 12 through 16 in your hand if the dealer's "up" card is a 7, 8, 9, 10, or ace.

There's a lot more to blackjack-playing strategy than the above, of course. So consider this merely as the bare bones of the game.

A final tip: Avoid insurance bets; they're sucker bait!

CRAPS

The most exciting casino action is always at the craps tables. Betting is frenetic, play fast-paced, and groups quickly bond yelling and screaming in response to the action.

THE TABLE   The craps table is divided into marked areas (Pass, Come, Field, Big 6, Big 8, and so on), where you place your chips to bet. The following are a few simple directions.

PASS LINE   A "Pass Line" bet pays even money. If the first roll of the dice adds up to 7 or 11, you win your bet; if the first roll adds up to 2, 3, or 12, you lose your bet. If any other number comes up, it's your "point." If you roll your point again, you win, but if a 7 comes up again before your point is rolled, you lose.

DON'T PASS LINE   Betting on the "Don't Pass" is the opposite of betting on the Pass Line. This time, you lose if a 7 or an 11 is thrown on the first roll, and you win if a 2 or a 3 is thrown on the first roll.

If the first roll is 12, however, it's a push (standoff), and nobody wins. If none of these numbers are thrown and you have a point instead, in order to win, a 7 will have to be thrown before the point comes up again. A "Don't Pass" bet also pays even money.

COME   Betting on "Come" is the same as betting on the Pass Line, but you must bet *after* the first roll or on any following roll. Again, you'll win on 7 or 11 and lose on 2, 3, or 12. Any other number is your point, and you win if your point comes up again before a 7.

DON'T COME This is the opposite of a "Come" bet. Again, you wait until after the first roll to bet. A 7 or an 11 means you lose; a 2 or a 3 means you win; 12 is a push, and nobody wins. You win if 7 comes up before the point. (The point, you'll recall, was the first number rolled if it was none of the above.)

FIELD This is a bet for one roll only. The "Field" consists of seven numbers: 2, 3, 4, 9, 10, 11, and 12. If any of these numbers is thrown on the next roll, you win even money, except on 2 and 12, which pay to 2 to 1 (at some casinos 3 to 1).

BIG 6 AND 8 A "Big 6 and 8" bet pays even money. You win if either a 6 or an 8 is rolled before a 7.

ANY 7 An "Any 7" bet pays the winner five for one. If a 7 is thrown on the first roll after you bet, you win.

"HARD WAY" BETS In the middle of a craps table are pictures of several possible dice combinations together with the odds the casino will pay you if you bet and win on any of those combinations being thrown. For example, if 8 is thrown by having a 4 appear on each die, and you bet on it, the bank will pay 10 for 1; if 4 is thrown by having a 2 appear on each die, and you bet on it, the bank will pay 8 for 1; if 3 is thrown, the bank pays 15 for 1. You win at the odds quoted if the exact combination of numbers you bet on comes up. But you lose either if a 7 is rolled or if the number you bet on was rolled any way other than the "Hard Way" shown on the table. In-the-know gamblers tend to avoid "Hard Way" bets as an easy way to lose their money. And note that the odds quoted are not 3 to 1, 4 to 1, or 8 to 1; here the key word is *for*—that is, 3 for 1 or 8 for 1.

ANY CRAPS Here you're lucky if the dice "crap out"—if they show 2, 3, or 12 on the first roll after you bet. If this happens, the bank pays 8 for 1. Any other number is a loser.

PLACE BETS You can make a "Place Bet" on any of the following numbers: 4, 5, 6, 8, 9, and 10. You're betting that the number you choose will be thrown before a 7 is thrown. If you win, the pay-off is as follows: 4 or 10 pays at the rate of 9 to 5; 5 or 9 pays at the rate of 7 to 5; 6 or 8 pays at the rate of 7 to 6. "Place Bets" can be removed at any time before a roll.

SOME PROBABILITIES Because each die has six sides numbered from 1 to 6, and craps is played with a pair of dice, the probability of throwing certain numbers has been studied carefully. Professionals have employed complex mathematical formulas in searching for the answers. And computers have data-processed curves of probability.

Suffice it to say that 7 (a crucial number in craps) will be thrown more frequently than any other number over the long run, for there are six possible combinations that make 7 when you break down the 1 to 6 possibilities on each separate die. As to the total possible number of combinations on the dice, there are 36.

Comparing the 36 possible combinations, numbers, or point combinations, run as follows:

>*2 and 12* may be thrown in *1 way* only.
>*3 and 11* may be thrown in *2 ways.*
>*4 and 10* may be thrown in *3 ways.*
>*5 and 9* may be thrown in *4 ways.*
>*6 and 8* may be thrown in *5 ways.*
>*7* may be thrown in *6 ways.*

So 7 has an advantage over all other combinations, which, over the long run, is in favor of the casino. You can't beat the law of averages.

KENO

This is one of the oldest games of chance. Originating in China, the game can be traced back to a time before Christ, when it operated as a national lottery. Legend has it that funds acquired from the game were used to finance construction of the Great Wall of China.

Keno was first introduced into the United States in the 1800s by Chinese railroad construction workers. Easy to play, and offering a chance to sit down and converse between bets, it is one of the most popular games in town—despite the fact that *the house percentage is greater than that of any other casino game!*

To play, you must first obtain a keno form, available at the counter in the keno lounge and in most Las Vegas coffee shops. In the latter, you'll usually find blank keno forms and thick black crayons on your table. Fill yours out, and a miniskirted keno runner will come and collect it. After the game is over, she'll return with your winning or losing ticket. If you've won, it's customary to offer a tip, depending on your winnings.

Looking at your keno ticket and the keno board, you'll see that it is divided horizontally into two rectangles. The upper half (in China the yin area) contains the numbers 1 through 40; the lower (yang) half contains the numbers 41 through 80. You can win a maximum of $50,000, even more on progressive games, though it's highly unlikely (the probability is less than a hundredth of a percent). Mark up to 15 out of the 80 numbers; bets range from about 70¢ on up. A one-number mark is known as a one-spot, a two-number selection is a two-spot, and so on. After you have selected the number of spots you wish to play, write the price of the ticket in the right-hand corner where indicated. The more you bet, the more you can win if your numbers come up. Before the game starts, you have to give the completed form to a keno runner or hand it in at the keno lounge desk, and pay for your bet. You'll get back a duplicate form with the number of the game you're playing on it. Then the game begins. As numbers appear on the keno board, compare them to the numbers you've marked on your ticket. After 20 numbers have appeared on the board, if you've won, turn in your ticket immediately for a payoff before the next game begins. Otherwise, you will forfeit your winnings, a frustrating experience to say the least.

On a straight ticket that is marked with one or two spots, all of your numbers must appear on the board for you to win anything. With a few exceptions, if you mark from 3 to 7 spots, 3 numbers must appear on the board for you to win anything. Similarly, if you mark 8 to 12 spots, usually at least 5 numbers must come up for you to win the minimum amount. And if you mark 13 to 15 spots, usually at least 6 numbers must come up for a winning ticket. To win the maximum amount ($50,000), which requires that all of your numbers come up, you must select at least 8 spots. The more numbers on the board matching the numbers on your ticket, the more you win. If you want to keep playing the same numbers over and over, you can replay a ticket by handing in your duplicate to the keno runner; you don't have to keep rewriting it.

In addition to the straight bets described above, you can split your ticket, betting various amounts on two or more groups of numbers. To do so, circle the groups. The amount you bet is then divided by the number of groups. You could, if you so desire, play as many as 40 two-spots on a single ticket. Another possibility is to play three groups of four numbers each as eight spots (any two of the three groups of four numbers can be considered an eight spot). It does get a little complex, since combination betting options are almost infinite. Helpful casino personnel in the keno lounge can assist you with combination betting.

POKER

Poker is *the* game of the Old West. There's at least one sequence in every western where the hero faces off against the villain over a poker hand. In Las Vegas poker is a tradition, although it isn't played at every casino.

There are lots of variations on the basic game, but one of the most popular is **Hold 'Em.** Five cards are dealt faceup in the center of the table and two are dealt to each player. The player uses the best five of seven, and the best hand wins. The house dealer takes care of the shuffling and the dealing and moves a marker around the table to alternate the start of the deal. The house rakes 1% to 10% (it depends on the casino) from each pot. Most casinos include the usual seven-card stud and a few have hi-lo split.

If you don't know how to play poker, don't attempt to learn at a table. Find a casino that teaches it in free gaming lessons.

Pai gow poker (a variation on poker) has become increasingly popular. The game is played with a traditional deck plus one joker. The joker is a wild card that can be used as an ace or to complete a straight, a flush, a straight flush, or a royal flush. Each player is dealt seven cards to arrange into two hands: a two-card hand and a five-card hand. As in standard poker, the highest two-card hand is two aces, and the highest five-card hand is a royal flush. The five-card hand *must* be higher than the two-card hand (if the two-card hand is a pair of sixes, for example, the five-card hand must be a pair of sevens or better). Any player's hand that is set incorrectly is an automatic loser. The object of the game is for both of the player's hands to rank higher than both of the banker's hands. Should one hand rank exactly the same as the banker's hand, this is a tie (called a "copy"), *and the banker wins all tie hands.* If the player wins one hand but loses the other, this is a "push," and no money changes hands. The house dealer or any player may be the banker. The bank is offered to each player, and each player may accept or pass. Winning hands are paid even money, less a 5% commission.

Caribbean stud poker is yet another variation on the basic game that is gaining in popularity. Players put in a single ante bet and are dealt five cards facedown from a single deck; they play solely against the dealer, who receives five cards, one of them face up. Players are then given the option of folding, or may call by making an additional bet that is double their original ante. After all player bets have been made, the dealer's cards are revealed. If the dealer doesn't qualify with at least an ace/king combination, players are paid even money on their ante and their call bets are returned. If the dealer does qualify, each player's hand is compared to the dealer's. On winning hands, players receive even money on their ante bets, and call bets are paid out on a scale according to the value of their hands. The scale ranges from even money for a pair, to 100 to 1 on a royal flush, although there is usually a cap on the maximum payoff that varies from casino to casino.

An additional feature of Caribbean stud is the inclusion of a progressive jackpot. For an additional side bet of $1, a player may qualify for a payoff from a progressive jackpot. The jackpot bet only pays off on a flush or better, but you can win on this bet even if the dealer ends up with a better hand than you do. The odds of hitting a royal flush for the entire progressive jackpot are astronomical, but considering that Caribbean stud has a house advantage that is even larger than the one in roulette, if you're going to play, you might as well toss in the buck and pray.

ROULETTE

Roulette is an extremely easy game to play, and it's really quite colorful and exciting to watch. The wheel spins and the little ball bounces around, finally dropping into one of the slots, numbered 1 to 36, plus 0 and 00. You can bet on a single number, a combination of numbers, or red or black, odd or even. If you're lucky, you can win as much as 35 to 1. The method of placing single-number bets, column bets, and others is fairly obvious. The dealer will be happy to show you how to "straddle" two or more numbers and make many other interesting betting combinations. Each player is given different-colored chips so that it's easy to follow the numbers you're on.

Some typical bets are indicated by means of letters on the roulette layout depicted here. The winning odds for each of these sample bets are listed. These bets can be made on any corresponding combinations of numbers.

SLOTS

You put the coin in the slot and pull the handle. What, you thought there was a trick to this?

Actually, there is a bit more to it. But first, some background. Old-timers will tell you slots were invented to give wives something to do while their husbands gambled. Slots used to be stuck at the edges of the casino and could be counted on one hand, maybe two. But now they *are* the casino. The casinos make more from slots than from craps, blackjack, and roulette combined. There are 115,000 slot machines (not including video poker) in the county alone. Some of these are at the airport, steps from you as you deplane. It's a just

Slot Clubs

If you play slots or video poker, it definitely pays to join a slot club. These so-called clubs are designed to attract and keep customers in a given casino by providing incentives—meals, shows, discounts on rooms, gifts, tournament invitations, discounts at hotel shops, VIP treatment, and (more and more) cash rebates. Join a slot club and soon you too will be getting those great hotel rate offers— $20-a-night rooms, affordable rooms at the luxury resorts, even free rooms. (This is one way to beat the high hotel rate system.) Of course, your rewards are greater if you play just in one casino, but your mobility is limited.

When you join a slot club (inquire at the casino desk), you're given something that looks like a credit card, which you must insert into an ATM-like device whenever you play. (Don't forget to retrieve your card when you leave the machine, as we sometimes do—though that may work in your favor if someone comes along and plays the machine without removing it.) The device tracks your play and computes bonus points.

Which slot club should you join? Actually, you should join one at any casino where you play, since even the act of joining usually entitles you to some benefits. It's convenient to concentrate play where you're staying; if you play a great deal, a casino hotel's

a matter of time before the planes flying into Vegas feature slots that pop up as soon as you cross the state line.

But in order to keep up with the increasing competition, the plain old machine, where reels just spin, has become nearly obsolete. Now, they are all computerized and have added buttons to push, so you can avoid carpal tunnel syndrome yanking the handle all night. (The handles are still there on many of them.) The idea is still simple: Get three (sometimes four) cherries (clowns, sevens, dinosaurs, whatever) in a row and you win something. Each machine has its own combination; some will pay you something with just one symbol showing; on most, the more combinations there are, the more opportunities for loot. Some will even pay if you get three blanks. Study each machine to learn what it does.

The **payback** goes up considerably if you bet the limit (from two to as many as 45 coins). But while the payoff can be much bigger, the odds *against* winning also go up when you put in the limit. (So slot-club benefits may be a factor in your accommodations choice. It may also now factor into your airline choice—National Airlines is affiliated with both Harrah's and the Rio, and you can accumulate slot club points when you fly with them. Consider, though, particularly if you aren't a high roller, the slot clubs Downtown. You get more bang for your buck, because you don't have to spend as much to start raking in the goodies.

One way to judge a slot club is by the quality of service when you enroll. Personnel should politely answer all your questions (for instance, is nickel play included? or is there a time limit for earning required points?) and be able to tell you exactly how many points you need for various bonuses.

Maximizing your slot-club profits and choosing the club that's best for you is a complex business. If you want to get into it in depth, order a copy of Jeffrey Compton's **The Las Vegas Advisor Guide to Slot Clubs** ($9.95 plus shipping), which examines just about every facet of the situation (☎ **800/244-2224**). Compton gives high ratings to the clubs at Caesars Palace, the Desert Inn, the Mirage, Treasure Island, the Flamingo Hilton, the Rio, the Sahara, Sam's Town, the Four Queens, the Golden Nugget, and Lady Luck.

if you hit something on a machine and realize your $25 win would have been $500 had you only put in more money, take a deep breath, stop kicking yourself, and remember you might not actually have hit that winning combination so easily had you bet the limit.)

Progressive slots are groups of machines where the jackpot gets bigger every few moments (just as lottery jackpots build up). Bigger and better games keep showing up; for example, there's Anchor Gaming's much-imitated **Wheel of Gold,** wherein if you get the right symbol, you get to spin a roulette wheel, which guarantees you a win of a serious number of coins. **Totem Pole** is the Godzilla of slot machines, a behemoth that allows you to spin up to three reels at once (provided you put in the limit). And of course, there's our personal favorite, **Piggy Bankin'.** This has an LED display on which a silly tune plays and a pig cavorts (at erratic times, he trots across the screen, oinks, giggles when you lose and imitates Elvis, among other playful actions). It's so much fun to watch, you start putting in the coins just to get the pig to move—forget about the money. But meanwhile, money is building up in the piggy bank, an extra bonus you win if you hit the right symbol.

Other gimmick machines include **Clear Winner,** where you can satisfy your curiosity about the inner workings of a slot machine, and **Rockin' Reels,** which looks like a jukebox. And, of course, there are always those **Big Giant Slot** machines, gimmicky devices found in almost every casino. They may not win as often as regular slots (though there is no definite word on it one way or the other), but not only are they just plain fun to spin, they often turn into audience participation gambling, as watchers gather to cheer you on to victory.

Are there surefire ways to win on a slot machine? No. But you can lose more slowly. The slots are on computer timers, and there are times when they are hitting and times when they are not. A bank of empty slots probably (but not certainly) means they aren't hitting. Go find a line where lots of people are sitting around with trays full of money. (Of course, yours will be the one that doesn't hit.) A good rule of thumb is that if your slot doesn't hit something in four or five pulls, leave it and go find another. It's not as though you won't have some choice in the matter. Also, each casino has some bank of slots that they advertise as more loose or with a bigger payback. Try these. It's what they want you to do, but what the heck.

SPORTS BOOKS

Most of the larger hotels in Las Vegas have sports book operations—they look a lot like commodities-futures trading boards. In some, almost as large as theaters, you can sit comfortably, occasionally in recliners and sometimes with your own video screen, and watch ball games, fights, and, at some casinos, horse races on huge TV screens. To add to your enjoyment, there's usually a deli/bar nearby that serves sandwiches, hot dogs, soft drinks, and beer. As a matter of fact, some of the best sandwiches in Las Vegas are served next to the sports books. Sports books take bets on virtually every sport. They are best during important playoff games or big horse races, when everyone in the place is watching the same event, shrieking, shouting, and moaning sometimes in unison. Joining in with a cheap bet (so you feel like you, too, have a personal stake in the matter) makes for bargain entertainment.

VIDEO POKER

Rapidly coming up on slots in popularity, video poker works the same way as regular poker, except you play against the machine. You are dealt a hand, you pick which cards to keep and which to discard, and then get your new hand. And, it is hoped, collect your winnings. Somewhat more of a challenge and more active than slots because you have some control (or at least illusion of control) over your fate, and they are easier than playing actual poker with a table full of folks who probably take it very seriously.

There are a number of varieties of this machine, with **Jacks Are Better, Deuces Wild,** and so forth. Be sure to study your machine before you sit down. (The best returns are offered on the **Jacks Are Wild** machines, when the payback for a pair of Jacks or better is two times your bet, and three times for three of a kind.) Some machines offer **Double Down:** After you have won, you get a chance to draw cards against the machine, with the higher card the winner. If you win, your money is doubled and you are offered a chance to go again. Your money can increase nicely during this time, and you can also lose it all very fast, which is most annoying. Technology is catching up with Video Poker, too. Now they even have touch screens, which offer a variety of different poker games, blackjack, and video slots—just touch your screen and choose your poison.

2 The Casinos

Casino choice is a personal thing. Some like to find their lucky place and stick with it, while others love to take advantage of the nearly endless choices Vegas offers. Everyone should casino-hop at least once to marvel (or get dizzy) at the decor/spectacle and the sheer excess of it all. But beyond decoration, there isn't too much difference. You've got your slot machines, gaming tables, big chandeliers.

Virtually all casinos make sure they have no clocks or windows—they do not want you to interrupt your losing streak by realizing how much time has passed. Of course, we've all heard the legend that Vegas casinos pump in fresh oxygen to keep the players from getting tired and wanting to pack it in. The veracity of this is hard to confirm, but we can only hope it's true, especially when we think of that time we looked up after a long stretch of gambling and discovered it was Thursday.

Don't be a snob, and don't be overly dazzled by the fancy casinos. Sometimes you can have a better time at one of the older places Downtown, where stakes are lower, pretensions are nonexistent, and the clientele are often friendlier.

What follows is a description of most of the major casinos in Vegas, including their level of claustrophobia, whether they have a Big Giant Slot Machine (it's a sucker bet, but we love them), and a completely arbitrary assessment based on whether we won there.

SOUTH STRIP

Excalibur. 3850 Las Vegas Blvd. S. ☎ **702/597-7777.**

As you might expect, the Excalibur casino is replete with suits of armor, stained-glass panels, knights, dragons, and velvet and satin heraldic banners, with gaming action taking place beneath vast iron-and-gold chandeliers fit for a medieval castle fortress. This all makes it fine for kitsch-seekers, but anyone hating crowds or sensitive to noise will hate it. The overall effect is less like a castle and more like a dungeon. A popular feature here is Circus Bucks, a progressive slot machine that builds from a jackpot base of $500,000; players can win on a $3 pull. A nonsmoking area is a plus. One of us won a lot of money here and refused to share it with the other, so our final judgment about the casino is, well, mixed.

Luxor Las Vegas. 3900 Las Vegas Blvd. S. ☎ **702/262-4000.**

More accessible than ever thanks to the addition of the air-conditioned people-mover from Excalibur, Luxor has been completely remodeled and, in our opinion, improved immeasurably. You enter through a giant temple gateway flanked by massive statues of Ramses. Gone is the space-wasting central area that used to contain the bathrooms, cashiers, and casino offices. This additional space gives the casino a much more airy feel, which gives it a low claustrophobia level. King Tut heads and sphinxes adorn slot areas. There's a nonsmoking slot area. The Gold Chamber Club offers rewards of cash, merchandise, meals, and special services to slot and table players. And sports action unfolds on 17 large-screen TVs and 128 personalized monitors in Luxor's race and sports book. We already felt inclined to like this casino thanks to a good run at blackjack, but the redesign has made it even more inviting.

Mandalay Bay. 3950 Las Vegas Blvd. S. ☎ **702/632-7777.**

"Elegant" gaming in a pre-fab, deliberate way, with a very high ceiling that produces a very low claustrophobia factor. Definitely the right place if you are looking for less hectic, less gimmick-intrusive play. Its layout makes it look airy, and it's marginally less confusing and certainly less overwhelming than many other casinos. There is a big, ultra-comfortable sports book (complete with armchairs that could well encourage a most relaxed gambler to fall asleep), including a live daily sports radio show.

MGM Grand. 3799 Las Vegas Blvd. S. ☎ **702/891-7777.**

The world's largest casino—at 171,500 square feet, we've been to countries that were smaller!—is divided into four themed areas, in a futile attempt to make it seem smaller. Many of the Wizard of Oz decorations have been removed, but spend an hour in here and you may feel like Dorothy after she got hit by the twister. One section features a high-roller slot area with machines that operate on coins valued at $100 and $500! The sports casino houses a big poker room, a state-of-the-art race and sports book, and the Turf Club Lounge. The MGM Grand Director's Club offers guests prizes ranging from comps and gifts to cash rebates.

Monte Carlo. 3770 Las Vegas Blvd. S. ☎ **702/730-7777.**

All huge ceilings and white-light interiors: Obviously, they are trying to evoke gambling in Monaco. While the decor shows lots of attention, it perhaps had too much attention. Bulbs line the ceiling, and everywhere you look is some detail or other. It's busy on both your eyes and your ears. So despite the effort put in, it's not a pleasant place to gamble. There's a large and comfortable race and sports book area, with its own cocktail lounge.

✪ **New York New York.** 3790 Las Vegas Blvd. S. ☎ **702/740-6969.**

Another theme-run-wild place: tuxes on the backs of gaming chairs, change carts that look like yellow cabs, and so forth, all set in a miniature New York City. It's all fabulous fun, but despite a low claustrophobia level (thanks to an unusually high ceiling), it is a major case of sensory overload akin to the reaction elicited by a first-time look at the Strip. This may prove distracting. Serious gamblers understandably may sniff at it all and prefer to take their business to a more seemly casino, but everyone else should have about the most Vegasy time they can.

Orleans. 4500 W. Tropicana Ave. ☎ **702/365-7111.**

This is not a particularly special gambling space, though it has a low claustrophobia level, but over the sound system they play Cajun and Zydeco music, so you can two-step while you gamble, which can make losing somewhat less painful. It has all the needed tables—blackjack, craps, and so forth—plus plenty of slots, including a Wheel of Fortune machine that works like those other roulette wheel slots, but in this case, actually plays the theme song from the TV show. It will even applaud for you if you win.

Tropicana. 3801 Las Vegas Blvd. S. ☎ **702/739-2222.**

The Trop casino is quite good-looking, and, yes, highly tropical, with gaming tables situated beneath a massive stained-glass archway and art nouveau lighting fixtures. In summer, it offers something totally unique: swim-up blackjack tables located in the hotel's stunning 5-acre tropical garden and pool area. Slot and table game players can earn bonus points toward rooms, shows, and meals by obtaining an Island Winners Club card in the casino.

MID-STRIP

✪ **Bally's Las Vegas.** 3645 Las Vegas Blvd. S. ☎ **702/739-4111.**

Bally's casino is one of the cleanest and best lit and definitely has that high-rent appeal. It's large (the size of a football field) with lots of colorful signage. The big ceiling makes for a low claustrophobia level. There's a Most Valuable Player Slot Club, offering members cash rebates, room discounts, free meals and show tickets, and invitations to special events, among other perks. The casino hosts frequent slot tournaments, and free gaming lessons are offered. There is not, however, a Big Giant Slot machine. For shame.

Barbary Coast. 3595 Las Vegas Blvd. S. ☎ **702/737-7111.**

The Barbary Coast has a cheerful 1890s-style casino ornately decorated with $2 million worth of gorgeous stained-glass skylights and signs, as well as immense crystal-dangling globe chandeliers over the gaming tables. It's worth stopping in just to take a look around when you're in the central "four corners" area of the Strip. The casino has a free Fun Club for slot players; participants earn points toward cash and prizes.

Bellagio. ☎ **888/987-6667.** 3600 Las Vegas Blvd. S.

The slot machines here are mostly encased in marble. How's that for upping the ante on classy? In all fairness, Bellagio comes the closest to re-creating the feel of gambling in Monte Carlo (the country, not the next-door casino), but its relentless good taste means this is one pretty forgettable casino. After all, we are suckers for a wacky theme and European class just doesn't cut it. Sure, there are good touches—we always like a high ceiling to reduce the claustrophobia index, and the place is laid out in an easy-to-navigate grid with ultra-wide aisles, so walking through doesn't seem like such a crowded collision course maze. (*Tip:* The main casino path is identified with black carpets.) The cozy sports book has individual TVs and entirely denlike leather chairs—quite, quite comfortable.

☉ Caesars Palace. 3570 Las Vegas Blvd. S. ☎ **702/731-7110.**

Caesars casino is simultaneously the ultimate in gambling luxury and the ultimate in Vegas kitsch. Cocktail waitresses in togas parade about, as you gamble under the watchful gaze of faux marble Roman statues. The very high ceiling makes for a very low claustrophobia level, especially thanks to the recent face-lift, which has lightened up the paint and made the whole casino much brighter. A notable facility is the state-of-the-art **Race and Sports Book,** with huge electronic display boards and giant video screens. (Caesars has sophisticated satellite equipment that can pick up the broadcast of virtually any sporting event in the world.) Slot players can accumulate bonus points toward cash back, gifts, gratis show tickets, meals, and rooms by joining the Emperors Club. It's a gorgeous and elegant place to gamble, but we've never won there, so we hate it.

Flamingo Hilton. 3555 Las Vegas Blvd. S. ☎ **702/733-3111.**

If you've seen the movie *Bugsy,* you won't recognize this as Mr. Siegel's baby. The Flamingo is in the middle of redoing its casino area, which is just as well, because right now it feels overly crowded, thanks to overall tight confines. It sprawls across a large space, meandering around corners, so it is very difficult to get out of. Actual daylight does stream in from windows and glass doorways on the Strip, however. Players Club slot bettors qualify for free meals, shows, rooms, and other play-based incentives. One of our favorite slot machines is here, but we won't tell you which one, to save it for ourselves. Sorry.

Gold Coast. 4000 W. Flamingo Rd. ☎ **702/367-7111.**

Adjacent to the Rio, this casino is not only well lit but totally unique in Vegas: It has windows! It's a little thing, but it made us really excited. They also had a higher ratio of video poker machines to slot machines, rather than the other way around.

Harrah's. 3475 Las Vegas Blvd. S. ☎ **702/369-5000.**

Confetti carpeting and fiber-optic fireworks overhead combine with murals and an overall Mardi Gras theme to make a festive environment. Does it help you win more? Who knows. But the different, better energy that has resulted from this recent, costly face-lift certainly couldn't hurt. Don't miss the "party pits," gaming-table areas where dealers are encouraged to wear funny hats, celebrate wins, and otherwise break the usual stern dealer facade. Singing, dancing, and the handing out of party favors have all been known to break out. Gambling is supposed to be fun, so enjoy it. Slot and table game players can earn bonus points toward complimentary rooms, meals, and show tickets by acquiring a Harrah's Gold Card in the casino.

Imperial Palace. 3535 Las Vegas Blvd. S. ☎ **702/731-3311.**

The 75,000-square-foot casino here reflects the hotel's pagoda-roofed Asian exterior with a dragon-motif ceiling and giant wind-chime chandeliers. There is a nonsmoking slot machine area separate from the main casino (as opposed to just another part of the room, at best, in other casinos), and a Breathalyzer for voluntary alcohol limit checks on your way to the parking lot (useful since there are nine bars on the casino premises). Visitors can get free Scratch Slotto cards for prizes up to $5,000 in cash (cards and free passes to the auto collection are distributed on the sidewalk out front). A gaming school offers lessons in craps and blackjack, and slot tournaments take place daily.

Maxim. 160 E. Flamingo Rd. ☎ **702/731-4300.**

This friendly but dimly lit facility (with some of the '70s frills) is the neighborhood bar of casinos. They have a racetrack game where you can place bets on little mechanical horses and jockeys—kind of a kid's toy for adults. Pick up a fun book here for a free $1,000 slot pull.

✪ **Mirage.** 3400 Las Vegas Blvd. S. ☎ **702/791-7111.**

Gamble in a Polynesian village in one of the prettiest casinos in town. It has a meandering layout, and the low ceiling makes for a medium claustrophobia level, but neither of these things is overwhelming. This remains one of our favorite places to gamble. Slot players can join the Club Mirage and work toward bonus points for cash rebates, special room rates, complimentary meals and/or show tickets, and other benefits. It's one of the most pleasant, and popular, casinos in town, so it's crowded more often than not.

The Rio. 3700 W. Flamingo Rd. ☎ **702/252-7777.**

This Brazilian-themed resort's 85,000-square-foot casino is, despite the presence of plenty of glitter and neon, very dark. It has about the highest claustrophobia rating of the major casinos. Its sports book feels a little grimy. The waitresses wear scanty costumes (particularly in the back), probably in an effort to distract you and throw your game off. Do not let them. The part of the casino in the new Masquerade Village is considerably more pleasant (the very high ceilings help) though still crowded, plus the loud live show adds still more noise. In an area called Jackpot Jungle, slot machines come equipped with TV monitors that present old movies and in-house information while you play. There are nonsmoking slot and gaming table areas.

Treasure Island. 3300 Las Vegas Blvd. S. ☎ **702/894-7111.**

Treasure Island's huge casino is highly themed. If you have ever been on Disney World's Pirates of the Caribbean and thought, "Gee, if only this were a casino," this is the place for you. Many people complain they don't like the atmosphere here, possibly because that very theme backfires. Slot club members can earn meals, services, show tickets, and cash rebates. Throughout the casino there is something called Slot 2000. Hit a button, and a video screen pops up showing a (female) casino worker, to whom you can talk. She will answer questions, send someone over with drinks, make reservations, and otherwise help make your time there better. If you win a jackpot, she will come on and congratulate you. No, she can't see you, so don't try to flirt. There are nonsmoking gaming tables in each pit.

Venetian. 3355 Las Vegas Blvd. S. ☎ **702/414-1000.**

"Tasteful" is the watchword in these days of classy Vegas gaming, and consequently, with the exception of more hand-painted Venetian art re-creations on parts of the ceiling, the Venetian's casino is interchangeable with those found at Mandalay Bay, the Monte Carlo, and to a certain extent, Bellagio. All that gleaming marble, columns, and such is very nice, but after a while, also a bit ho-hum. Besides, this is Vegas, and we want our tacky theme elements, by gosh. The lack thereof, combined with poor signage, may be why this casino is so hard to get around—every part looks exactly the same. It's not precisely claustrophobic, but it can be confusing. Plus, there is no (at this writing) Big Giant Slot machine. On the other hand, we made a killing at blackjack, so we love the place. You can access the casino directly from the St. Mark's Square re-creation out front.

NORTH STRIP

Circus Circus. 2880 Las Vegas Blvd. S. ☎ **702/734-0410.**

This vast property has three full-sizes casinos that, combined, comprise one of the largest gaming operations in Nevada (more than 100,000 square feet). More importantly, they have an entire circus midway set up throughout, so you are literally gambling with trapeze stunts going on over your head. The other great gimmick is the slot machine carousel—yep, it turns while you spin the reels. Unfortunately, it is crowded, noisy, and there are lots of children passing through. That, plus some low ceilings (not in the Big Top, obviously), make for a very high claustrophobia rating, though the new Commedia del'Arte clown motif has upgraded its appearance. The Ringmaster Players Club offers slot/video poker and table players the opportunity to earn points redeemable for cash, discounted rooms and meals, and other benefits.

✪ **Desert Inn.** 3145 Las Vegas Blvd. S. ☎ **702/733-4444.**

Possibly the most genuinely elegant casino in Vegas, it's also one of the smallest for a major hotel. They don't care—they are looking for one good James Bond figure, rather than the masses. Crystal chandeliers here replace the usual neon glitz, and gaming tables are comfortably spaced. The ambience is reminiscent of intimate European gaming houses and is downright quiet. Some might find this almost creepy. Others may find it a huge relief. Since there are fewer slot machines here than at most major casinos, there's less noise in ringing bells and clinking coins. The very high ceiling gives it a nonexistent claustrophobia rating.

The Riviera. 2901 Las Vegas Blvd. S. ☎ **702/734-5110.**

The Riviera's 100,000-square-foot casino, one of the largest in the world, offers plenty of opportunities to get lost and cranky. A wall of windows lets daylight stream in (most unusual), and the gaming tables are situated beneath gleaming brass arches lit by recessed, pink neon tubing. The casino's Slot and Gold (seniors) clubs allow slot players to earn bonus points toward free meals, rooms, and show tickets. Nickeltown is just that—nothin' but nickel slots and video poker. The race and sports book here offers individual monitors at each of its 250 seats, and this is one of the few places in town where you can play the ancient Chinese game of *sic bo* (a fast-paced dice game resembling craps).

The Sahara. 2535 Las Vegas Blvd. S. ☎ 702/737-2111.

This is one place where there seem to be more tables than slots and video poker machines. It also has good deals like $1 craps, but with that comes the kind of people who are drawn by $1 craps—belligerent drunks and other fun-killing folks. When we were last there, they had a whole row of Piggy Bankin' machines that were all paying off, so we were happy. The Sahara runs frequent slot tournaments and other events, and its slot club, Club Sahara, offers cash rebates and other perks.

The Stardust. 3000 Las Vegas Blvd. S. ☎ 702/732-6111.

Always mobbed, this popular casino features 90,000 square feet of lively gaming action, including a 250-seat race and sports book with a sophisticated satellite system and more than 50 TV monitors airing sporting events and horse-racing results around the clock. Adjacent to it is a sports handicapper's library offering comprehensive statistical information on current sporting events. Stardust Slot Club members win cash rebates, with credit piling up even on nickel machines; free rooms, shows, meals, and invitations to special events are also possible bonuses. If you're a novice, avail yourself of gratis gaming lessons. We usually do well there, so even though it's a little loud, we like it. Check out those $1 slots just inside the front door—they've been very good to us.

The Stratosphere. 2000 Las Vegas Blvd. S. ☎ 702/380-7777.

Originally set up to evoke a world's fair but ending up more like a circus, the Stratosphere redid the whole area in order to make it more appealing for the many adults who were staying away in droves. The newly redone facility aims for class but doesn't necessarily achieve it. It's not that it fails, it just no longer has any identity at all. They heavily advertise their high payback on certain slots and video poker: 98% payback on dollar slots and 100% payback on quarter video poker (if you bet the maximum on each). We can't say we noticed a difference, but other people around us were winning like crazy. There's a test area for new slot games, a Harley slot area with motorcycle-seat stools, and a high-roller slot room ($5 minimum bet) where chairs move up and down and can vibrate to give you a back massage while you play. The Stratosphere Players Club sponsors frequent tournaments, and its members can earn points toward gifts, VIP perks, discounted room rates, meals, and cash rebates.

EAST OF THE STRIP

✪ **Hard Rock Hotel & Casino.** 4455 Paradise Rd. ☎ **702/693-5000.**

Where Gen X goes to gamble. The Hard Rock has certainly taken casino decor to a whole new level. The attention to detail and the resulting playfulness is admirable, if not incredible. Gaming tables have piano keyboards at one end; some slots have Fender guitar fret boards as arms; gaming chips have band names and/or pictures on them; slot machines are similarly rock-themed (check out the Jimi Hendrix machine!); and so it goes. The whole thing is set in the middle of a circular room, around the outskirts of which are various rock memorabilia in glass cases. Rock blares over the sound system, allowing boomers to boogie while they gamble. A bank of slots makes gambling an act of charity: Environmentally committed owner Peter Morton (the Hard Rock's motto is "Save the Planet") donates profits from specified slots to organizations dedicated to saving the rain forests. A Back Stage Pass allows patrons to rack up discounts on meals, lodging, and gift-shop items while playing slots and table games. The race and sports book here provides comfortable seating in leather-upholstered reclining armchairs. All this is genuinely amazing, but the noise level is above even that of a normal casino and we just hated it. It's worth looking at anyway.

✪ **Las Vegas Hilton.** 3000 Paradise Rd. ☎ **702/732-7111.**

The casino has two parts, thanks to the space-themed portion adjacent to the Star Trek Experience. In an area designed to look like a space port, you find space-themed slot machines, many of which have no handles—just pass your hand through a light beam to activate. You'll find other gimmicks throughout the casino (though already some have been dropped since the recent opening), including urinals that give you an instant "urinalysis"—usually suggesting this is your lucky day to gamble. We do like a well-designed space in which to lose our money. Over in the original casino section,

Austrian crystal chandeliers add a strong touch of class. The casino is actually medium-sized, but it does have an enormous sports book—at 30,500 square feet, the world's largest race and sports book facility. It, too, is a luxurious precinct equipped with the most advanced audio, video, and computer technology available, including 46 TV monitors, some as large as 15 feet across. In fact, its video wall is second in size only to NASA's. The casino is adjacent to the lobby, but is neither especially loud nor frantic. By joining Club Magic, a slot club, you can amass bonus points toward cash prizes, gifts, and complimentary rooms, meals, and show tickets.

DOWNTOWN

Binion's Horseshoe. 128 E. Fremont St., between Casino Center Blvd. and First St. ☎ **702/382-1600.**

Professionals who know, say that "for the serious player, the Binions are this town." Benny Binion could neither read nor write, but boy, did he know how to run a casino. His venerable establishment has been eclipsed over the years, but it claims the highest betting limits in Las Vegas on all games (probably in the entire world, according to a spokesperson). It offers single-deck blackjack and $2 minimums, 10-times odds on craps, and high progressive jackpots. We especially like the older part of the casino here, which—with its flocked wallpaper, gorgeous lighting fixtures, and gold-tasseled burgundy velvet drapes—looks like a turn-of-the-century Old West bordello. Unfortunately, all this adds up to a very high claustrophobia level.

California Hotel/Casino. 12 Ogden Ave., at 1st St. ☎ **702/385-1222.**

The California is a festive place filled with Hawaiian shirts and balloons. This friendly facility actually provides sofas and armchairs in the casino area—an unheard-of luxury in this town. Players can join the Cal Slot Club and amass points toward gifts and cash prizes, or participate in daily slot tournaments. Gaming facilities include a keno lounge, sports book, blackjack tables, craps, roulette, minibaccarat, pai gow poker, Let-It-Ride, Caribbean stud, and slot and video poker machines. This is the first place we found our favorite Piggy Bankin' machines.

Fitzgeralds. 301 Fremont St., at 3rd St. ☎ **702/388-2400.**

They recently redid their casino in greens and golds, and the overall effect is not quite as tacky as you might expect. In fact, it's rather friendly, and with a medium to low claustrophobia level. The casino is actually two levels: From the upstairs part you can access a balcony from which you get an up-close view of the Fremont Street Experience. Their mascot, Mr. O'Lucky (a costumed leprechaun), roams the casino. You don't have to be nice to him. The Fitzgerald Card offers slot players gifts, meals, and other perks for accumulated points.

Four Queens. 202 Fremont St., at Casino Center Blvd. ☎ **702/385-4011.**

The Four Queens is New Orleans–themed, with turn-of-the-century-style globe chandeliers, which make for good lighting and a low claustrophobia level. It's small, but the dealers are helpful, which is one of the pluses of gambling in the more manageably sized casinos. The facility boasts the world's largest slot machine: More than 9 feet high and almost 20 feet long, six people can play it at one time! It's the Mother of all Big Giant Slot machines, and frankly, it intimidates even us. Here is also the world's largest blackjack table (it seats 12 players). The Reel Winners Club offers slot players bonus points toward cash rebates.

Golden Nugget. 129 E. Fremont St., at Casino Center Blvd. ☎ **702/385-7111.**

Frankly, this is not the standout that other casino properties owned by Steve Wynn are. It goes for luxury, of course, but so much is crammed into so little space that the only feeling that emerges is one of overcrowding. That's not to say we didn't like it, because we won a lot of money here. And compared to most other Downtown properties, this is the most like the Strip. It has a much cleaner and fresher feeling, in an area filled with dingy, time-forgotten spaces. Slot players can earn bonus points toward complimentary rooms, meals, shows, and gifts by joining the 24 Karat Club.

Jackie Gaughan's Plaza Hotel/Casino. 1 Main St., at Fremont St. ☎ **702/386-2110.**

This is old Vegas, with an attempt at '60s glamour (think women in white go-go boots). Now it's a little worn. Gaming facilities include a keno lounge (featuring double keno), race and sports book, blackjack, craps, roulette, baccarat, Caribbean stud, pai gow poker, poker, pan, Let-It-Ride, and slot/video poker machines. Cautious bettors will appreciate the $1 blackjack tables and penny slots here.

Lady Luck. 206 N. 3rd St., at Ogden Ave. ☎ **702/477-3000.**

Even though Lady Luck is an older casino with the anticipated drop in glamour, it's surprisingly cheerful and with a low to medium claustrophobia level. Decorations give it a festive quality, and cocktail waitresses push drink carts, to mix you up something right on the spot. The Mad Money Slot Club offers scrip, cash, meals, accommodations, and prizes as incentives. Liberal game rules are attractive to gamblers.

✪ **Main Street Station.** 200 N. Main St., between Fremont St. and I-95. ☎ **702/387-1896.**

Part of a long-closed old hotel that has been recently renovated and reopened to great success, this is the best of the Downtown casinos, at least in terms of comfort and pleasant environment. Even the Golden Nugget, nice as it is, has more noise and distractions. The decor here is, again, classic Vegas/old-timey (Victorian-era) San Francisco, but with extra touches (check out the old-fashioned fans above the truly beautiful bar) that make it work much better than other attempts at the same. Strangely, it seems just about smoke-free, perhaps thanks in part to a very high ceiling. The claustrophobia level is zero.

8

Shopping

*U*nless you're looking for souvenir decks of cards, Styrofoam dice, and miniature slot machines, Las Vegas is not exactly a shopping mecca. It does, however, have several noteworthy malls that can amply supply the basics. And many hotels also offer comprehensive, and sometimes highly themed, shopping arcades, most notably Caesars Palace and the Venetian (details below). You might consider driving **Maryland Parkway,** which runs parallel to the Strip on the east and has just about one of everything: Target, Toys R Us, several major department stores, Tower Records, major drugstores (in case you forgot your shampoo and don't want to spend $8 on a new one in your hotel sundry shop), some alternative-culture stores (tattoo parlors and hip clothing stores), and so forth. It goes on for blocks.

1 The Malls

Boulevard Mall. 3528 S. Maryland Pkwy., between Twain Ave. and Desert Inn Rd. ☎ **702/732-8949.** Mon–Fri 10am–9pm, Sat 10am–8pm, Sun 11am–6pm.

The Boulevard is the largest mall in Las Vegas. Its 144-plus stores and restaurants are arranged in arcade fashion on a single floor occupying 1.2 million square feet. Geared to the average consumer (not the carriage trade), it has anchors like Sears, JC Penney, Macy's, Dillard's, and Marshalls. Other notables include The Disney Store, The Nature Company, a 23,000-square-foot Good Guys (electronics), The Gap, Gap Kids, The Limited, Victoria's Secret, Colorado (for outdoor clothing and gear), Howard and Phil's Western Wear, and African and World Imports. There's a wide variety of shops offering moderately priced shoes and clothing for the entire family, books and gifts, jewelry, and home furnishings, plus more than a dozen fast-food eateries. In short, you can find just about anything you need here. There's free valet parking.

DFS Galleria. 3057 Las Vegas Blvd. S, just north of the Desert Inn. ☎ **702/731-6446.** Daily 10:30am–midnight.

If the words *duty-free shopping* are sacred to you, then come here for a collection that includes Estee Lauder, Burberry, Cartier, Bulgari, Dendi, Bally, Ferragamo, Coach, Le Sport, and Christian Dior. Note that it's contained in a mall that caters to an Asian clientele, so there are some interesting import stores plus a very good dim sum restaurant.

Fashion Show Mall. 3200 Las Vegas Blvd. S., at the corner of Spring Mountain Rd. ☎ **702/369-0704.** Mon–Fri 10am–9pm, Sat 10am–7pm, Sun noon–6pm.

This luxurious and centrally located mall, one of the city's largest, opened in 1981 to great hoopla. Designers Adolfo, Geoffrey Beene, Bill Blass, Bob Mackie, and Pauline Trigere were all on hand to display their fashion interpretations of the "Las Vegas look."

The mall comprises more than 130 shops, restaurants, and services. It is anchored by Neiman-Marcus, Saks Fifth Avenue, Macy's, Robinsons-May, and Dillard's. Other notable tenants: Abercrombie and Fitch, The Disney Store, The Walt Disney Gallery, The Discovery Channel Store, Lillie Rubin (upscale women's clothing), The Gap, Benetton, Uomo, Banana Republic, Victoria's Secret, Caché, Williams Sonoma Grand Cuisine, The Body Shop, Mondi (upscale women's clothing), Waldenbooks, Louis Vuitton, and Sharper Image. There are several card and book shops, a wide selection of apparel stores for the whole family (including large sizes and petites), 9 jewelers, 21 shoe stores, and gift and specialty shops. There are dozens of eating places (see chapter 6 for specifics). Valet parking is available, and you can even arrange to have your car hand washed while you shop.

Galleria at Sunset. 1300 W. Sunset Rd., at Stephanie St., just off I-515 in nearby Henderson. ☎ **702/434-0202.** Mon–Sat 10am–9pm, Sun 11am–6pm.

This upscale 1 million-square-foot shopping center, 9 miles southeast of Downtown Las Vegas, opened in 1996, with performing Disney characters on hand to welcome shoppers and a nighttime display of fireworks. The mall has a Southwestern motif, evidenced in the use of terra-cotta stone, interior landscaping, cascading fountains, and skylights; eight 20-foot hand-carved pillars flank the main entrance. Anchored by four department stores—Dillard's, JC Penney, Mervyn's California, and Robinsons-May—the Galleria's 110 emporia include branches of The Disney Store, The Gap/Gap Kids/Baby Gap, The Limited and The Limited Too, Eddie Bauer, Miller's Outpost, Ann Taylor, bebe, Caché,

Compagnie International, Lane Bryant, Lerner New York, Victoria's Secret, The Body Shop, B. Dalton, and Sam Goody. In addition to shoes and clothing for the entire family, you'll find electronics, eyewear, gifts, books, home furnishings, jewelry, and luggage here. Dining facilities include an extensive food court and two restaurants.

The Meadows. 4300 Meadows Lane, at the intersection of Valley View and U.S. 95. ☎ **702/878-4849.** Mon–Fri 10am–9pm, Sat–Sun 10am–7pm.

Another immense mall, The Meadows comprises 144 shops, services, and eateries, anchored by four department stores: Macy's, Dillard's, Sears, and JC Penney. In addition, there are 15 shoe stores, a full array of apparel for the entire family (including maternity wear, petites, and large sizes), an extensive food court, and shops purveying toys, books, CDs and tapes, luggage, gifts, jewelry, home furnishings (The Bombay Company, among others), accessories, and so on. Fountains and trees enhance the Meadows's ultramodern, high-ceilinged interior, and a 1995 renovation added comfortable conversation/seating areas and made the mall lighter and brighter. It is divided into five courts, one centered on a turn-of-the-century carousel (a plus for kids). A natural history–themed court has a "desert fossil" floor, and an entertainment court is the setting for occasional live musical and dramatic performances. You can rent strollers at the Customer Service Center.

2 Factory Outlets

Las Vegas has a big factory outlet center just a few miles past the southern end of the Strip (See Belz Factory Outlet World below). If you don't have a car, you can take a no. 301 CAT bus from anywhere on the Strip and change at Vacation Village to a no. 303. Dedicated bargain hunters may want to make the roughly 40-minute drive along I-15 to the Fashion Outlet at Primm (☎ **888/424-6898**), right on the border of California and Nevada. On your left is a large factory outlet with some designer names prominent enough to make that drive well worth while; Kenneth Cole, Donna Karen, even Prada, among several others, plus Williams Sonoma.

Belz Factory Outlet World. 7400 Las Vegas Blvd. S., at Warm Springs Rd. ☎ **702/896-5599.** Mon–Sat 10am–9pm, Sun 10am–6pm.

Belz houses 145 air-conditioned outlets, including a few dozen clothing stores and shoe stores. It offers an immense range of merchandise at savings up to 75% off retail prices. Among other emporia, you'll find Adolfo II, Casual Corner, Levi's, Nike, Dress

Barn, Oshkosh B'Gosh, Leggs/Hanes/Bali, Esprit, Aileen, Bugle Boy, Carters, Reebok, Spiegel, Guess Classics, Oneida, Springmaid, We're Entertainment (Disney and Warner Bros.), Bose (electronics), Danskin, Van Heusen, Burlington, Royal Doulton, Lennox (china), Waterford (crystal), and Geoffrey Beene here. There is also a carousel.

3 Hotel Shopping Arcades

Just about every Las Vegas hotel offers some shopping opportunities. The following have the most extensive arcades. The physical spaces of these shopping arcades are always open, but individual stores keep unpredictable hours. *Note:* The Forum Shops at Caesars and the Grand Canal shops at the Venetian—as much a sightseeing attraction as a shopping arcade—are in the must-see category.

Bally's   Bally's **Avenue Shoppes** number around 20 emporia offering pro team sports apparel, toys, clothing (men's, women's, and children's), logo items, gourmet chocolates, liquor, jewelry, nuts and dried fruit, flowers, handbags, and T-shirts. In addition, there are several gift shops, three restaurants, art galleries, and a pool-wear shop. There are blackjack tables and slot and video poker machines right in the mall, as well as a race and sports book. You can dispatch the kids to a video arcade here while you shop.

Bellagio   The Via Bellagio collection of stores isn't as big as some of the other mega-hotel shopping arcades, but here it's definitely quality over quantity. It's a veritable roll call of glossy magazine ads: Armani, Prada, Chanel, Tiffany, Hermès, Fre Leighton, Gucci, and Moschino. That's it. You need anything else? Well, yes—money. We can't even afford the oxygen in these places. If you can, good for you, you lucky dog. (Actually, we've discovered affordable, good-taste items in every store here, from Tiffany's $30 silver key chains to $100 Prada business card holders.) A nice touch is a parking lot by the far entrance to Via Bellagio, so you need not navigate the great distance from Bellagio's main parking structure, but can simply pop in and pick yourself up a little something.

Caesars Palace   Since 1978, Caesars has had an impressive arcade of shops called the **Appian Way.** Highlighted by an immense white Carrara-marble replica of Michelangelo's *David* standing more than 18 feet high, its shops include the aptly named Galerie Michelangelo (original and limited-edition artworks), jewelers (including branches of Ciro and Cartier), a logo merchandise shop, and several shops for upscale men's and women's clothing. All in all, a respectable grouping of hotel shops, and an expansion is in the works.

But in the hotel's tradition of constantly surpassing itself, in 1992 Caesars inaugurated the fabulous ✪ **Forum Shops,** an independently operated 250,000-square-foot Rodeo-Drive-meets-the-Roman-Empire affair complete with a 48-foot triumphal arch entranceway, a painted Mediterranean sky that changes as the day progresses from rosy-tinted dawn to twinkling evening stars, acres of marble, lofty scagliola Corinthian columns with gold capitals, and a welcoming goddess of fortune under a central dome. Its architecture and sculpture span a period from 300 B.C. to A.D. 1700. Storefront facades, some topped with statues of Roman senators, resemble a classical Italian streetscape, with archways, piazzas, ornate fountains, and a barrel-vaulted ceiling. The "center of town" is the magnificent domed Fountain of the Gods, where Jupiter rules from his mountaintop surrounded by Pegasus, Mars, Venus, Neptune, and Diana. And at the Festival Fountain, seemingly immovable "marble" Animatronic statues of Bacchus (slightly in his cups), a lyre-playing Apollo, Plutus, and Venus come to life for a 7-minute revel with dancing waters and high-tech laser-light effects. The shows take place every hour on the hour. Even if you don't like shopping, it's worth the stroll just to giggle.

More than 70 prestigious emporia here include Louis Vuitton, Plaza Escada, Bernini, Christian Dior, A/X Armani Exchange, bebe, Caché, Gucci, Ann Taylor, and Gianni Versace, along with many other clothing, shoe, and accessory shops. Other notables include a Warner Brothers Studio Store (a sign at the exit reads THATIUS FINITUS FOLKUS), The Disney Store, Kids Kastle (beautiful children's clothing and toys), Rose of Sharon (classy styles for large-sized women), Sports Logo (buy a basketball signed by Michael Jordan for $695!), Field of Dreams (more autographed sports memorabilia), Museum Company (reproductions ranging from 16th-century hand-painted Turkish boxes to ancient Egyptian scarab necklaces), West of Santa Fe (western wear and Native American jewelry and crafts), Antiquities (neon Shell gas signs, 1950s malt machines, Americana; sometimes "Elvis" is on hand), Endangered Species Store (ecology-themed merchandise), Brookstone (one-of-a-kind items from garden tools to sports paraphernalia), and Victoria's Secret. There's much more, including jewelry shops and art galleries.

And as if that weren't enough, in 1998 the Forum Shops added an extension. The centerpiece is a giant **Roman Hall,** featuring a

50,000-gallon circular aquarium and another fountain that also comes to life with a show of fire (don't stand too close—it gets really hot), dancing waters, and Animatronic figures as the mythical continent of Atlantis rises and falls every hour. The production values are much higher than the Bacchus extravaganza, but it takes itself more seriously, so the giggle factor remains. The hall is also the entrance to the Race for Atlantis IMAX 3-D ride.

In this shopping area, you will find a number of significant stores, including a DKNY, Emporio Armani, Niketown, Fendi, Polo for Ralph Lauren, Guess, Virgin Megastore, and FAO Schwarz. Do go see the latter, as it is fronted by a gigantic Trojan horse, in which you can clamber around, while its head moves and smoke comes out its nostrils. We love it. Also in the shops is Wolfgang Puck's Chinois, a Cheesecake Factory, and a Caviartorium, where you can sample all varieties of the high-priced fish eggs.

Circus Circus   There are about 15 shops between the casino and Grand Slam Canyon, offering a wide selection of gifts and sundries, logo items, toys and games, jewelry, liquor, resort apparel for the entire family, T-shirts, homemade fudge/candy/soft ice cream, and, fittingly, clown dolls and puppets. At Amazing Pictures you can have your photo taken as a pinup girl, muscle man, or whatever else your fantasy dictates. Adjacent to Grand Slam Canyon, there is a new shopping arcade themed along a European village, with cobblestone walkways and fake woods and so forth, decorated with replicas of vintage circus posters. It's much nicer than what the tacky Circus Circus has had before. Among the stores are Marshall Russo, Headliners, The Sweet Tooth, and Carousel Classics.

Excalibur   The shops of **"The Realm"** for the most part reflect the hotel's medieval theme. Dragon's Lair, for example, features items ranging from pewter swords and shields to full suits of armor, and Merlin's Mystic Shop carries crystals, luck charms, and gargoyles. Other shops carry more conventional wares—gifts, candy, jewelry, women's clothing, and Excalibur logo items. A child pleaser is Kids of the Kingdom, which displays licensed character merchandise from Disney, Looney Tunes, Garfield, and Snoopy. Wild Bill's carries western wear and Native American jewelry and crafts. And at Fantasy Faire you can have your photo taken in Renaissance attire.

Flamingo Hilton   The **Crystal Court** shopping promenade here accommodates men's and women's clothing/accessories stores, gift shops, and a variety of other emporia selling jewelry, beachwear,

Southwestern crafts, fresh-baked goods, logo items, children's gifts, toys, and games.

Harrah's Harrah's has finished up a massive new renovation that includes a new shopping center called **Carnivale Court.** It's entirely outdoors and features live entertainment strolling around, plus a show at night with fireworks and circus-type acts. Among the store highlights is a Ghirardelli Chocolate store, a branch of the famous San Francisco–based chocolate company. Other stores include On Stage (a CD and video store) and Carnival Corner (gourmet foods and cigars). You might also swing into the hotel and examine the artwork found in **The Art of Gaming**—all gambling-related artwork.

Luxor Hotel/Casino **Giza Galleria** is a new 20,000-square-foot shopping arcade with eight full shops. Most of the stores emphasize clothing. Adjacent is the Cairo Bazaar, a trinket shop.

MGM Grand The hotel's **Star Lane Shops** include more than a dozen upscale emporia lining the corridors en route from the monorail entrance. The Knot Shop carries designer ties by Calvin Klein, Gianni Versace, and others. El Portal features luggage and handbags—Coach, Dior, Fendi, Polo Ralph Lauren, and other exclusive lines. Grand 50's carries *Route 66* jackets, Elvis T-shirts, photos of James Dean, and other mementos of the 1950s. MGM Grand Sports sells signed athletic uniforms, baseballs autographed by Michael Jordan, and the like; it is the scene of occasional appearances by sports stars such as Floyd Patterson and Stan Musial. You can choose an oyster and have its pearl set in jewelry at The Pearl Factory. Other Star Lane Shops specialize in movie memorabilia, Betty Boop merchandise, *EFX* wares, children's clothing, decorative magnets, MGM Grand logo items and Las Vegas souvenirs, seashells and coral, candy, and sunglasses. Refreshments are available at a Häagen-Dazs ice-cream counter and Yummy's Coffees and Desserts.

In other parts of the hotel, retail shops include a *Wizard of Oz* gift shop, Front Page (for newspapers, books, magazines, and sundries), a spa shop selling everything from beachwear to top-of-the-line European skin care products, a liquor store, a candy store, Kenneth J. Lane jewelry, and Marshall Rousso (men's and women's clothing). In addition, theme-park emporia sell Hollywood memorabilia, cameras and photographic supplies, MGM Grand and theme-park-logo products, toys, fine china and crystal, animation cels, collectibles (limited-edition dolls, plates, figurines), Hollywood-themed clothing and accessories, and western wear. At Arts and Crafts you can watch artisans working in leather, glass, wood, pottery, and other materials, and at Photoplay Gallery you can have your picture taken as *Time* magazine's man or woman of the year.

Monte Carlo   An arcade of retail shops here includes Bon Vivant (resort wear for the whole family, dress wear for men), Crown Jewels (jewelry, leather bags, crystal, Fabergé eggs, gift items), a florist, logo shop, jeweler, food market, dessert store, and Lance Burton magic paraphernalia shop.

The Rio   The new 60,000-square-foot **Masquerade Village** is a nicely done addition to the Rio. It's done as a European village, and is 2 stories, featuring a wide variety of shops including the nation's largest Nicole Miller, Speedo, and the N'awlins store, which includes "authentic" voodoo items, Mardi Gras masks, and so forth. It's attached to a cafe that sells beignets (from Cafe Du Monde mix) and chicory coffee.

The Riviera   The Riviera has a fairly extensive shopping arcade comprising art galleries, jewelers, a creative photographer, and shops specializing in women's shoes and handbags, clothing for the entire family, furs, gifts, logo items, toys, phones and electronic gadgets, and chocolates.

Sam's Town   Though Sam's Town does not contain a notably significant shopping arcade, it does house the huge **Western Emporium** (almost department-store size), selling western clothing for men and women, boots (an enormous selection), jeans, belts, silver and turquoise jewelry, Stetson hats, Native American crafts, gift items, and old-fashioned candy. You can have your picture taken here in period western costume. Open daily at 9am; closing hours vary.

Stratosphere   Shopping is no afterthought here. The internationally themed second-floor **Tower Shops** promenade, which will soon house 40 stores, is entered via an escalator from the casino. Some shops are in "Paris," along the Rue Lafayette and Avenue de l'Opéra (there are replicas of the Eiffel Tower and Arc de Triomphe in this section). Others occupy Hong Kong and New York City streetscapes. Already-extant emporia include The Money Company (money-motif items from T-shirts to golf balls), a T-shirt store, a magic shop, Key West (body lotions and more), Victoria's Secret, a magnet shop, Norma Kaplan (for glitzy/sexy women's footwear), an electronics boutique, a logo shop, and several gift shops. There are branches of Jitters (a coffeehouse) and Häagen-Daz, and the stores are supplemented by cart vendors.

Treasure Island Treasure Island's shopping promenade—doubling as a portrait gallery of famed buccaneers (Blackbeard, Jean Lafitte, Calico Jack, Barbarosa)—has wooden ship figureheads and battling pirates suspended from its ceiling. Emporia here include the Treasure Island Store (your basic hotel gift/sundry shop, also offering much pirate-themed merchandise, plus a section devoted to Calvin Klein clothing), Loot 'n' Booty, Candy Reef, Captain Kid's (children's clothing), and Damsels in Dis'Dress (women's sportswear and accessories). The Mutiny Bay Shop, in the video-game arcade, carries logo items and stuffed animals. In the casino are the Buccaneer Bay Shoppe (logo merchandise) and the Treasure Chest (a jewelry store; spend those winnings right on the spot). And the Crow's Nest, en route to the Mirage monorail, carries Cirque du Soleil logo items. Cirque du Soleil and *Mystère* logo wares are also sold in a shop near the ticket office.

Venetian The **Grand Canal Shoppes** are a direct challenge to Caesars's shopping eminence. Like the Forum Shops, you stroll through a re-created Italian village—in this case, more or less Renaissance-era Venice, complete with a painted, cloud-studded blue sky overhead, and a canal right down the center on which gondoliers float and sing. Pay them ($6 to $8) and you can take a lazy float down and back, serenaded by your boatsman (actors hired especially for this purpose and with accents perfect enough to fool Roberto Begnini). As you pass by, under and over bridges, flower girls will serenade you and courtesans will flirt with you, and you may have an encounter with a famous Venetian or two, as Marco Polo discusses his travels, and Casanova exerts his famous charm. The stroll (or float) ends at a miniature (though not by all that much) version of St. Mark's Square, the central landmark of Venice. Here, plans are to have more opera singers, strolling musicians, glass blowers, and other bustling marketplace activity. It's all most ambitious and beats the heck out of Animatronic statues. The Shoppes are accessible directly from outside via a grand staircase, whose ceiling features more of those impressive hand-painted art re-creations. It's quite smashing. The Venetian's "Phase Two" hotel addition will some day adjoin the Shoppes at the far end of St. Mark's Square.

Oh, the shops themselves? The usual high- and medium-end brand names: Sephora (France's leading perfume and cosmetics shop), Jimmy Choo (Princess Diana's favorite shoe maker), Mikimoto, Movado, Davidoff, Lana Marks, Kieselstein-Cord, Donna Karan, Oliver & Col, Ludwig Reiter, Kenneth Cole, Ann

Taylor, BCBG, bebe, Banana Republic, Rockport, and more, plus Venetian glass and paper makers. At the entrance is a 55,000-square-foot Warner Bros. complex that will include a restaurant along with retail shops and screening rooms.

4 Vintage Clothing

The Attic. 1018 S. Main St. ☎ **702/388-4088.** Daily 10am–6pm. MC, V.

Sharing a large space with **Cafe Neon,** a coffeehouse that also serves Greek-influenced cafe food (so you can raise your blood sugar again after a long stretch of shopping), and a comedy club stage, and upstairs from an attempt at a weekly club (as of this writing, the Saturday night Underworld), The Attic has plenty of clothing choices on many racks. During a recent visit, a man came in asking for a poodle skirt for his 8-year-old. They had one.

Buffalo Exchange. 4110 S. Maryland Pkwy., at Flamingo, near Tower Records. ☎ **702/791-3960.** Mon–Sat 11am–7pm, Sun noon–6pm. MC, V.

This is actually part of a chain of such stores spread out across the western United States. If the chain part worries you, don't let it—this merchandise doesn't feel processed. Staffed by plenty of incredibly hip alt-culture kids (ask them for what's happening in town during your visit), it is stuffed with dresses, shirts, pants, and so forth. Like any vintage shop, the contents are hit and miss; you can easily go in one day and come out with 12 fabulous new outfits, but you can just as easily go in and come up dry. It is probably the most reliable of the local vintage shops.

5 Reading Material: Used Books, Comics & a Notable Newsstand

USED BOOKS

Dead Poet Books. 3858 W. Sahara Ave., corner of Valley View, near Albertson's. ☎ **702/227-4070.** Mon–Sat 10am–6pm, Sun noon–5pm. AE, DISC, MC, V.

Eliot? Byron? Tennyson? None of the above. Actually, the dead poet in question was a man from whose estate the owners bought their start-up stock. He had such good taste in books, they "fell in love with him" and wanted to name the store in his memory. Just one problem—they never did get his name. So they just called him "the dead poet." He wasn't a poet, but surely anyone with such fine taste in books must have been one in his soul. His legacy continues in this book-lover's haven.

A LAS VEGAS SPECIALTY STORE

Gambler's Book Shop. 630 S. 11th St., just off Charleston Blvd. ☎ **800/ 522-1777** or 702/382-7555. Mon–Sat 9am–5pm.

Here you can buy a book on any system ever devised to beat casino odds. Owner Edna Luckman carries more than 4,000 gambling-related titles, including many out-of-print books, computer software, and videotapes. She describes her store as a place where "gamblers, writers, researchers, statisticians, and computer specialists can meet and exchange information." On request, knowledgeable clerks provide on-the-spot expert advice on handicapping the ponies and other aspects of sports betting. The store's motto is "knowledge is protection."

COMIC BOOKS

Alternative Reality Comics. 4800 S. Maryland Pkwy. ☎ **702/736-3673.** Mon–Sat 11am–7pm, Sun noon–6pm.

The place in Vegas for all your comic-book needs. They have a nearly comprehensive selection, with a heavy emphasis on the underground comics. But don't worry—the superheroes are here, too.

6 Antiques

Antiques in Vegas? You mean really old slot machines, or the people playing the really old slot machines?

Actually, Vegas has quite a few antique stores—nearly two dozen, of consistent quality and price, nearly all located within a few blocks of each other. We have one friend, someone who takes interior design very seriously, who comes straight to Vegas for most of her best finds (you should see her antique chandelier collection!).

To get there, start in the middle of the 1600 block of East Charleston Boulevard and keep driving east. The little stores, nearly all in old houses dating from the '30s, line each side of the street. Or you can stop in at **Silver Horse Antiques,** 1651 E. Charleston Blvd. (☎ **702/385-2700**), and pick up a map to almost all the locations, with phone numbers and hours of operation.

For everything under one roof, try **Sampler Shops Antique Mall,** 6115 W. Tropicana Ave (☎ **702/368-1170**). Open Monday to Saturday 10am to 6pm, Sunday noon to 6pm. Over 200 small antique shops sell their wares in this mall, which offers a diversity of antiques ranging from exquisite Indian bird cages to Star Wars memorabilia (let's not call those sorts of items "antiques" but rather "nostalgia").

7 Wigs

Serge's Showgirl Wigs. 953 E. Sahara Ave. #A-2. ☎ **702/732-1015.** Mon–Sat 10am–5:30pm.

Oh, you probably thought all those showgirls just naturally had bountiful thick manes. If you have a desire to look like a showgirl yourself (and why not?), come to Serge's, which for 23 years has been supplying Vegas wiggy needs, with over 2,000 wigs to choose from. Wigs range in price from $130 to over $1,500, depending on quality and realness, and you can pick from Dolly Parton's wig line or get something custom-made. They also make hairpieces and toupees, and carry hair-care products. If these prices are too rich to bring your fantasy alive, right across the way is **Serge's Showgirl Wigs outlet,** with prices running from a more reasonable $60 to $70.

9

Las Vegas After Dark

*Y*ou will not lack for things to do at night in Vegas. It is a town that truly comes alive only at night. Don't believe us? Just look at the difference between the Strip during the day, when it's kind of dingy and nothing special, and at night when the lights hit and the place glows in all its glory. Night is when it's happening in this 24-hour town. In fact, most bars and clubs don't even get going until close to midnight. That's because it's only around then that all the restaurant workers and people connected with the shows get off the clock and can go out and play themselves. It's extraordinary. Just sit down in a bar at 11pm; it's empty. You might well conclude it's dead. Return in 2 hours and you'll find it completely full and jumping.

But you also won't lack for things to do before 11pm. There are shows all over town, ranging from traditional magic shows to cutting-edge acts like *Mystère.* The showgirls remain, topless and otherwise; Las Vegas revues are what happened to vaudeville, by the way, as chorus girls do their thing in between jugglers, comics, magicians, singers, and specialty acts of dubious category. Even the topless shows are tame; all that changes is the already scantily clad showgirls are even more so.

Every hotel has at least one lounge, usually offering live music. The days of fabulous Vegas lounge entertainment, where sometimes the acts were of better quality than the headliners (and headliners like Sinatra would join the lounge acts on stage between their own sets), are gone. Most of what remains is homogeneous and bland, and serves best as a brief respite or background noise. On the other hand, finding the most awful lounge act in town can be rewarding on its own.

Vegas still attracts some dazzling headliner entertainment in its showrooms and arenas. Pavarotti inaugurated Mandalay Bay's Arena, with Bob Dylan doing the same for the House of Blues, and Cher opened up the Venetian with a rare live performance. It's also going to be the center of the entertainment universe on New Year's

Eve, 1999, as we head into the millennium. Barbara Streisand will be doing perhaps her last U.S. show ever at the MGM Grand, while Rod Stewart will be headlining the Rio, and Harry Connick Jr. will be playing the Mirage. It is still a badge of honor for comedians to play Vegas, and there is almost always someone of marquee value playing one showroom or the other.

Of course, if you prefer alternative or real rock music, your choices are less limited than they used to be. More rock bands are coming through town, attracted to either the House of Blues, the Hard Rock Hotel's Joint, or the Huntridge Theater, so that means you can actually see folks like Marilyn Manson and Beck in Vegas. But otherwise, the alternative club scene in town is no great shakes.

If you want to know what is playing here during your stay, consult the local free alternative papers: the *Las Vegas Weekly,* formerly *Scope* Magazine (biweekly, with great club and bar descriptions in their listings) and *City Life* (weekly, with no descriptions but comprehensive listings of what's playing where all over town). Both can be picked up at restaurants, bars, record and music stores, and hep retail stores.

Admission to shows runs the gamut, from about $19 for *An Evening at La Cage* (a female impersonator show at the Riviera) to $80 and more for top headliners or *Siegfried and Roy.* Prices usually include two drinks or, in rare instances, dinner.

To find out who will be performing during your stay, and for up-to-date listings of shows (prices change, shows close), you can call the various hotels featuring headliner entertainment, using toll-free numbers. Or call the **Las Vegas Convention and Visitors Authority** (☎ **702/892-0711**) and ask them to send you a free copy of *Showguide* or *What's On in Las Vegas* (one or both of which will probably be in your hotel room).

In addition to the listings below, consider the **Fremont Street Experience,** described in chapter 6.

1 What's Playing Where

Below is a list of the major production shows playing at press time in Las Vegas. In the following section we've reviewed some of the major ones.

- **Bally's:** ✪ *Jubilee!* (Las Vegas–style review)
- **Bellagio:** ✪ **Cirque du Soleil's** *O* (unique circus meets performance art theatrical experience)

- **Excalibur:** *Tournament of Kings* (medieval-themed review)
- **Flamingo Hilton:** *Forever Plaid* (off-Broadway review featuring '60s music) and *The Great Radio City Spectacular* (Las Vegas–style review featuring the Radio City Music Hall Rockettes)
- **Harrah's:** *Spellbound* (magic review)
- **Imperial Palace:** *Legends in Concert* (musical impersonators)
- **Jackie Gaughan's Plaza:** *Kenny Kerr's Boylesque* (female impersonators)
- **MGM Grand:** ✪ *EFX* (special-effects review featuring Tommy Tune)
- **The Mirage:** ✪ *Siegfried and Roy* (magical extravaganza)
- **Monte Carlo:** ✪ *Lance Burton: Master Magician* (magic show and review)
- **Riviera Hotel:** *An Evening at La Cage* (female impersonators), *Crazy Girls* (sexy Las Vegas–style review), and *Splash* (aquatic review)
- **Stardust:** *Enter the Night* (Las Vegas–style review)
- **Stratosphere Tower:** *American Superstars* (an impression-filled production show) and *Viva Las Vegas* (Las Vegas–style review)
- **Treasure Island:** ✪ **Cirque du Soleil's** *Mystère* (unique circus performance)
- **Tropicana:** *Folies Bergère* (Las Vegas–style review)

2 The Major Production Shows

This category covers production shows major and minor.

American Superstars. Stratosphere, 2000 Las Vegas Blvd. S. ☎ **800/99-TOWER** or 702/380-7711.

One of the increasing number of celebrity impersonator shows (cheaper than getting the real headliners), *American Superstars* is one of the few where said impersonators actually sing live. Five performers do their thing; celebs impersonated vary depending on the evening. A typical Friday night featured Gloria Estefan, Charlie Daniels, Madonna, Michael Jackson, and Diana Ross and the Supremes. (And recently they added the Spice Girls—the catty among us will notice the impersonators have better figures than the real Girls.) The performers won't be putting the originals out of work anytime soon, but they aren't bad. Actually, they are closer in voice than in looks to the celeb in question (half the black performers were played by white actors), which is an unusual switch for Vegas impersonators. The "Charlie Daniels" actually proved to be a fine fiddler in his own right and was the hands-down crowd favorite. The live band actually had a look-alike of their own: Kato Kaelin on drums (it's good that he's getting work). The youngish crowd (by Vegas standards) included a healthy smattering of children and seemed to find no faults with the production. The action is also shown on two large, and completely unnecessary, video screens flanking the stage, so you don't have to miss a moment.

- **Showroom Policies:** Smoking not permitted; maître d' seating.
- **Price:** Admission $22.95 includes tax.
- **Show Times:** Sun–Tues at 7pm; Wed, Fri, and Sat at 7 and 10pm. Dark Thurs.
- **Reservations:** Up to 3 days in advance.

✪ *Chicago.* Mandalay Bay, 3950 Las Vegas Blvd. S. ☎ **877/632-7400** or 702/632-7580.

The first of what we hope will be a wave of legitimate theater, though the jury is still out on the success of this experiment (if this production has closed by the time you read this, that may be the answer). It's the story of sassy and scandalous 1930s Chicago showgirls Roxie and Velma, who find nothing, including a trial for murder, a setback in their relentless quest for fame. This is the same revival of Kander and Ebbs's musical that recently won a number of Tony Awards, featuring Bob Fosse's erotic and daring choreography (as re-created and embellished by Ann Reinking, who won one of those Tony Awards for her efforts). When it opened, it featured highly acclaimed performing names such as Chita Rivera and Ben Vereen, plus German chanteuse Ute Lemper. Regardless of the cast, it's a hugely entertaining show, with a timely, clever, humorous plot, and production numbers that captivate even those who normally cringe during musicals. Given the rather slapdash nature of most productions in town, we really want to encourage more entertainment like this. However, even if this should not settle into a long run, the state-of-the-art theater (whose posh lobby evokes classic old theaters) it's housed in, with steep stadium seating that gives every patron a good view, should be a terrific place to see any subsequent show.

- **Showroom Policy:** Nonsmoking with preassigned seating.
- **Price:** $55–$65 (does not include tax, drink, or gratuity).
- **Show Times:** Tues, Thurs, Fri, and Sun at 7:30pm; Wed and Sat at 7 and 10:30pm. Dark Mon.
- **Reservations:** Can charge up to a month before show.

✪ **Cirque du Soleil's** *Mystère.* Treasure Island, 3300 Las Vegas Blvd. S.
☎ **800/392-1999** or 702/894-7722.

The in-house ads for *Mystère* (say miss-*tair*) say "Words don't do it justice," and for once, that's not just hype. The show is so visual that trying to describe it is a losing proposition. And simply calling it a circus is like calling the Hope Diamond a gem, or the Taj Mahal a building. It's accurate, but something seems a little left out of the description.

Cirque du Soleil began in Montréal as a unique circus experience, not only shunning the traditional animal acts in favor of gorgeous feats of human strength and agility, but also adding elements of the surreal and the absurd. The result seems like a collaboration between Salvador Dalí and Luis Buñuel, with a few touches by Magritte and choreography by Twyla Tharp. Mirage Resorts has built them their own theater, an incredible space with an enormous dome and superhydraulics that allow for the Cirque performers to fly in space. Or so it seems.

While part of the fun of the early Cirque was seeing what amazing stuff they could do on a shoestring, seeing what they can do with virtually unlimited funds is spectacular. Unlike, arguably, other artistic ventures, Cirque took full advantage of their new largesse, and their art only rose with their budget. The show features one simply unbelievable act after another (seemingly boneless contortionists and acrobats, breathtakingly beautiful aerial maneuvers), interspersed with Dadaist, commedia dell'arte clowns, and everyone clad in costumes like nothing you've ever seen before. All this and a giant snail. The show is dreamlike, suspenseful, funny, erotic, mesmerizing, and just lovely. At times, you might even find yourself moved to tears. However, for some children, it might be a bit too sophisticated and arty. Even if you've seen Cirque before, it's worth coming to check out, thanks to the large production values. It's a world-class show, no matter where it's playing. That this is playing in Vegas is astonishing.

- **Showroom Policies:** Nonsmoking with preassigned seating.
- **Price:** $70 per person (tax, drink, and gratuity extra).
- **Show Times:** Wed–Sun at 7:30 and 10:30pm. Dark Mon and Tues.
- **Reservations:** You can reserve by phone via credit card up to 7 days in advance (do reserve early since it often sells out).

✪ **Cirque du Soleil's** *O.* Bellagio, 3600 Las Vegas Blvd. S. ☎ **888/488-7111** or 702/693-7722.

♟ Family-Friendly Shows

Appropriate show for kids, all described in this chapter, include the following:

- **Tournament of Kings** at Excalibur *(see p. 174)*
- **Siegfried and Roy** at the Mirage *(see p. 183)*
- **Lance Burton** at the Monte Carlo *(see p. 182)*
- **EFX** at the MGM Grand *(see p. 178)*
- **Cirque du Soleil's Mystère** at Treasure Island *(see p. 176)*

How to describe the indescribable wonder and artistry of Cirque du Soleil's latest and most dazzling display? An Esther Williams–Busby Berkley spectacular on peyote? A Salvador Dalí painting come to life? A stage show by Fellini? The French troupe has topped itself with this production—and not simply because it's situated its breathtaking acrobatics in, on, around, and above a 1½-million-gallon pool (*eau*—pronounced O—is French for water)—though there is that. Even without those impossible feats, this might be worth the price just to see the presentation, a constantly shifting dreamscape tableau that's a marvel of imagination and staging. If you've seen *Mystère* at Treasure Island or other Cirque productions, you'll be amazed that they've once again raised the bar to new heights without losing any of the humor or stylistic trademarks, including the sensuous music. If you've never seen a Cirque show, prepare to have your brain turned inside out.

- **Showroom Policies:** Nonsmoking with preassigned seating. No tank tops, shorts, or sneakers. Attendees are asked to be seated half an hour before show time. Please do—you will be tremendously annoyed and distracted by those who come late.
- **Price:** General admission $90 and $100 (tax included).
- **Show Times:** Fri–Tues at 7:30 and 10:30pm. Dark Wed and Thurs.
- **Reservations:** Tickets may be purchased by the general public 28 days in advance, 90 days for guests of Mirage Resorts.

✪ *Danny Gans: The Man of Many Voices.* Rio Suites, 3700 W. Flamingo Rd. ☎ **800/PLAY-RIO** or 702/252-7777.

That Danny Gans' one-man variety act sells out nightly with nothing more than a back-up band and a few props is a tribute to his charisma and appeal. Gans is "the man of many voices"—over 400 of them—and his show features impressions of 80 different celebrities. The emphasis is on musical impressions (everyone from Sinatra to Springsteen), with some movie scenes (Hepburn and Tracy from *On Golden Pond,* Tom Hanks in *Forrest Gump*) and weird, fun duets (Michael Bolton and Dr. Ruth) thrown in. A stand out is "The Twelve Months of Christmas" sung by 12 different celebrities (Paul Lynde, Clint Eastwood, Woody Allen). Gans' vocal flexibility is impressive, though his impersonations are hit and miss—only some of them would fool the celebrity's mother. Truth be told, he's better than his current material, which has a weakness for obvious jokes and mawkish sentimentality. Still, he's a consistent crowd-pleaser and the lack of bombast can be a refreshing change of pace.

Note: At press time, Danny Gans is set to leave the Rio in late 1999, and to move to the Mirage in April, to a brand new showroom built just for him. Ticket prices and times will probably change, so call the Mirage box office for information.

•**Showroom Policies:** Nonsmoking with maître d' seating.
   • **Price:** $99 (including tax, two drinks, and gratuities).
   • **Show Times:** Tues, Wed, and Fri–Sun at 7:30pm. Dark Mon and Thurs.
   • **Reservations:** Tickets can be ordered up to 30 days in advance.

✪ *EFX*. MGM Grand, 3799 Las Vegas Blvd. S. ☎ **800/929-1111** or 702/891-7777.

EFX's $40 million makeover has used its money wisely, updating the classic Vegas revue into essentially a live-action version of the modern over-the-top Strip hotels. It's not so much cheese anymore, as expensive and occasionally jaw-dropping cheese. Which is not to say it's bad—quite the opposite. As we write this (but possibly not by the time you read this) it stars Broadway musical perennial Tommy Tune, and has reverted to a revue nominally linked around "Tommy's dreams," which conveniently dovetail with already existing production numbers involving King Arthur and Merlin, Houdini, HG Wells, and PT Barnum. This implies that regardless of which star takes it over in the future, it will remain roughly the same, delivering set pieces of better-than-usual dancing, magic, singing, acrobatics, and illusion. And, of course, special effects (*EFX* is the movie industry term for same). The sets are lavish, beyond belief; the costumes and some of the acting show the Cirque influence (faintly Grand Guignol); and the choreography is considerably more imaginative and fresh than any other such show in town. The songs are somewhat bland, but sung almost totally live, and some prove surprisingly hummable. And the effects (flying saucers and cast members, fire-breathing dragons, 3-D time travel, lots of explosions) show where the money is. Cranks may occasionally spot wires, and sometimes said effects are a little painful on the eyes and ears (and they overdo it on the fog machine). The ticket price isn't cheap, so it might be worth taking the less-expensive seats in the mezzanine, as the view is just as good from there.

- **Showroom Policies:** Nonsmoking with preassigned seating.
- **Price:** $51.50–$72.
- **Show Times:** Tues–Sat at 7:30 and 10:30pm. Dark Sun and Mon.
- **Reservations:** You can reserve by phone any time in advance.

Enter the Night. The Stardust, 3000 Las Vegas Blvd. S. ☎ **800/824-6033** or 702/732-6111.

It's kind of cute how the Stardust has tried to stage a full-sized top-less revue on a small- to medium-sized stage. Okay, maybe not *cute,* but the production does seem to be busting at its seams, and it never quite reconciles its aspirations with its reality. There is no plot or point to this; the theme is "enter the night" (of course) and about the passion and mystery that will then ensue, but the songs and ac-tions are vague as to how this is supposed to come about. Instead, what you get is one of those "why is that girl parading around in her underwear?" sort of shows. It's a question that can be quite relevant, depending on your seats, since a circular catwalk extends into the audience; some seats are perched right on the rail edge of this, vir-tually squashing the occupant's face into a showgirl's midriff. In fact, some of those topless breasts could put out an eye. (Besides, it spoils the illusion when you are close enough to see all that pancake makeup.) Your seat placement is worth noting for this reason, if you don't want to be that up close and personal with a virtually naked total stranger. Others might pay extra.

Anyway, it's a revue, featuring songs about listening to your heart, dancing (the Space Age Viking dance number was a camp high-light), and one blonde (presumably Aki, "Showgirl for the 21st Cen-tury") in a flesh-colored G-string performing nearly *nude en pointe* ballet. All this is delivered with a Mickey Mouse Club enthusiasm, which is a bit disconcerting when half the performers are partially naked. There is also nearly naked ice skating, which was actually better than you might think; the skaters are very good and make use of the world's tiniest patch of ice in dramatic and resourceful ways. They were also a huge crowd pleaser, as was the delightful Argentinean gaucho act.

- **Showroom Policies:** Nonsmoking with preassigned seating.
- **Price:** Most seats $30, booths $35–$45 (includes tax, two drinks, and gratuity).
- **Show Times:** Tues, Wed, Thurs, and Sat at 7:30 and 10:30pm; Sun and Mon at 8pm. Dark Fri.
- **Reservations:** You can reserve up to a month in advance by phone.

An Evening at La Cage. Riviera Hotel and Casino, 2901 Las Vegas Blvd. S. ☎ **800/634-3420** or 702/734-9301.

No, not inspired by the French movie or the recent American re-make, or even the Broadway musical. Actually, it's more the stage show from *Priscilla, Queen of the Desert.* Female impersonators dress up as various entertainers (with varying degrees of success) to lip-synch to said performers' greatest hits (with varying degrees of success). Celebs lampooned can include Cher, Bette Midler, Judy Garland, Whitney Houston, Dionne Warwick, and, intriguingly, Michael Jackson. A Joan Rivers impersonator, looking not unlike the original but sounding (even with the aid of, oddly, a constant echo) not at all like her, is the hostess, delivering scatological phrases and stale jokes. They do make the most of a tiny stage with some pretty stunning lighting, though the choreography is bland. Still, it's a crowd pleaser—one couple was back for their fourth (all comped) visit.

- **Showroom Policies:** Nonsmoking with maître d' seating.
- **Price:** $27.72 and $35.96 (includes two drinks; gratuity extra).
- **Show Times:** Wed–Mon at 7:30 and 9:30pm, with an extra show at 11:15pm Wed and Sat. Dark Tues.
- **Reservations:** Tickets can be purchased at the box office only, in advance if you wish.

The Great Radio City Spectacular. Flamingo Hilton, 3555 Las Vegas Blvd. S. ☎ **800/221-7299** or 702/733-3333.

This is the wholesome showgirls show. If you aren't familiar with the venerable Rockettes tradition, the short black-and-white film on their history that opens the production will get you up to date. It also sets the stage for the big entrance by the ladies, arguably the world's best-known chorus line. There is a headliner who accompanies them—

this star changes frequently. As of this writing, it was Paige O'Hara, the voice of Belle from Disney's *Beauty and the Beast.* Regardless of who it is, the star's musical numbers are interspersed with a variety of dance productions by the Rockettes that serve as a veritable history of dance, ranging from tap to '40s swing, waltzes, *March of the Wooden Soldiers,* and the like. Of course, the signature Rockettes' high-kicking line is worked into at least half the numbers. That's their greatest hit—if O'Hara remains with the show, you can count on seeing her do hers, from the aforementioned *Beauty and the Beast.* The variety acts are standard Vegas: a juggler who keeps up a disturbing David Helfgott–like banter under his breath and a magician who tries too hard.

- **Showroom Policies:** Nonsmoking with maître d' seating.
- **Price:** Dinner show based on main-course price ($52.50 and up includes tax and gratuity). Cocktail show $42.50 (includes tax, two drinks, and gratuity).
- **Show Times:** Dinner show Sat–Thurs at 7:45pm, cocktail show Mon and Sat only at 10:30pm.
- **Reservations:** You can reserve by phone 2 weeks in advance.

✪ *Jubilee!* Bally's, 3645 Las Vegas Blvd. S. ☎ **800/237-7469** or 702/ 739-4567.

A classic Vegas spectacular, crammed with singing, dancing, magic, acrobats, elaborate costumes and sets, and, of course, bare breasts. It's a basic review, with production numbers featuring homogenized versions of standards (Gershwin, Cole Porter, some Fred Astaire numbers) sometimes sung live, sometimes lip-synched, and always accompanied by lavishly costumed and frequently topless showgirls. Humorous set pieces about Samson and Delilah and the sinking of the *Titanic* (!) show off some pretty awesome sets (and they were doing the *Titanic* long before a certain movie and recent attendees claimed the ship-sinking effect on stage here was a better production value than the one in the movie), while the finale features aerodynamically impossible feathered and bejeweled costumes and headpieces designed by Bob Mackie. So what if the dancers are occasionally out of step, and the action sometimes veers into the dubious (a Vegas-style revue about a disaster that took more than 1,000 lives?) or even the inexplicable (a finale praising beautiful and bare-breasted girls suddenly stops for three lines of "Somewhere Over the Rainbow"?). With plenty of rhinestones and nipples on display, this is archetypal Vegas entertainment and the best of those presently offered.

- **Showroom Policies:** Nonsmoking with preassigned seating.
- **Price:** $49.50 and up (tax included, drinks extra).
- **Show Times:** Sun–Wed at 8pm, Thurs and Sat at 8 and 11pm. Dark Fri.
- **Reservations:** You can reserve up to 6 weeks in advance.

✪ *Lance Burton: Master Magician.* Monte Carlo, 3770 Las Vegas Blvd. S. ☎ **800/311-8999** or 702/730-7000.

Magic acts are a dime a dozen in Vegas of late. Along with impersonator acts, they seem to have largely replaced the topless showgirls of yore. Most seem more than a little influenced by the immeasurable success of Siegfried and Roy. So when someone pops up who is original—not to mention charming and, yes, actually good at his job—it comes as a relief.

Monte Carlo dumped a lot of money into building the lush Victorian music hall–style Lance Burton Theater for the star, and it was worth it. Handsome and folksy (he hails from Lexington, Kentucky), Burton is talented and engaging, for the most part shunning the big-ticket special effects that seem to have swamped most other shows in town. Instead, he offers an extremely appealing production that starts small, with "close-up" magic. These rather lovely tricks, he tells us, are what won him a number of prestigious magic competitions. They are truly extraordinary. (We swear that he tossed a bird up in the air, and the darn thing turned into confetti in front of our eyes. Really.) Burton doesn't have patter, per se, but his dry, laconic, low-key delivery is plenty amusing and in contrast to other performers in town who seem as if they have been spending way too much time at Starbucks. He does eventually move to bigger illusions, but his manner follows him—he knows the stuff is good, but he also knows the whole thing is a bit silly, so why not have fun with it? Accompanying him are some perky showgirls, who border on the wholesome, and talented comic juggler Michael Goudeau. The latter is a likable goofball who instantly wins you over (or should) when he juggles three beanbag chairs. All this and extremely comfortable movie theater–style plush seats with cup holders. And for a most reasonable price.

- **Showroom Policies:** Nonsmoking with preassigned seating.
- **Price:** $40 and $45 (includes tax, drinks extra).
- **Show Times:** Tues–Sat at 7:30 and 10:30pm. Dark Sun and Mon.
- **Reservations:** Tickets can be purchased 60 days in advance.

Legends in Concert. Imperial Palace, 3535 Las Vegas Blvd. S. ☎ **702/ 794-3261.**

It's a crowd pleaser, which is probably why it's been running since May 1983. Arguably the best of the Vegas impersonator shows (though it's hard to quantify such things), *Legends* does feature performers live, rather than lip-synching. Acts vary from night to night (in a showroom that could use a face-lift) on a nice, large stage with modern hydraulics but twinkle lighting that is stuck in a *Flip Wilson Show* time warp. The personal touches here include scantily clad (but well-choreographed) male and female dancers, and an utterly useless green laser. When we went, the performers included Neil Diamond (whose "America" was accompanied by red-, white-, and blue-clad showgirls covered in flags of all nations), an actual piano-playing Elton John, the Blues Brothers (a reasonable John Belushi, but a not-even-close Dan Ackroyd), and the inevitable Diana Ross, Four Tops, and the young, thin Elvis (who performs hits from the fat, old Elvis years). The latter, by the way, was preceded by a reverent multimedia presentation (the stage also has video screens that show not only the live action, but also clips by the real celebs). Best of all, Wayne Newton was there. Yes, the *real* one. During the Blues Brothers bit, the band showed a rare display of spontaneity. When one audience member called out a request for "country," they actually broke into the theme from *Rawhide*. Maybe it was a planned moment, but we were impressed that it didn't seem that way.

- **Showroom Policies:** Nonsmoking, with maître d' seating.
- **Price:** $34.50 (includes two drinks or one Polynesian cocktail such as a mai tai or zombie; tax and gratuity extra).
- **Show Times:** Mon–Sat at 7:30 and 10:30pm. Dark Sun.
- **Reservations:** You can make reservations by phone up to 2 weeks in advance.

✪ **Siegfried & Roy.** The Mirage, 3400 Las Vegas Blvd. S. ☎ **800/963-9634** or 702/792-7777.

A Vegas institution for more than 2 decades, illusionists Siegfried and Roy started as an opening act, became headliners at the Frontier, and finally were given their own $30 million show and $25 million theater in the Mirage. They (and their extensive exotic animal menagerie) have amply repaid this enormous investment by selling out every show since. No wonder the Mirage has them booked "until the end of time."

But while the spectacle is undeniable (and the money right on the stage), the result is overproduced. From the get go, there is so much light, sound, smoke, and fire; so many dancing girls, fire-breathing dragons, robots, and other often completely superfluous effects; not to mention an original (and forgettable) Michael Jackson song, that it overwhelms the point of the whole thing. Or maybe it's *become* the point of the whole thing. The magic, which was the Austrian duo's original act, after all, seems to have gotten lost. Sometimes literally. The tricks are at a minimum, allowing the flash pots, lasers, and whatnot to fill out the nearly 2-hour show. More often than not, when a trick is actually being performed, our attention was elsewhere, gawking at an effect, a showgirl, or something. Only the gasps from the audience members who actually happened to be looking in the right place let us know we missed something really neat.

Tellingly, the best part of the show is when all that stuff is switched off, and Siegfried and Roy take the stage to perform smaller magic and chat with the audience. The charm that helped get them so far shines through, and spontaneity is allowed to sneak in. The white tigers are certainly magnificent, but they don't do much other than get cuddled (charmingly) by Roy and badly lip-synch to pretaped roars. The duo is clearly doing something right, judging from the heartfelt standing ovations they receive night after night. But more than one couple was heard to say it was not the best show they had seen, and also to express a feeling that it was overpriced. At these ticket costs (essentially $90 *per person!*) almost anything is. Go if you can't live without seeing a true, modern Vegas legend, but one can find better entertainment values in town.

- **Showroom Policies:** Nonsmoking with preassigned seating.
- **Price:** $89 (includes two drinks, souvenir brochure, tax, and gratuity).
- **Show Times:** Fri–Tues at 7:30 and 11pm, except during occasional dark periods. Dark Wed and Thurs.
- **Reservations:** Tickets can be purchased 3 days in advance.

3 Piano Bars

In addition to the establishments listed below, consider the ultra-elegant Palace Court Terrace Lounge, adjoining the **Palace Court restaurant at Caesars** (see chapter 5). This romantic piano bar has a stained-glass skylight that retracts for a view of open starlit sky. Off the lounge is an intimate crystal-chandeliered, European-style casino

Wayne Newton's Top-10 Favorite Lounge Songs

Wayne Newton is the consummate entertainer. He has performed more than 25,000 concerts in Las Vegas alone, and in front of more than 25 million people worldwide. Wayne has received more standing ovations than any other entertainer in history. Along with his singing credits, his acting credits are soaring—one of his more recent credits is *Vegas Vacation.* Make sure you catch him playing at the MGM Grand. No trip to Vegas is complete without seeing the "King of Las Vegas."

1. "You're Nobody, Til Somebody Loves You" (*You don't have a body unless somebody loves you!*)
2. "Up a Lazy River" (*or "Up Your Lazy River!"*)
3. "Don't Go Changin' (Just the Way You Are)" (*The clothes will last another week!*)
4. "Having My Baby" (*Oh God!*)
5. "The Windmills of My Mind" (*A mind is a terrible thing to waste!*)
6. "The Wind Beneath My Wings" (*Soft and Dry usually helps!*)
7. "Copacabana"
8. "When the Saints Go Marching In"
9. "I Am, I Said" (*Huh?!*)
10. "The Theme from the Love Boat" (*or "Would a Dingy Do?"*)

for high-stakes players only. **Gatsby's** at the MGM Grand (see chapter 5) also has a sophisticated and stunning adjoining piano bar as does the **Brown Derby.** And **Cafe Nicolle** (see chapter 5) has a small but agreeable genuine piano bar.

Alexis Park Resort: Pisces Bistro. 375 E. Harmon Ave. ☎ **702/796-3300.** No cover or minimum.

Alexis Park offers live music nightly from 8pm until about midnight; a versatile pianist and vocalist perform everything from show tunes to oldies to Top 40. Light fare is available.

The Bar at Times Square. 3790 Las Vegas Blvd. S., in New York New York. ☎ **702/740-6969.**

If you are looking for a quiet piano bar, this is not the place for you. Smack in the middle of the Central Park part of the New York New

York casino, every night two pianos are going strong, and the young hipster, cigar-smoking crowd overflows out the doors. It always seems to be packed with a singing, swaying, drinking throng full of camaraderie and good cheer—or at least, booze. Hugely fun, provided you can get a foot in the door. And yes, every night, right outside, the ball on top drops at midnight, for a little auld lang syne.

Carriage House: Kiefer's. 105 E. Harmon Ave. ☎ **702/739-8000.** No cover or minimum.

This rooftop restaurant has a plushly furnished adjoining piano bar/ lounge. Windowed walls offer great views of the Las Vegas neon skyline, making this a romantic setting for cocktails and hors d'oeuvres. There's piano music Thursday to Saturday 7 to 11pm.

Club Monaco. 1487 E. Flamingo Rd., between Maryland Pkwy. and Tamarus St. (on your right as you come from the Strip; look for the LA-Z-BOY Furniture Gallery). ☎ **702/737-6212.** No cover or minimum.

This low-key, sophisticated piano bar—its walls lined with oil paintings of icons such as Elvis, Bogart, James Dean, and Marilyn Monroe (not to mention Rodney Dangerfield, finally getting respect)— is a romantic setting for cocktails and classic piano-bar entertainment. There's a small dance floor. Friday and Saturday a talented vocalist is on hand as well. Club Monaco is far from a meat market, but it is a relaxed atmosphere in which to meet people. The crowd is over 30. A menu offers salads, burgers, steak sandwiches, pastas, and gourmet appetizers such as oysters Rockefeller and escargot-stuffed mushrooms. Open 24 hours.

4 Other Bars

In addition to the venues listed below, consider hanging out, as the locals quickly began doing, at **Aureole, Red Square,** and the **House of Blues,** all in Mandalay Bay. You might also check out the incredible nighttime view at the bar atop the **Stratosphere**—nothing beats it. There's also the **Viva Las Vegas Lounge** at the Hard Rock Hotel, where every rock-connected person in Vegas will eventually pass through.

Holy Cow. 2432 Las Vegas Blvd. S., at Sahara Ave. ☎ **702/732-COWS.**

Okay, so maybe you go to serious bars for serious drinking, but anyplace with a giant bovine on the roof and an extensive cow theme on the inside can't be all bad. Cows are everywhere—cow paintings, cow-motif lighting fixtures, a "sidewalk of fame" of cow hoof prints outside, even slot machines called (irresistibly) "Moolah"—so if you are heifer-a-phobe, stay away. The microbrew pub upstairs offers a free tour, or you can taste its four hand-crafted microbrews: pale ale, wheat beer, brown ale, and a monthly changing brewmaster's special, which sometimes contains the word *blueberry* in it. Pub grub is also offered, which they assure us requires only one stomach to consume.

✪ **Main Street Station: Triple 7 Brew Pub.** 200 Main St. ☎ **702/387-1896.**

Yet another of the many things the new(ish) Main Street Station hotel has done right. Stepping into its microbrew pub feels like stepping out of Vegas. Well, maybe, except for the dueling piano entertainment. Part modern warehouse look (exposed pipes, microbrew fixtures visible through exposed glass at back, very high ceiling), but with a hammered tin ceiling that continues the hotel's Victorian decor, this is a look more appropriate to North Beach in San Francisco. Dare we say it? The result produces an environment that is a bit on the yuppified side, but escapes being pretentious. And frankly, it's a much-needed modern touch for the Downtown area. They have their own brewmaster, a number of microbrews ready to try, and if you are feeling like a quick bite, there is also an oyster and sushi bar, plus fancy burgers and pizzas. It can get noisy during the aforementioned piano duel act, but otherwise casino noise stays out. And Downtown being all too heavy on the old Las Vegas side (which is fine for a time but not *all* the time), this is good for a suitable breather.

✪ **Peppermill's Fireside Lounge.** 2985 Las Vegas Blvd. S. ☎ **702/735-7635.**

Walk through the classic Peppermill's coffee shop (not a bad place to eat, by the way) on the Strip, and you land in its dark, plush, cozy lounge. A fabulously dated view of hip, it has low, circular banquette seats, fake floral foliage, low neon, and electric candles. But best of all is the water and fire pit as the centerpiece—a piece of kitsch thought long vanished from the earth, which attracts nostalgia buffs like moths to flames. It all adds up to a cozy, womblike place. Perfect for crashing down a bit after some time spent on the hectic Strip. The enormous, exotic froufrou tropical drinks (including the signature basketball-sized margaritas) will ensure that you sink into that level of comfortable stupor.

Pink E's. 3695 W. Flamingo Rd. ☎ **702/252-4666.**

Sick of the attitude at Club Rio? (And well you should be.) Escape directly across the street to Pink E's, where the theme is pink. You were expecting maybe seafoam? Anyway, at least one regular described this as "the only place to go if you are over 25 and have a brain." And like pink. Because everything here is: the many pool tables, the Ping-Pong tables, the booths, the lighting, the lava lamp on the bar, and even the people. In its own way, it's as gimmick-ridden as The Beach dance club (see below), but surely no one would put out a pink pool table in all seriousness? Yeah, it's a ludicrous heresy, but don't you want to play on one? Anyway, Pink E's offers retro diner food and a deejay on weekends. The dress code basically translates to "no gangsta wannabe wear." Go, but wear all black just to be ornery.

Sand Dollar Blues Lounge. 3355 Spring Mountain Rd., at Polaris. ☎ **702/ 871-6651.**

The kind of funky, no decor (think posters and beer signs), atmosphere-intensive, slightly grimy, friendly bar you either wish your town had or wish it had something other than. Just up the road from Treasure Island, this is a great antidote to artificial Vegas. Attracting a solid mix of locals and tourists (employees claim the former includes everything from bikers to chamber of commerce members), the Sand Dollar features live blues (both electric and acoustic, with a little Cajun and zydeco thrown in) every night. The dance floor is tiny and often full. The minimal cover always goes to the band. Depending on your desires, it's either refreshingly not Las Vegas, or just the kind of place you came to Vegas to escape.

Sky Lounge (at the Polo Towers). 3745 Las Vegas Blvd. S. ☎ **702/ 261-1000.**

It may not quite be the view offered by the Stratosphere's bar, but it's pretty darn good and easier to get to. You see too much of the Holiday Inn Boardwalk directly across the street and not quite enough of the MGM Grand to the left, but otherwise there are no complaints. The decor is too modern (heavy on '80s black and purple), but overall the place is quiet (especially during the day) and civil. A jazz vocal/piano performs at night (when the views are naturally best). The atmosphere produced by all this is classic Vegas in the best sense (with only a slight touch of necessary kitsch). Worth a trip for an escape from the mob, though you won't be the only tourist fighting for window seats.

Tom & Jerry's. 4550 S. Maryland Pkwy. and Harmon Ave. ☎ **702/ 736-8550.**

The dull exterior belies what is inside: a lively bar with three different rooms, each with its own entirely different feel and atmosphere.

Decidedly catering to the UNLV crowd (it's right across the street, after all), it prides itself on being ethnically diverse and holding no pretensions. "Drink cheap, be loose, have fun" is the owner's motto, and the result is a bar more enjoyable than the words "college bar" might make you think. Each room has its own ambience; the first is indeed a basic college bar, with a mural homage to UNLV wrapping its walls. The next room serves as the dance area, where cover bands (Prince, Beastie Boys) and reggae groups play all nights but Sunday and Monday. The back room is a pool hall with 20 tables. Most nights feature some kind of $1 drink specials, plus weekly beer busts and other such tempting offers. There's a moderate cover that changes week to week.

Tommy Rocker's. 4275 Industrial Blvd. ☎ **702/261-6688.**

Tommy Rocker is the owner—surely he wasn't born with that name—and he plays his club every Friday and Saturday nights, mixing bar band standards with '80s and '90s hits. It's a one-man show, with Strip musicians dropping by after their own shifts are done. (Occasionally, local bands are permitted to play as well.) Sort of like the inside of a Quonset hut painted black, his vaguely beach-frat-party-themed club has become the home for local and out-of-town Parrot Heads (Jimmy Buffet fans, for those not in the know), with the result that the crowd is 5 to 10 years past their heavy college drinking days. The large bar dominates the middle of the room; there are two pool tables and a grill for ordering food, plus an espresso machine.

5 Dance Clubs

In addition to the options listed below, country music fans might want to wander on over to **Dylan's,** 4660 Boulder Hwy. (☎ **702/451-4006**), and **Rockabilly's,** 3785 Boulder Hwy. (☎ **702/641-5800**). Not far from each other, both offer country music (live and otherwise) and line dancing, with free dance lessons.

✪ The Beach. 365 S. Convention Center Dr., at Paradise Rd. ☎ **702/731-1925.** Cover $10 and up Fri–Sat and special events.

If you are a fan of loud, crowded, 24-hour party bars filled with tons of good-looking fun-seekers, then bow in this direction, for you have found Mecca. This huge tropical-themed (hence the whole "Beach" thing) nightclub is right across the street from the Convention Center and is, according to just about anyone you ask, the "hottest" club in the city. It's a two-story affair with five separate bars downstairs and another three up. Just in case walking the 20 feet to the closest one is too much of an effort, they also have bikini-clad women serving beer out of steel tubs full of ice (they also roam the floor with shot belts). Also downstairs is the large 2-story dance floor, which dominates the center of the room and is built around a full-service bar at one end. Upstairs, there are balconies overlooking the dance floor, pool tables, darts, foosball, pinball, and various other arcade games plus slot machines, video poker, and a sports book. The crowd is aggressively young and pretty, more men than women (70/30 split), and about 60% tourist, which is probably why the place can get away with charging a $10 cover. Party people look no further. There's free valet parking, and if you've driven here and become intoxicated, they'll drive you back home at no charge.

Club Rio. Rio Suites, 3700 W. Flamingo Rd. ☎ **702/252-7777.** As advertised: Cover $10 for men, local women free, out-of-state women $5—but frequently when we went by on a weekend night, the cover was $20 for everyone.

This is the hottest night spot in Vegas (along with The Beach) as of this writing, but apparently made so by people who don't mind long lines, restrictive dress codes, attitudinal door people, hefty cover charges, and bland dance music. Waits can be interminable and admittance denied thanks to the wrong footwear or shirt. Once inside, you find a large, circular room, with a spacious dance floor taking up much of the space. Giant video screens line the upper parts of the walls, showing anything from shots of the action down below to catwalk footage. Comfy circular booths fill out the next couple of concentric circles; these seem mostly reserved, and when empty they leave the impression that the place isn't very full—so why the wait? Music on a recent visit included a Madonna medley and the perennial "Celebration," not the most au courant of tunes. The total effect is of a grown-up, not terribly drunken, frat and sorority mixer.

☼ Drink. 200 E. Harmon Ave., at Koval Lane. ☎ **702/796-5519.** Cover $10 after 10pm ($15–$25 when major artists are performing); women are admitted free Tues night. No minimum.

Where Gen X Vegas hangs out. Decor is hip, which in this case means an odd mix of industrial warehouse, peeling plaster, and brick country cottage exterior; somehow, it works. Soundproofing is impressive; you can literally pass from the hard-rock room to the dance room with only a second's worth of the two overlapping into each other. (Of course, getting there can be a problem—the hallways from room to room are narrow and bottlenecks frequent. Be patient.) A recent stroll through the hard-rock room heard a mix of retro and more current rock. The different sounds mean different appeals for different rooms; thus something for everyone. Despite a young, fashion-conscious crowd, it's friendlier than you would imagine, and surprisingly enough, there is virtually no attitude. (If you go there after Club Rio, the difference in attitude is almost palpable.) Of the nightly dance clubs, this is the one to go to, unless a hip quotient frightens you. Open daily 8pm to 5am. Self-parking is free, valet parking $3.

Ra. Luxor Las Vegas, 3900 Las Vegas Blvd. S. ☎ **702/262-4000.** Cover $10 for men, $5 for women; higher for concerts and special events.

The futuristic Egyptian-themed Ra is the new hot spot in Vegas. It has that Vegas "we're a show and an attraction" vibe, but is still not overly pretentious and the staff are friendly, which is a rare thing for a hot club. It might be worth it to go just to gawk at the heavy gilt decor. Current dance music (mostly techno) is on the soundtrack. The later you go, the more likely the mid- to upper 20s clientele will be entirely local.

✪ **rumjungle.** Mandalay Bay, 3950 Las Vegas Blvd. S. ☎ **702/632-7408.** Cover $15 after 10:30pm. Dinner daily 5:30–11pm. Nightclub Sun–Wed 11pm–2am, Thurs–Sat 11pm–4am.

Now, normally our delicate sensibilities wince at such overkill, and consider efforts such as this to be trying just a bit too hard, but surprisingly, rumjungle really is the great amount of fun it so blatantly tells you it wants to be. From the fire-wall entrance that gives way to a wall of water, to a 2-story bar full of the largest collection of rum varieties anywhere, each bottle illuminated with a laser beam of light, to go-go girls dancing and prancing between said bottles of wine, to dueling congos, to the food that all comes skewered on swords, it's all a bit much, but it works, really it does. Get there early (before 10pm) to avoid lines/guest lists/the cover charge, and consider having dinner; it's costly, but it's multicourse, all-you-can-eat, flame-pit-cooked Brazilian food, and for the amount (plus what it would cost you to enter the club), it's a good deal. Then dance it all off all night long.

Studio 54. MGM Grand Hotel, 3799 Las Vegas Blvd. S. ☎ **702/891-1111.** Cover $10 for men Sun–Thurs, $20 Fri–Sat; free for women.

The legendary Studio 54 has been resurrected here in Las Vegas, but with all the bad elements and none of the good ones. Forget Truman, Halston, and Liza doing illegal (or at least) immoral things in the bathroom stalls; that part of Studio 54 remains but a fond memory. However, the snooty, exclusive door attitude has been retained. Hooray. Red-rope policies are all well and good if you are trying to build a mystique in a regular club, but for a tourist attraction, where guests are likely to be one-time-only (or at best, once a year), it's obnoxious. Oddly, this doesn't lead to a high-class clientele; of all the new clubs, this is the most touristy and trashy. If the real Studio 54 were this boring, no one would remember it today.

Utopia. 3765 Las Vegas Blvd. S., in the Epicenter. ☎ **702/736-3105.** Cover varies.

According to *Scope* magazine, Utopia is "less a discotheque and more a revolution"—which is an apt description, considering that in Las Vegas, underground once-a-week nightclubs usually disappear in a matter of weeks. Utopia is still going strong (as of this writing), despite the death (in a car accident) of its founder, Aaron Britt. The music is progressive house, tribal, trance, techno, and rave. The atmosphere is industrial, foggy, and heavy with lasers and other dazzling visuals. A cool and outrageous crowd fills three rooms with fun, peace, and love, in a heart-pounding, techno way. It's for the tragically hip, but isn't it good to know they are out there in Vegas?

6 Strip Clubs

No, not entertainment establishments on Las Vegas Boulevard South. This would be the other kind of "strip." Yes, people come to town for the gambling and the wedding chapels, but the lure of Vegas doesn't stop there.

Cheetah's. 2112 Western Ave. ☎ **702/384-0074.** Cover $10. MC, V (but cash preferred—they have an ATM machine). Topless.

This is the strip club used in the movie *Showgirls,* but thanks to the magic of Hollywood and later renovations by the club, only the main stage will look vaguely familiar to those few looking for Nomi Malone. The management believes, "If you treat people right, they will keep coming back," so the atmosphere is friendlier than at other clubs. They "encourage couples—people who want to party—to come here. We get a 21 to 40 aged party kind of crowd," the manager told us. And indeed there is a sporty, frat-bar feel to the place. (Table dance $10, couch dance $20. Open 24 hours.

Club Paradise. 4416 Paradise Rd. ☎ **702/734-7990.** $10 cover, 2-drink minimum (drinks $4.50 and up). MC, V. Unescorted women allowed. Topless.

Two Strippers Give 9 Strip-Bar Etiquette Tips

Brittany and Kitty each have several years' experience working in strip bars, so they know what they're talking about. And they both really are sweet girls, honest.

1. Bathe.
2. Don't lie and say you never go into these places.
3. Don't take off your wedding ring—we can still see the mark it leaves.
4. Don't ask if we take credit cards. Bring cash!
5. Don't fall asleep—just because we are open 24 hours, we aren't a hotel.
6. Don't wear wool pants—they scratch.
7. Don't ask for our phone number.
8. Don't lick us. We're not Popsicles.
9. Don't forget: We aren't dumb strippers. We are a lot smarter than you think.

Possibly the nicest of the strip clubs (the outside looks a lot like the Golden Nugget), Club Paradise seems like a hot nightclub where most of the women happen to be topless. The glitzy stage looks like something from a miniature showroom, and the place is relatively bright by strip-club standards. Not too surprisingly, they get a very white-collar crowd here. The result is not terribly sleazy, which may please some and turn off others. The club says it is "women-friendly," and indeed there were a few couples, including one woman who was receiving a lap dance herself—and didn't seem too uncomfortable. Lap dance $20. Open Monday to Friday 4pm to 6am and Saturday and Sunday 6pm to 6am.

Glitter Gulch. 20 Fremont St. ☎ **702/385-4774.** No cover, 2-drink minimum (drinks $5.75). Topless.

Right there in the middle of the Fremont Street Experience, Glitter Gulch is either an eyesore or the last bastion of Old Las Vegas, depending on your point of view. It also had a brief moment of tabloid fame in 1999 when "Suddenly Susan" actor David Strickland came here for one last hurrah (lap dances were involved, as well as "News Radio's" Andy Dick) before committing suicide in an adult motel on the Strip. The inside is modern enough: black light and bubble fountains, arranged around a runway strip. As you enter, you are assigned your own (overly clothed) waitress who escorts you to your table. They also offer limo service to the hotels. There is even a line of souvenir clothing. Given such services and its convenient location, this is the perfect place for the merely curious—you can easily pop in, check things out, goggle and ogle, and then hit the road, personal dignity intact. Table dance $20. Open Sunday to Thursday noon to 4am, Friday to Saturday noon to 6am.

Olympic Gardens. 1531 Las Vegas S. Blvd. ☎ **702/385-8987.** Cover $15 (includes 2 drinks). AE, DISC, MC, V (they have an ATM machine). Unescorted women allowed. Topless.

Possibly the largest of the strip clubs, this almost feels like a family operation, thanks to the middle-aged women handling the door. They also have a boutique selling lingerie and naughty outfits. The crowd is a mix of 20s to 30s blue-collar guys and techno geeks. Table dance $20, more in VIP room. Open Monday to Sunday 2pm to 6am.

Index

See also separate Accommodations, Restaurants, and Buffets indexes, below.

ACCOMMODATIONS

RESTAURANTS

BUFFETS